The Essential Guide for
Experienced Teaching Assistants

The *Essential Guide* for
Experienced Teaching Assistants

Meeting the National Occupational
Standards at Level 3

ANNE WATKINSON

with contributions by John Acklaw,
Graham Beeden, Peter Nathan
and Ann Reilly

David Fulton Publishers
London

David Fulton Publishers Ltd
The Chiswick Centre, 414 Chiswick High Road, London W4 5TF
www.fultonpublishers.co.uk

David Fulton Publishers is a division of Granada Learning, part of ITV plc.

First published 2003
10 9 8 7 6 5 4 3

British Library Cataloguing in Publication Data
A catalogue record for this book is available from the British Library.

ISBN 1 84312 009 7

Typeset by Mark Heslington, Scarborough, North Yorkshire
Printed and bound in Great Britain by Ashford Colour Press.

Contents

Preface

This book aims to provide the underpinning knowledge to support teaching assistants in all phases of schooling when undertaking study at an advanced level. It contains practical examples of TAs at work and references to other texts which will give the reader further information about the work of TAs at this level. It actively engages the reader in activities, giving the theoretical background to their school based work. The suggested reading at the ends of chapters enables the reader to extend their reading if they are interested in any particular aspect and so helps the development of reflective practice. It gives insight and information about learning in general as well as pupils' individual needs. It explores curriculum based areas and teaching skills which will enable the reader to support pupils, teachers, the curriculum and the school more effectively.

Hopefully, it will enable TAs to operate more independently, to use their increasing knowledge and confidence, always ensuring that they develop their practice in partnership with class teachers, who retain the responsibility for the teaching and learning of the pupils. Also, it emphasises that TAs are team members, supporting the school, and must be supported by the school. It is important that any TA studying at this level has the opportunity to discuss the contents with a teacher mentor, to increase their understanding of the subject matter and its implications for practice, and to make sure that any changes in practice they would like to make are in line with the policies and practice of the school.

The book can be used to support NVQs or other TA awards at Level 3 and is related to the competencies described in National Occupational Standards (NOS) at Level 3 and also provides a reference handbook for established TAs who, not wanting to go on to teaching as a career, just want to be 'a really good TA'. For those who do wish to continue into higher education, it will provide a stepping stone to the kind of critical and reflective study strategies needed for such progression.

Acknowledgements

I would like to thank:

- my friends and colleagues who contributed chapters; I could not have written the book without them: John Acklaw, Chartered Educational Psychologist, for Chapter 8; Graham Beeden, Numeracy Consultant for Slough LEA, for Chapter 13; Peter Nathan, Educational Consultant with Public Private Associates, for Chapter 9; Ann Reilly, Literacy Consultant for Slough LEA, for Chapter 12;
- the Employers' Organisation for Local Government (formerly known as the Local Government Training Organisation) for their permission to reproduce the Values and Principles of the National Occupational Standards;
- Maldon Primary School staff, children and parents for permission to use the photographs taken in their school;
- the many schools and TAs whose practice and friendship have been a constant inspiration throughout my work with them;
- Margaret Haigh of David Fulton Publishers for her encouragement and help while preparing the book;
- my husband, Frank, for his endless patience, domestic help and support with my ICT systems.

List of abbreviations

A Level	Advanced level
ALS	Additional Literacy Support
BSP	Behaviour Support Plan
DfES	Department for Education and Skills
DT	Design and technology
EAL	English as an additional language
ELS	Early Literacy Support
EMA	Ethnic Minority Achievement
ERA	Education Reform Act
FLS	Further Literacy Support
GCSE	General Certificate of Secondary Education
HLTA	Higher Level Teaching Assistant
ICT	Information and communication technology
IEP	Individual Education Plan
INSET	In-service education and training (for teachers)
IQ	Intelligence quotient
LEA	Local education authority
LGNTO	Local Government National Training Organisation
LSA	Learning support assistant
NC	National Curriculum
NLNS	National Literacy and Numeracy Strategies
NLS	National Literacy Strategy
NNS	National Numeracy Strategy
NOS	National Occupational Standards
NQT	Newly qualified teacher
NVQ	National Vocational Qualification
Ofsted	Office for Standards in Education
OMS	Oral and mental starter
OU	Open University
PPA	Planning, preparation and assessment
PE	Physical education
PMLD	Profound and multiple learning difficulties
PSHE	Personal, social and health education

QCA	Qualifications and Curriculum Authority
QTS	Qualified Teacher Status
RE	Religious education
SAT	Standard Assessment Task or Test
SDP	School Development Plan
SEN	Special educational needs
SENCO	Special educational needs coordinator
SLD	Severe learning difficulties
SMART	Specific, measurable, achievable, realistic and time-bound
STAC	Specialist Teacher Assistant Certificate
SWOT	Strengths, weaknesses, opportunities and threats
TA	Teaching assistant
ZPD	Zone of proximal development

1 Introduction

The reason for this book

Teaching assistants (TAs) are being recognised as increasingly important in the life of schools. The recent government initiatives for raising standards by supporting teachers and reducing their workload (DfES 2002a; DfES 2002b) have highlighted the value of the role in all phases. There are still problems of parity across employers, both in conditions of service and in pay, but the government continues to put in resources for the recruitment, training and support of systems for professional and career development, including facilitating pathways to teaching for those who wish it. Indeed, a continuous framework of development for TAs from recruitment through induction, Levels 2 and 3 of the National Occupational Standards (NOS) and the higher level teaching assistant (HLTA) standards to Qualified Teacher Status (QTS) is being developed at the time of writing (DfES and TTA 2003).

This book uses the term 'teaching assistant' as the preferred Department for Education and Skills (DfES) generic term for all those who support teaching and learning in the classroom, and the references to the National Curriculum (NC) are for that in use in England. Note that Acts of Parliament and codes of practice are sometimes changed for use in the countries of the United Kingdom other than England.

The NOS are divided into units, where 'a unit of competence represents an activity which can be undertaken by one individual, and which has real meaning in the workplace' (Fisher 1995: 23). Some of these are considered essential for any TA in any kind of school and these units would be considered 'mandatory' if taking a National Vocational Qualification (NVQ). This book will cover all the possible units for Level 3, as it is impossible to determine who would want information on which units. At Level 3, obtaining the NVQ would require showing evidence for the four mandatory units and six of the 19 optional units. The units are detailed in Table 1.1, along with chapter references for relevant material in this book.

The standards themselves are not reproduced in this book; you must get hold of a copy for yourself from the Employers' Organisation (EO) (www.lg-employers.gov.uk). You need to go through 'Skills and development' to 'teaching/classroom assistants' to 'download the standards'. This organisation now subsumes the Local Government National Training Organisation (LGNTO), which drew up the standards. The relevant NOS references for Level 3 are given in square brackets in the text. The NOS values and principles are reproduced in full at the end of this book in the Appendix.

In order to use this book effectively you should have had at least one year's experience in the job, and possibly have studied for a Level 2 qualification already. It is to be hoped that TAs working at this level would have at least General Certificate of Secondary Education (GCSE) English and mathematics to a Grade C or an equivalent, in order to undertake support of pupils in the classroom. Level 3 'is designed to be applicable to experienced teaching /classroom assistants and/or those whose working role calls for competence across a varied range of responsibilities' (LGNTO 2001 Level 3: 2). Some of the units are common to both level standards – managing behaviour, ICT, pupil safety, security, health and well-being, for instance – and some of the Level 3 units contain elements from the Level 2 units. While you could undertake assessment without attending any training or course and use this book as your guide, you would be ill-advised to do so. The level of knowledge and understanding is deemed to be equivalent to that of advanced (A) level examinations and requires that you are reflective, thinking, able to offer critical comment and use your judgement. You need therefore to have colleagues you can debate issues with. You should also ensure there is someone in your school who knows you are undertaking assessment, to share your ideas and feelings – an in-school mentor – even if you are not being assessed by a member of your own staff. Many of the standards refer to practice in your own school and schools vary so. In working at Level 3, you must understand your limitations but also recognise your competence and operate with initiative to carry out your designated role. You must know when to refer to other people and what difficulties you need help with. You should be able to contribute what you know, and do what you can to help others, particularly those less experienced.

This cannot be an exhaustive text; you will need to have access to a library, although most of the books referred to should be available in your staffroom library or be owned by some of the teachers. At an advanced level, it is to be expected that you will read wider than any one prescribed textbook. Evidence of such critical reading should be part of the assessment procedure for an award at this level.

The structure of the book

This book is not based directly on the standards, but on a more holistic and fundamental approach to the role and personal development of the TA. It follows the structure of the Level 2 book (Watkinson 2003), based on the four strands of TA work: supporting the school, the pupils, the teachers and the curriculum. As each standards unit can stand alone, there is some repetition between units as published. Do not use them as a tick list; it would be very time consuming and tedious. Assessors and centres carrying out the awards

Table 1.1 Level 3 units and elements with chapter references

Unit number	Unit title	Element number	Element title	Main chapter sources
3-1	Contribute to the management of pupil behaviour	3-1.1	Promote school policies with regard to pupil behaviour	7
		3-1.2	Support the implementation of strategies to manage pupil behaviour	7
3-2	Establish and maintain relationships with individual pupils and groups	3-2.1	Establish and maintain relationships with individual pupils	3
		3-2.2	Establish and maintain relationships with groups of pupils	3
3-3	Support pupils during learning activities	3-3.1	Provide support for learning activities	5, 10
		3-3.2	Promote independent learning	6
3-4	Review and develop your own professional practice	3-4.1	Review your own professional practice	2, 14
		3-4.2	Develop your professional practice	14
3-5	Assist in preparing and maintaining the learning environment	3-5.1	Help prepare the learning environment	5, 10
		3-5.2	Prepare learning materials for use	5, 10
		3-5.3	Monitor and maintain the learning environment	11
3-6	Contribute to maintaining pupil records	3-6.1	Contribute to maintaining pupil records	11
		3-6.2	Contribute to maintaining the record keeping system	11
3-7	Observe and report on pupil performance	3-7.1	Observe pupil performance	11
		3-7.2	Report on pupil performance	11
3-8	Contribute to the planning and evaluation of learning activities	3-8.1	Contribute to the planning of learning activities	5, 10
		3-8.2	Contribute to the evaluation of learning activities	5, 10
3-9	Promote pupils' social and emotional development	3-9.1	Support pupils in developing relationships with others	3, 7
		3-9.2	Contribute to pupils' development of self-reliance	6
		3-9.3	Contribute to pupils' ability to recognise and deal with emotions	6
3-10	Support the maintenance of pupil safety and security	3-10.1	Support the maintenance of pupil safety and security	7
		3-10.2	Minimise risks arising from health emergencies	7
3-11	Contribute to the health and well-being of pupils	3-11.1	Support pupils in adjusting to a new setting	7
		3-11.2	Support pupils in maintaining standards of health and hygiene	7
		3-11.3	Respond to signs of health problems	7
3-12	Provide support for bilingual/ multilingual pupils	3-12.1	Support the development of the target language	9
		3-12.2	Help bilingual/multilingual pupils to access the curriculum	9
3-13	Support pupils with communication and interaction difficulties	3-13.1	Enable pupils with communication and interaction difficulties to participate in learning activities	8
		3-13.2	Help pupils with communication and interaction difficulties to develop relationships with others	8

Table 1.1 Continued

Unit number	Unit title	Element number	Element title	Main chapter sources
3-14	Support pupils with cognition and learning difficulties	3-14.1	Support pupils with cognition and learning difficulties	8
		3-14.2	Help pupils with cognition and learning difficulties to develop effective learning strategies	8
3-15	Support pupils with behavioural, emotional and social development needs	3-15.1	Support the behaviour management of pupils with behavioural, emotional and social development needs	8
		3-15.2	Help pupils with behavioural, emotional and social development needs to develop relationships with others	8
		3-15.3	Help pupils with behavioural, emotional and social development needs to develop self-reliance and self-esteem	8
3-16	Provide support for pupils with sensory and/or physical impairment	3-16.1	Enable pupils with sensory and/or physical impairment to participate in learning activities	8
		3-16.2	Implement structured learning programmes for pupils with sensory and/or physical impairment	8
3-17	Support the use of information and communication technology in the classroom	3-17.1	Prepare ICT equipment for use in the classroom	10
		3-17.2	Support the use of ICT equipment	
3-18	Help pupils develop their literacy skills	3-18.1	Help pupils develop their reading skills	12
		3-18.2	Help pupils develop their writing skills	12
		3-18.3	Help pupils develop their speaking and listening skills	12
3-19	Help pupils develop their numeracy skills	3-19.1	Help pupils to develop their understanding and use of number	13
		3-19.2	Help pupils to understand and use shape, space and measures	13
3-20	Help pupils to access the curriculum	3-20.1	Provide literacy support to help pupils access the curriculum	12
		3-20.2	Provide numeracy support to help pupils access the curriculum	13
3-21	Support the development and effectiveness of work teams	3-21.1	Contribute to effective team practice	3, 4
		3-21.2	Contribute to the development of the work team	3, 4
3-22	Develop and maintain working relationships with other professionals	3-22.1	Work effectively with other professionals	4
		3-22.2	Maintain effective working relationships with other professionals	4
3-23	Liaise effectively with parents	3-23.1	Share information with parents about their children	4
		3-23.2	Share the care of children with their parents	4

should have cross-referenced the performance criteria to indicate where one activity can show evidence for competence in several units.

As this is a reference book, you need not read it page by page, but use the index to find what you need, read that bit, do any associated activities and make any notes for your own future reference. Discuss the reading with others in the school or on your course and remember anything you feel is important to use in your daily work. Chapter 2 starts from you, and following some of the ideas in that chapter will immediately give you evidence for a unit in the standards.

It is essential that all that you do in school fits in with school policy and culture, and that you play your part as a member of staff. So the book starts with the importance of relationships, particularly with the pupils, and then looks at the importance of being part of a team. It deals with whole-school issues – the policies and procedures which will underpin your work. It examines in some depth aspects of children's development which affect their learning and looks at supporting pupils, firstly in general and then those with special educational needs (SEN) and those for whom English is an additional language (EAL). Later chapters consider how what you do will support teachers in the classroom and particular aspects of the curriculum. You will need access to specialist texts for guidance on supporting pupils with special needs or specific curriculum areas.

There are some activities for you to try, some lists of questions, suggestions for resources or areas of study, and these are set out in boxes. Some of the examples of practice are fictional, but all of them are based on good practice that I have seen in the many schools I have worked in or visited. Even where the stories are factual, all the names have been changed to preserve the participants' anonymity. After you have tried out the ideas for yourself, you will begin to recognise other examples of good practice within your own school and should begin to write scenarios of your own.

Questions to ask yourself as you start

- To whom can you turn in school to act as a mentor while you read this book and/or study for a Level 3 qualification?
- With whom can you discuss issues outside the school, bearing in mind the need for confidentiality?
- Where might you find further reading or study materials in your locality?
- Is there a local group or network to which you can belong?
- What do you know about the practices of and around TAs in other schools?
- What do you know about national initiatives and associations which could support you in your job?
- Who can tell you about local courses and qualifications and whether you can get financial help, or advise you on career and professional development?
- What does the local education authority (LEA) provide? Where are the local colleges?

Essential reading

LGNTO (2001) *Teaching/Classroom Assistants National Occupational Standards.* London: Local Government National Training Organisation.

Some further reading

DfEE (1998a) *Teachers Meeting the Challenge of Change* (Green paper). London: DfEE.

DfEE (2000a) *Working with Teaching Assistants: A Good Practice Guide.* London: DfEE.

DfES (2002a) *Developing the Role of School Support Staff* (Consultation DfES/0751/2002). London: Department for Education and Skills.

DfES (2002b) *Time for Standards* (Proposals DfES/0751/2002). London: Department for Education and Skills.

DfES and TTA (2003) *Standards for Higher Level Teaching Assistants: Consultation Document April 2003.* London: Department for Education and Skills and Teacher Training Agency.

Ofsted (2002) *Teaching Assistants in Primary Schools: An Evaluation of the Quality and Impact of their Work* (HMI 434). London: Ofsted.

Useful website

www.lg-employers.gov.uk

2 | Starting with yourself – continuous personal and professional development

Study skills

Whatever your intentions, whether you want to take an accredited course, eventually train to be a qualified teacher, or just consolidate your position as a really good TA, you must consider yourself as a learner, continually developing. This may even be written into your job description. You need to develop ways of personal organisation, reviewing your experiences to date, addressing any wishes or needs for development and developing or honing your study skills. There is more detail about study skills in the Level 2 book (Watkinson 2003). A Level 3 qualification will require some sustained study at an advanced level. You should be able to read through your own work and be critical, not only of content but also of style and use of vocabulary. You should be developing a breadth of educational vocabulary and use some of the jargon with understanding. Make notes as you read; small 'Post-its' are very useful to mark pages you want to come back to, or quote, rather than pencil underlining.

When you read:

Do you understand what the passage/chapter/book is about?
Think why a particular passage attracts your attention.
Does it ring true with something in your experience?
Make a note of your experience as well as a note of the thought in the reading.
Do you disagree with the comments? Then think why.
Do you want to talk with someone else about an aspect of what you have read?
Will it change what you do in your work at school, how you behave or what you think of certain practices? Why? How?

Keeping materials together

You need a ring binder accompanied by card pocket files to collect things together – a portfolio. Do construct a personal file for yourself if you do not have one already, with a section for your personal details and a section for your school's details. Use later sections for your progress in your job and any procedure of review within your school. Any course of study will need its own file, and any accreditation process will need a separate one which will be submitted to the assessors or examiners. Material can be photocopied from your personal file or a course file, if it is relevant to the accreditation you are seeking. Just remember, you cannot be assessed on materials which you have obtained from elsewhere, handouts or photocopies of pages from books, as these are the work of other people, unless you annotate them with notes about how these points are relevant to you.

Do ensure, if you put any notes regarding pupils in your portfolio, that you anonymise or depersonalise them; that is, you should refer to the pupil by a fictitious name or just a letter. This also applies to any references to pupils or people in any assignments which you undertake. Keep a diary or notebook with these thoughts from the beginning. When you are looking for evidence, photocopy the page, highlight the relevant passage and put a reference to the NOS unit, element and section or a qualification item reference in the margin. This book is set out in that fashion, the bracketed numbers referring to the 2001 NOS (LGNTO 2001). For example, by having details of the main roles and responsibilities within your school and filling in section 2 of a personal file you would have evidence for Unit 4 element 1, underpinning knowledge point iv, set out in this book as [4.1:iv]. All the induction materials are matched to the NOS at Levels 2 and 3, and the resultant mapping can be found on the DfES resources website (www.teachernet.gov.uk/teachingassistants).

Personal qualities

Knowing yourself, your experiences, expertise, strengths and weaknesses and how this can all be used to make a contribution to your school is found in three places in the NOS [8.1:8; ix & x]. In the section below on review, you need to reflect on this list and consider your strengths and weaknesses and whether you can make any changes.

Some things to consider:

- Sensitivity to others, their feelings, aspirations, what interests them and what makes them work better, whether it is pupils or other staff, will enable you to enhance their strengths as well as developing your own.
- Empathy with the situation of others, especially for all those who are learning – staff and pupils: you should be a learner yourself.
- Respect for others' beliefs and background, a commitment to the school in which you are employed.
- Having an outgoing personality, without dominating, which enables you to make friends, share ideas and contribute to the teams within the school.

- Having interpersonal skills, accepting pupils and people even if their behaviour is unacceptable; knowing how to be assertive without being aggressive, express yourself without being unpleasant, have your say without being rude (watch out for eye contact, posture, voice control and hand gestures; they can all indicate your feelings).
- Being approachable or available means that people will look to you to help – the essence of your job [3.1:5].
- Being comforting to those in distress (note: there are ways of doing this appropriately; see the section on child protection in Chapter 7).
- Being able to go one step further than that required in any job always 'oils the wheels' of the organisation, accepting reasonable challenges.
- Having good manners, a careful and responsible attitude to the job not only sets a good example to pupils but shows that you are someone who understands the importance of education and caring for others; avoid blaming people.
- Patience will be needed when working with slower children and kindness for those who are struggling.
- Developing the intrapersonal skills of self-awareness, appropriate self-confidence, reflection, contemplation, compromise.
- Developing creativity, enabling yourself and others to innovate, encouraging independence in others, particularly pupils.
- Recognising stress in yourself or others, developing the ability to cope with it or seek help.

You also need to know your academic qualities, what kind of learner you are and what you do not know and need to find out about. You need to recognise your own skills and levels of knowledge and understanding, and what of these is needed to fulfil your appointed role [4.1:1]. You must understand how your own experiences and achievement contribute to those of others [4.1:2]. Knowing yourself also includes knowing 'how to maintain your own health and safety' when dealing with pupils and 'your own capabilities to deal with an emergency' [10.2:vi]. It is your responsibility to share any health problems you have that might affect your work with your line manager, and that applies to emotional problems as well [10.3:vi; 11.2:x & 3:viii].

Professional knowledge

The school

You need details of the place in which you work, the context for your job, and you must understand the principles which underlie effective communication and collaboration [8.2:i]. You have to work within the legal context of the school and the school's own policies. You should familiarise yourself with all the main roles and responsibilities within the school and how you fit into any hierarchy. Figure 2.1 shows a possible primary school hierarchy. Since the pupil learners are the main purpose of the establishment, instead of looking at the

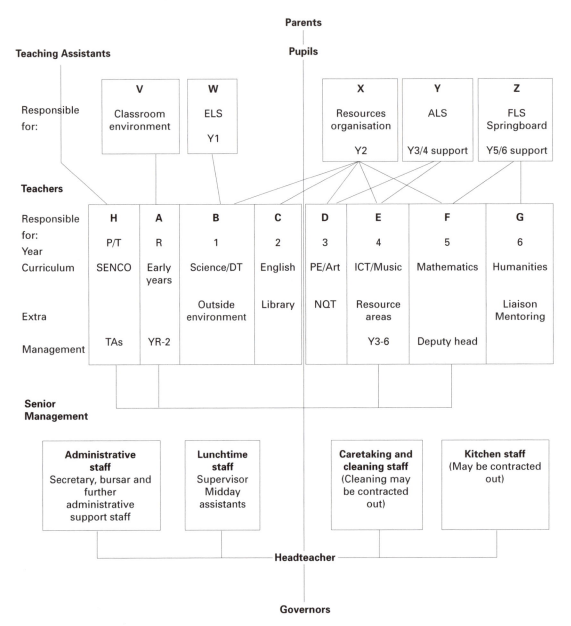

Figure 2.1 A possible primary school responsibility tree

headteacher as top of the pile this example puts the pupils at the top. It clearly shows the potential complexity of the responsibility routes.

Secondary schools have a variety of management structures for TAs. Most have been traditionally organised through the SEN department, with TAs working directly with individual pupils under the SEN coordinator (SENCO). More recently, the wider role of TAs being recognised, some schools have allocated TAs to each subject department, with liaison routes through the SENCO. A few schools have allocated their TAs to year groups, hoping to get the best of both worlds; the SEN and the curriculum support. It remains to be seen how these variations work out in practice.

Compile a responsiblity tree for your own school [4.1:iv]

Find out who the senior managers are and for what are they responsible.
Who has responsibility for:
    Leading each NC subject, religious education (RE), personal, social and health education (PSHE), and citizenship?
    SEN – does the SENCO and what that entails line manage all the TAs? If not, who does?
    Pastoral care of pupils?
    Gifted and able pupils?
    Maintaining the various resource areas such as the library, the information and communication technology (ICT) equipment, the outside study areas, the reception area and displays?
    Clubs or extra-curricular activities?
    Health, safety and security?
Who represents the staff on the governing body, especially the support staff?
Who liaises with visiting therapists, community leaders, local businesses, other local schools, pre-schools or colleges?
Who runs the parents' association (assuming there is one)?

Your job

Your job description should state what you are required to do to support pupils, teachers, the school and the curriculum; to whom and for what you are responsible; and what the school will do to support you. It is important that you understand your job description as to where your responsibilities start and finish [4.1:iii; 4.1:2:iii]. It should define not only your direct role but also your role and responsibilities with regard to health, safety and security and there is much more about this in later chapters [10.1:iii]. You should always be working under the direction of a teacher, whether or not that teacher is actually present in the room with you. The final responsibility for the learning of the pupils in the school is that of a qualified teacher, whether or not you have planned the activity, prepared the materials, carried out the task and fed back what happened; whether or not it is decided that you can liaise directly with the parent, or contribute to an assessment report on the pupil. Several of the standards refer to you working within the limitations of your knowledge, understanding and skills, or within the limits of your job description. It is important that you know yourself and your capabilities and do not try to undertake more than you can do, and that you only undertake things for which you have been made responsible. Nevertheless, it is hoped that you are intelligent and at Level 3 can use your initiative where appropriate. If you feel this involves more than you were originally employed for, talk with your line manager. In most cases senior staff will be delighted when people offer to do more, but it could be that it is actually someone else's job already, or it is inappropriate for reasons which only they can see. People working at Level 3 competence, with such jobs specified in their job description, should be paid more than those working at Level 2 competence, who are contracted to do jobs with less responsibility. This may be a problem. With the new single status agreements made between the LEA as employers and the unions, grades of pay should be clearly matched to levels of responsibility. Ask questions if you are troubled about any of this, but beware; depending on the personnel history in your school, you could be opening up a 'can of worms'.

In looking at your own job description and the responsibility tree you have drawn up, see where your role lies in respect to others and track how any one person contributes to the learning of pupils [8.2:ii]. For some this will be direct and obvious – for those of you who work in the classroom in lessons with the pupils – but for some roles in school it will seem less obvious. Some of you will be midday assistants as well as TAs and will quickly realise, as you learn more about school curricula and how pupils learn, that midday assistants contribute greatly in two particular areas. One is the obvious one, that of enabling those in direct contact with pupils in class to have a well-earned break and come back to afternoon school refreshed and prepared; but the other is that in helping pupils with table manners, socialising, cooperating, sometimes emotional traumas or physical mishaps, or enabling them to understand fair play, taking turns, using game rules, you are enabling pupils to learn life skills, crucial in their development and ability to make the most of their classroom experiences. Without site managers and cleaners, the learning environment would soon deteriorate; without office staff, the teachers could not cope with the outside world and thus would not be able to teach (any small school headteacher with class responsibility and few administrative hours will affirm this with feeling!).

Often standards or job descriptions talk of 'appropriate' support or help. You have to find out what this means for you in your situation, by asking. Too often in the past things have been left to people's intuition, but it need not be so. Explicit instructions can be given and do help to prevent misunderstandings.

Self-review

Part of your responsibility as an adult is that you are now responsible for your own development. You not only want to do your best as a basically competent TA, but you want to develop to be recognised for your experience and advanced competencies [4.1:i]. It is up to you to decide what you want to do, what responsibilities you want to take on in future and what you need to do to maintain your present circumstances, if that is where you wish to be. This self-analysis is part of being employed, and needs to be updated regularly [4.2:3]. There are many mothers over the last forty years who have come through the playgroup movement since its inception, to help in schools, to be employed in schools and find they are capable of taking not only basic examinations but degree courses and going on to become teachers, even headteachers. There are others who recognise such pathways are not for them; they realise the work involved, the academic strengths needed, the responsibility and time involved in such development are too great; in their words they just want to be a good TA. An acronym that is used commonly is that you undertake a SWOT analysis – looking at your Strengths and Weaknesses, but also reflecting on your Opportunities and any Threats which would prevent your development.

You can complete a checklist such as that below and add it to your personal professional portfolio [4.1:v].

Constituents of the self-review:

- Successes and appreciation from others
- Job satisfaction and lack of it – fulfilling your existing job description
- Relationships with pupils, colleagues and others associated with the school
- Understanding of the learning process and special educational needs
- Teaching skills and contribution to the learning objectives of the teachers
- Relevant curriculum knowledge and understanding
- Contributions to pastoral and physical care and behaviour management
- Understanding of and contributions to school life
- Professional development opportunities taken: training, courses, meetings attended, personal study undertaken, in school or out of school
- Setting and achieving of any personal targets
- Areas for change, development or improvement – adjustments to job description, and career development issues or ideas. (Watkinson 2002: 85).

Compare what you do and think with the thoughts of others and formulate a concept of good practice [4.1:4].

The above paragraphs assume that all goes smoothly in career development, whether moving upwards or expanding understanding at a desired level. Of course, this is not always so. Sometimes you will make mistakes, your relationships with other staff could become sour or difficult, or personal circumstances intervene in work-based situations – you may have a bereavement or other emotional problems, you may have developed a serious illness, or a close member of the family has, or you could have money problems. You may just find that the demands being put upon you are too great for your ability. You might feel you need more communication about something – this is quite common for support staff, as historically they were left out of staff meetings. Whatever the problem, you need to think whom to tell and share it with, or what you can do about it [4.2:4]. Letting relationships fester is no solution. Coping with domestic problems beyond your control will be sympathetically listened to; ideas for improving the working practices in which you are involved should be listened to, provided you are tactful and constructive.

Also, circumstances change, and alter what you are capable of [4.1:6]. Having children dependent on you makes a lot of difference to your time commitments. If you have a family, they do grow up and may release you to undertake more responsibility or a new course. This means you have to review your personal objectives [4.2:5]. Not only that, the educational scene is constantly changing with new initiatives, ideas for teaching and learning, new resources. The school circumstances may change. The building of a new estate in your neighbourhood can radically alter not only the number of pupils attending the school, but also the nature of the background of those pupils. The installation of a new industry or the closing of a large factory can create all sorts of problems as well as opportunities for different qualities in staff. The arrival of one new pupil with particular SEN can alter the opportunities for yourself.

Case study

Margaret, a TA in a small village primary school, had started work in the school as a volunteer when her children started school. She loved the job and showed capability and enthusiasm. When the opportunity to pay Margaret for a few hours a week came, she was taken on the staff. A young girl started at the school, Jane, who was a wheelchair user. Jane needed 'full time' (25 hours a week) cover in order that her physical needs could be catered for. Margaret was offered the job. By that time her own children were old enough to enable her to undertake these longer hours. Jane later needed first an electric typewriter to help her write and then a laptop computer. Margaret had been a typist before her marriage, and adapted the reading scheme words to a typing tutor and taught Jane proper keyboard skills at a time when the other pupils were learning to use a pencil. She taught herself computer skills. As soon as any courses became available for TAs she asked to go on them, particularly ones with special needs included in them. She even asked to go on courses which were supposed to be for teachers, and with the cooperation of the school and the tutors did so, to the benefit of all concerned. Later, as Jane got older, Margaret had to decide whether she would go on to Jane's secondary school with her or change her job. She decided her village and family affiliations came first, and also that Jane's need for independence would be best served by her having various adult carers, not just one. While this meant changes in Margaret's role, becoming a general TA rather than one with SEN specialities, Margaret started to organise the school's ICT resources and became an invaluable trouble shooter and source of expertise. She never went on to higher education, of which she was quite capable, deeming herself 'too old' (her words!). In her retirement she promised herself to undertake a GCSE course in mathematics, understanding of which she felt she was lacking.

Being a reflective practitioner

Pollard (2002) in his book *Reflective Teaching*, explores many ways for teachers to look at their own practice. While much of the book is unnecessary for a TA there are some useful bits to read. Some schools have a copy of this in the staffroom or a teacher may have one. Just read the first chapter and the beginning page of the other chapters. The first page of each chapter is a diagram showing the contents of the chapter. Some of these sections may interest you to read or even follow up with your mentor or class teacher. The author believes Dewey's characteristics of 'reflective action', as distinct from 'routine action', can be applied to teaching. These are:

1. an active concern with the intention and consequence of your actions;
2. your action (or teaching) is a cyclical or spiral process, where you continually monitor, evaluate and revise your practice;
3. the need to develop competence;
4. attitudes of open-mindedness (listening to others), responsibility, and whole-heartedness (energy and enthusiasm);
5. judgement and insight;
6. collaboration and dialogue which lead to professional development and personal fulfilment;
7. an ability to be creative with materials or frameworks developed by others.

Barber (1996: 181) says,

Information on its own is nothing. Information only provides access to power when it is linked with reason and thought. For information to be useful, people must make selections from it. To connect diverse strands of it together, to ask intelligent questions of it and to reject parts of it which, though they are there on the screen, in the book or on the paper, appear inaccurate. Even then, thought and information need to be linked in a chain of reasoned argument.

Developing a questioning attitude, making connections, arguing with reasons all takes a bit of practice. It is not about being argumentative or confrontational for the sake of it.

Developing a constructively critical view

- Try reading the same account of an event in two different daily newspapers, preferably broadsheets rather than tabloids. Formulate your own views on the subject, then look at their editorials and see how they have slanted their views and see if you agree with them – or not.
- When you next watch a film or a play, think about it afterwards. Why do you like it? What did you not like – the story, the acting, the location, the length? Would you recommend someone to go and see it and why? What would you do differently if you made the film?
- If you have the time(!) you could join a book reading group. They usually meet once a month, after all reading the same book, and discuss just these sorts of question. Ask at your local library if you are interested in this kind of thing.

A reflective practitioner examines their learning, achievement and aspirations, identifies areas for development, undertakes research and can justify their actions and conclusions. This is hard and it really helps if you have another view on your practice and people with whom to discuss your ideas and feelings [4.1:vi]. Use the NOS and any other models from your reading or experience to compare with your ideas and actions [4.1:ii]. A review of your practice against what is required in your job description is an appraisal, sometimes called a professional development review. If such a process does not seem to be the norm in your school, actively seek out other people to share and comment on your work [4.1:5].

Appraisal – involving others in feedback

Appraisal – or professional review – is a formal opportunity for TAs to discuss their performance and professional needs with their line manager. Appraisal is meant to be a dialogue, with the person appraised and the appraiser both contributing freely. Some (many?) TAs may not be familiar with this process, and it may need to be made clear in advance that an appraisal is not some form of one-way report delivered by the manager. The appraiser should clearly acknowledge what the TA does well, and provide an opportunity for the appraised to raise any problems or concerns that they may have about the way their job is developing or what they are expected to do.

(DfEE 2000a: 34)

Your appraisal is an opportunity to revisit the job description and see if it still applies. It is a time to assess your training needs and any queries you might have about performing at Level 3, having responsibilities that reflect your competence, and where you need to concentrate to gain evidence of further competence. It should be a time to discuss your self-review – you only have to share what you want to share with another person – and maybe decide which form of accreditation for any training you might undertake would be best suited to you and the school circumstances. You can also discuss what kind of contribution you could make to the life of the school, or any developments or initiative with which the school is involved [4.1:viii]. Any notes you have made in your personal/professional portfolio will be useful, and any records of training you have undertaken, meetings you have been to and thoughts you have had. If certain courses are agreed which mean you making changes to your timetable or not getting paid, both of you must take that into account. The school will also have priorities, particularly for their budget and may or may not be able to support you financially in any agreed process, but they should provide general support, opportunities and resources for any targets that you jointly set at the end of the appraisal dialogue. Together you can match your skills, knowledge and understanding and your potential for development against the school policies and objectives. The school will have a development plan (SDP) which will have set priorities for the year ahead and allocated funds to support them. It will also have to take account of any government initiatives or directions; for instance, the introduction of the National Literacy and Numeracy Strategies (NLNS) made considerable difference not only to schools but to the work of TAs [4.2:5]. National moves towards greater inclusion of those with special educational needs affected the use of TAs, resource provision and training opportunities, both in special schools and mainstream ones. You need to keep yourself informed of what is going on in your school, in the local education authority (LEA), and nationally [4.2:v]. Your personal objectives and school objectives have to be balanced [4.1:vii; 4.2:iv]. Also, you should agree a time to review those targets. The process is cyclical, probably on an annual programme [4.1:3].

Some schools recognise that equal opportunities in employment mean that if teachers are observed at work, so should support staff be. If this is done, you should be quite clear when it is happening, as should the class teacher in whose class you are working at the time. You should be able to see any notes made and discuss any comments at the dialogue time. The dialogue should be done in paid time, in a comfortable private place, even off the premises if you both agree. The only record of the meeting that should be made is when and where the observation and dialogue have taken place and any outcomes, targets or training programmes that are agreed. Appropriate targets are often described as being SMART: specific, measurable, achievable, realistic and time-bound [4.2:1]. Unrealistic vague targets, which could only be achieved after a lot of changes or considerable time, are useless.

While the school should provide this review system, you must take account of what is said about your performance, discuss any targets suggested for you constructively, and carry out any agreed programme to the best of your ability. You should keep a record of ideas and opportunities offered and those which you have come across [4.1:7]. Schools know it is in their own best interest to have highly competent and trained staff, and recognise the low pay scales on which many of you operate, so will help with fees if they can. The government Standards Fund allocated to school for training is for all staff, not just teachers. It is always worth discussing finance at your review.

Do also remember that you do not have to depend on your school line manager for personal or professional debate and support. Your school may have appointed a mentor for you within the school – someone to go to for such debate outside any formal review process. The class teacher with whom you feel greatest rapport may help; if you are on any course, the tutor is usually willing to discuss matters; if you are undertaking an NVQ assessment, the assessor should discuss your progress and ideas and plan ahead with you. Some courses, such as the Open University Specialist Teacher Assistant Certificate (OU STAC) course, formally pair students, and part of the course is set round visits to your paired colleague's school. Such pairing often creates lasting friendships as well as an opportunity for professional debate. When sharing information about your school, any staff or pupils, do remember to ensure that confidentiality is maintained.

Questions to ask yourself

- Do you have a personal professional portfolio? If not, construct one for yourself.
- Do you have an up-to-date job description? If not, why not?
- Have you had an appraisal? If not and you have worked in the school for more than a year, why not?
- Have you found out about the main roles and responsibilities of others in your school?
- What have you read lately? Did you share your comments on it with anyone?
- Why do you want to work with children or young people?
- What value systems do you adhere to? Are they the same as those of the school in which you work? Keep this in mind as you read further.

Essential reading

DfEE (2000a) *Working with Teaching Assistants: A Good Practice Guide*. London: DfEE.

Fox, G. (1998) *A Handbook for Learning Support Assistants*. London: David Fulton Publishers.

LGNTO (2001) *Teaching/Classroom Assistants National Occupational Standards*. London: Local Government National Training Organisation.

Some further reading

Balshaw, M. (1999) *Help in the Classroom*, 2nd edn. London: David Fulton Publishers.

Balshaw, M. and Farrell, P. (2002) *Teaching Assistants: Practical Strategies for Effective Classroom Support*. London: David Fulton Publishers. (Especially Chapters 7 and 12.)

Barber, M. (1996) *The Learning Game: Arguments for an Education Revolution*. London: Victor Gollancz.

DfEE (2000b) *Teaching Assistant File: Induction Training for Teaching Assistants*. London: Department for Education and Employment.

DfES (2001a) *Teaching Assistant File: Induction Training for Teaching Assistants in Secondary Schools*. London: Department for Education and Skills.

Freeman, R. and Meed, J. (1993) *How to Study Effectively*. London: National Extension College and Collins Educational Ltd.

Lorenz, S. (1998) *Effective In-class Support*. London: David Fulton Publishers.

Northledge, A. (1990) *The Good Study Guide*. Milton Keynes: The Open University.

Pollard, A. (2002) *Reflective Teaching: Effective and Evidence-informed Professional Practice*. London and New York: Continuum. (Especially Chapter 1.)

Watkinson, A. (2002) *Assisting Learning and Supporting Teaching*. London: David Fulton Publishers.

Watkinson, A. (2003) *The Essential Guide for Competent Teaching Assistants: Meeting the National Occupational Standards at Level 2*. London: David Fulton Publishers.

Useful websites

www.lg-employers.gov.uk
www.teachernet.gov.uk/teachingassistants

3 Relationships

The basic principles of good relationships

There are some principles which underlie good relationships whether they are professional or social: treating others as you would like to be treated, having respect for the other person or people in the relationship. They are built on a sensitivity to differences and an ability to make compromises and cooperate.

Effective relationships are helped by:

- a mutual accountability, whether doing the asking or being asked to complete a task of some kind;
- mutual trust;
- qualities such as punctuality, truthfulness, honesty, and reliability, building up the necessary trust;
- a recognition of your own mistakes – apologise and learn from them;
- effective communication [2.1:i; 8.2:i & 21.2:i]. This means not only listening, but also giving clear, appropriate and if possible unambiguous instructions or messages; even simple things like not mumbling when in doubt will help;
- being explicit (politely) about needs and misunderstandings; implicit messages can be misunderstood, causing hurt or delay. Write things down for yourself and others where you can, being as accurate and concise as possible;
- assertiveness without aggression;
- positive attitudes such as trying to see the good in people or pupils, trying to understand, smiling where you can; for instance, ask for things or give instructions in a positive not a negative manner;
- good manners – try to thank for things wherever possible, without being a 'creep';
- cooperation and collaboration rather than conflict [21.1:i] – although this does not mean always agreeing with others;
- avoidance of damaging conflict and unnecessary confrontation – aggression and attention seeking do not get the same results as cooperation;
- sharing problems, and not allowing worries to fester;

- common aims, objectives or goals – such as in a fundraising group, or a group trying to put on a play – which make people recognise the importance of burying differences to 'get the show on the road' [8.2:1];
- shared values or similar backgrounds;
- frequency of contact, helping people to get to know each other more, both what the common interests might be and what areas of potential disagreement there might be, and therefore how to avoid them;
- a lack of cliques, where groups of people become inward looking and exclusive;
- celebrating differences – the ability to speak more than one language, cook different dishes, have a differing style of dress or home furnishing, or read different books is something to be proud of, share or show an interest in.

Consider two relationships you know well, one a close relative and the other a work relationship. Look at each in the light of the above list.

- Are they different? How? [2.1:iv]
- Do you agree with the list?
- If not, where do you differ?
- Can you add to the list?

It is not important that all relationships conform with one person's list (mine or yours) but that you consider what makes things work well for you and what does not, then try to make them all work well.

Your relationships with the pupils in your care are crucial. Also, teamwork in schools is important; you cannot work in isolation, nor can other members of staff. You need to understand how your relationships with other members of staff enable the whole school to work better.

Take a copy of the organisational chart or tree of the school staff which you have built up from reading the previous chapter.

Circle the people with whom you come into contact daily, weekly and termly, even yearly, with different colours. This will give you an idea of where to concentrate your efforts in making sure relationships are effective.

Take two more colours and track the paths of your line management and accountability through the tree. Are they the same?

With whom do you have informal contact, and with whom do you have more formal meetings?

The climate and ethos of the school is largely reflected in the kind of relationships which develop. This climate is important in creating a learning environment which is supportive, and effective, not just operating in a shell of a building with paper policies. Leadership, not just from the headteacher but from all those who have responsibilities, sets the standards for how the school operates. The leaders can consult, supervise and show by example; they can respect others' contributions and delegate. You may be a leader in a small field for which you have responsibility, such as organising a resource area, or working with a group of pupils. What kind of leader are you? Collaborative cultures take more effort and time on the part of everyone in them, but have been found to produce more effective organisations. They prevent fragmentation of jobs and duplication, and this has a beneficial effect on pupils.

Learning and interpersonal intelligence

In the section on learning you will find more about the theory of multiple intelligences, suggested by Howard Gardner. He makes the case for human beings having different kinds of intelligence and nominates seven different types. Subsequent psychologists have suggested other dimensions than these seven. They are not discrete 'things' in the head but ways of thinking. Each of us has varying capabilities, and they are not fixed. We can recognise them, develop them and use them. Along with linguistic, musical, logico-mathematical, spatial, and bodily kinaesthetic Gardner proposes interpersonal and intrapersonal intelligences or skills or capabilities. These refer to our ability to relate to other people and to understand ourselves. By recognising what we find easy or hard – some people find music helpful when learning, some find mathematics and logic hard – we can see how to help our own ways of learning by utilising methods we find easy, or where we can concentrate effort on things we find difficult.

Having good interpersonal intelligence means that you find relationships with other people easy, you are sensitive to atmosphere and willing to cooperate or share [2.1:i & ii]. You may, however, be shy or have other traits which mean you find working with other people difficult. With the research that has been done on learning, following the ideas of multiple intelligences, have come ideas on how to recognise your strengths and weaknesses, and how aspects can be utilised or developed.

> Interpersonal intelligence makes use of core capacities to recognize and make distinctions among *others'* feelings, beliefs and intentions. Early in development, this intelligence is seen in the ability of young children to discriminate among the individuals in their environment and discern others' moods. In its most developed forms, interpersonal intelligence manifests itself in the ability to understand, act on and shape others' feelings and attitudes for good or otherwise.
>
> (Gardner *et al.* 1996: 211)

You can also see that interpersonal abilities need to utilise aspects of all the other 'intelligences'. They are, according to Smith (1996), highly developed in teachers, among others. To work in a school with pupils and the other staff, you will need to develop this area if you do not feel it is well developed in you already.

A person with a well developed interpersonal intelligence will enjoy paired and small group activities and collaborative learning. They will enjoy exercises which require looking at issues from a number of human perspectives, empathising, devising class rules – agreeing roles and responsibilities, interviewing adults other than teachers and participating in conflict management games.

(Smith 1996: 57)

Lazear (1994: 19), building on this concept of intelligences, gives some activities to help develop and use interpersonal skills:

Exercises to Stimulate Interpersonal Intelligence

- Get a partner to try to reproduce a complex shape or design you have drawn simply by describing how to make it. These are the rules: (1) Give verbal instructions only. (2) Your partner may not look at the drawing. (3) Your partner may ask you any question. (4) You may not look at what your partner is drawing.
- Explore different ways to express encouragement and support for other people (for example, facial expressions, body posture, gestures, sounds, words, and phrases).
- Practice giving encouragement and support to others around you each day.
- Practice listening deeply to someone who is expressing a view with which you disagree. Cut off the tendency to interpret what the person is saying and to express your own views. Force yourself to stay focused on what the person is saying. Try to paraphrase his or her thoughts to verify your own understanding.
- Volunteer to be part of a team and watch for positive and negative team behavior (positive team behavior includes the things that help the team work together and be successful; negative behavior includes the things that impair the team's efforts).
- Try disciplined people-watching, guessing what others are thinking and feeling, their backgrounds, professions, and so on, based on nonverbal clues (for example, dress, gestures, voice tone, colors, and so on). When possible (and appropriate!), check your accuracy with the person.

You can see that by practising some of these skills yourself, and with your family, and the pupils with whom you work, family life and decision making can be enhanced, and sophisticated proceedings such as school councils can result. Developing good interpersonal skills will enable your own personal and working life to be more fulfilled and help the pupils with whom you work to grow up into communicative, more confident adults [21.2:i]. You will be an effective team player and member of the school community.

Working with pupils

This has two aspects – your relationship with the pupils with whom you work, and your facilitation of their relationships with each other. It could develop into you listening and even advising them about their relationships with other adults or pupils outside the group, but this is really more about counselling. Some TAs are interested in this aspect of school work and undertake proper counselling training and are recognised by senior managers for these skills. The new proposals for support staff working with teachers include aspects of this work with pupils. It can be time consuming and challenging but very valuable if the pupils come from family circumstances where time is not made for anyone to listen to their concerns. Even if you are simply asked to run a circle time group you should still undertake appropriate training to ensure you do not make the situation worse.

When working with individual children your relationship with them is important. It should be a professional one, friendly, receptive to their ideas and suggestions, but enabling them to carry out the teacher's intentions. The aim is to increase the pupils' independence not their dependency on you [15.1:xi]. It feels good to be wanted and sometimes tempting to be a substitute parent or pal, but do keep a watch on this. Schools as a whole are *in loco parentis* but you must consider your personal purpose and role. Sometimes, that role includes carrying out intimate procedures for pupils, such as dealing with incontinence or menstruation. You must be familiar with the school's policies on child protection, confidentiality and health and safety. A pupil may, as a result of having a close relationship with you, reveal circumstances occurring out of school which may be quite harmless and interesting but could indicate matters which you should refer to someone else. Do read the child protection notes in Chapter 7 carefully if you have not studied them at Level 2.

It is interesting to consider how the pupils see you. Why not ask? You should be providing a role model for them, and for some pupils this may be different from their out-of-school relationships. This could be particularly important, for instance, if you are male and a pupil you are working with has a single-parent mum.

Considering the relationship you have with your pupils in groups is not necessarily about managing those groups. Check all the items mentioned above in thinking about relationships in general and apply them to the pupils you work with.

Good relationships with pupils [15.2:3]

Do you:

- listen to what they have to say [9.2:1; 15.3:1]?
- question them to explain more if you do not understand?
- try to see their point of view?
- give positive feedback and encouragement [8.2:vi]?
- facilitate their ability to contribute to a game or discussion?
- encourage them to cooperate when working in groups [9.1:1]?
- explain rules and how they can be observed?
- ensure each one in a group can take part appropriately, that each has a turn?
- enable the pupils to recognise and learn from their mistakes without losing face?
- make goals, aims or targets explicit and praise when they are reached [16.2:xiv]?
- look for similarities and celebrate differences?
- share joys and problems, yours and the pupils – establish rapport and understanding?
- look for opportunities to promote self-reliance, self-esteem and self-confidence [9.2:5; 15.3:2]?
- always show respect and good manners to all the pupils you work with?
- show a consistent and positive role model to the pupils in your relationships within the school [9.1:2 & v]?

You need to consider the age and stage of development of pupils when you are working with them. The stage may not be related to their learning ability or age, as home backgrounds and opportunities for seeing and participation in situations with good relationships will differ widely. The role models offered and the experiences of social behaviour will differ from family to family. Many children come from homes where games are not played, even simple card or board games. This is not necessarily a sign of a deprived home, for many wealthy parents are too busy with their jobs or social activities to spend time with their children. Having a different language from other pupils or yourself will inhibit communication, as will lack of appropriate vocabulary, which may be due to background or learning problems. The behaviour of others in a family or group can influence group dynamics and prevent good relationships developing. Peer pressure, members of the family needing or demanding attention through illness can divert adults in the family from giving attention where it should be; disruptive or even very noisy groups or family members can all influence the ways in which pupils develop their own interpersonal skills. Some pupils may have communication and interaction problems and need special help. Some of you may be working in speech and language units. The SENCO should be able to help you if there are pupils with SEN.

Photograph 1   Consulting the SENCO in the SEN resource area

Young children coming to school for the first time may have particular problems with relationships, and those changing schools, from a small rural primary to a large comprehensive, or from a school near home to one a bus ride away or even to a boarding school, will also be vulnerable. For these groups of children and young people it is about moving from the known surroundings to the unknown and from probably small, more intimate relationships to a much wider world. Young children are very self-centred, and see themselves as the link to everyone else, but a normal pupil at the end of Key Stage 2 has a much greater understanding of the 'give and take' of normal relationships. 'Only children' may find sharing and taking turns for adult attention more difficult than those from families with more children. Children with changing relationships between their parents or carers will have a different view of adult relationships from those from more stable backgrounds [15.2:2].

While this section is not focusing on sexual relationships or sex education, those of you working in secondary schools will be working with young people exploring this aspect of their lives, and may well have to deal with the results of sexual relationships, whether they are going well or not. If you have a close working relationship with a pupil, it may well be to you they bring their questions about sex and the problems of their love life. You do need to know the sex education policy of your school, whether you can enter into debates about HIV and AIDS or contraception, and where you should direct the older pupils for more specific advice.

There is some very useful material on the importance of working with children about their relationships in the *Health for Life* books, used in many primary schools for their health education materials. Book 2 (Williams *et al.* 1989: 260–3) gives some useful background on various developmental aspects of relationships and the emotions and feelings experienced by children aged 5 to 11 as explored in investigations of 22,603 children in 11 LEAs. This book also gives many pages of ideas for exploring feelings and relationships with Key Stages 1 and 2 pupils. You should not do these with pupils on your own, only as part of activities directed by a teacher, but there is much to make you think about how these difficult areas can be explored sensitively [9.3:2]. The book gives worksheets and questions for all these ages, and many of those for older primary children could be adapted for secondary pupils who are experiencing problems. They focus on five main areas – special people, friends and friendship, feelings, memories and growing up, and special places [9.3:iv].

Take every opportunity to play games of all sorts, in play activities in class with little ones, in the playground or as part of group activities. They help explain the purpose of rules, taking turns and competing without becoming aggressive. Just spending time talking with a pupil or group of pupils can be productive; communication is vital to good relationships. If pupils are not used to this – leading solitary lives with their own television, videos and computers, not participating in family meal times – they have to develop the skills needed [9.1:iii; 9.2:1]. The popularity of texting and chat rooms may well be explained by the lack of personal communication in homes [15.2:1; 18.3:6].

Also consider the environment in which you are working or playing with pupils. Noise, space, comfort, even lighting can all create a sense of well-being or anxiety. Hunger or disruption can affect what you are doing. You cannot influence the pupils' backgrounds or what is going on outside school to make them behave well towards each other, but you can listen and try to understand [9.1:iv]. They may be being bullied on the way home or even abused at home. Even if you live in the community and know the family, it is not your place to interfere at that level. If you have concerns, you must share them with a teacher, even the named teacher for child protection if you feel your knowledge warrants it [9.3:4]. You are a member of the school staff; you must be guided by the school protocols and policies, particularly regarding confidentiality [9.3:5]. Sometimes you need time to get pupils' confidence, but do ensure that you are not creating a dependency which is detrimental to the long-term independence of the pupils concerned. Relationships of all kinds have to be built but also sustained. All the factors that prevent the development of interpersonal skills before you meet the pupils could affect your relationships [2.1:ix].

Looking at group dynamics

Ask for a time to observe a group at work on a collaborative task or playing.
Draw a map of where each member of the group is standing or sitting.
Then for a period of ten minutes or a quarter of an hour

Either: make a list of members and tally when each member speaks

Or: draw a line on your map each time someone speaks, showing the line of communication

Or: tape-record the conversation, noting who is speaking each time so that you can transcribe the tape later

Or: look out for all the incidence of non-verbal communication.

- Did any one person dominate? Why?
- Did anyone not contribute at all? Why?
- Was there any off-task activity or discussion? Why?
- Did any outside things influence what was going on?
- Did it matter where the group members were placed?
- Did the group break into any sub-groups? Why? Did it help the task?
- What sort of intervention, if any, would have made things work better?
- Was it an appropriate activity for group work?

Relationships with teachers – partnership

The relationship between you and the teacher in whose class you are working is a working relationship which may even become a friendship. The teacher takes the responsibility and it may seem at first glance to be a boss–worker or power relationship. They just tell you what to do and you get on with it. You will have been working long enough in schools to realise that this is a very superficial way of viewing how you need to work together. Nevertheless, it is important that you take time to make the working relationship a human relationship; teachers and TAs should form a partnership based on understanding each others' roles, purposes and limitations. You need to talk with and listen to the teachers you work with, spend out-of-class contact time with them, if only in the corridor on the way to or leaving a lesson. Normal chat about the weather, families, homes or hobbies can cement relationships and prove to each partner that the other is human. The school should allow you to use the same staffroom as the teachers, although this is occasionally a problem where space is at a premium. Similarly, cloakrooms, toilet areas, car parks all provide common ground for beginning conversations. On top of this, the school should ensure that you both have non-class contact time to discuss curriculum matters and pupils' needs properly, to plan together what needs to be done.

You will find, even in the same school, that each teacher has their own characteristics, and you as a TA are likely to work with several in a week, and possibly even in a day. Many schools have realised that allowing the teacher and TA continuous time together, even in some cases allocating one TA per class in a primary school, has a beneficial effect on working relationships. On the other hand, varied experiences and working with different adults can increase your understanding of the different ways of tackling similar problems, giving you a range of ideas of how to operate. You must be seen to be an example of good working relationships not only by any assessor for a Level 3 accreditation but also by the pupils, for they will note subconsciously that this is how grown-ups work together, resolve their problems and hopefully enjoy their time together [9.1:2].

Whatever you do in school should be under the direction of a qualified teacher [8.1:iii]. The status conferred on them by their qualifications does mean taking responsibility for the learning of pupils whether in a class or a subject. You will often find yourself doing tasks that include teaching or working with a small group out of the sight of the class teacher. Whatever the situation, however, that teacher still takes responsibility for the progress of the pupils and ensuring that your role with them is as effective as possible. This can create tensions with the teacher; either you feel underused or you are given more responsibility than you feel comfortable with. The new regulations proposed for using support staff to relieve the teachers' workload (DfES 2002b) indicate that, whatever level you are working at, there will still be supervision of your work, and ultimate responsibility for teaching and learning of pupils will be with the teacher. The main problem seems to lie where communication and relationships with the teacher under whom you are working are not good. It takes two to make a partnership, even where one is in charge, so part of the responsibility for making this work for the good of the pupils is with you [8.2:4]. Do make time to discuss any problem or concern with the relevant person. It could be to do with your job description, the space you have been allotted to keep your things, your timetable or contract, or the pupils or materials with which you are working. If there is a real problem you must seek out your line manager, and if that is the same person then a senior manager or headteacher.

The case studies which Lacey (2001) quotes are taken from a study which she undertook of learning support assistants (LSAs) in special schools. Read the chapter about teacher and TA partnerships (pp. 100–12). She concludes (p. 112) by saying

> The partnerships between teachers and assistants that are effective, have to struggle in the face of many adversities. When they work, the partners are supportive of each other and of the children. They have sufficient time to plan and evaluate how best to work as well as efficient systems for communications ... This partnership appears to be built upon mutual respect and trust, support of each other and a shared understanding of how to meet pupils' learning needs. It is underpinned by clear lines of communication, commitment to providing planning time and the security of a permanent job supported by a career structure and relevant training. Nothing less is sufficient.

If you work with children who have severe or profound and multiple learning difficulties (SLD or PMLD) or work in a special school you will find the report *On a Wing and Prayer* (Lacey 1999) also very helpful reading. She (Lacey 2001: 103) gives an audit for partners wishing to look at how they spend their time together, developed by a group of teachers and assistants:

- Estimate how much time you spend together planning, reporting back, in meetings and in children's reviews in an average week.
- Make a note of the sort of topics covered.
- Gather together any planning and record sheets you use. Describe your roles in specific lessons.
- Estimate how long you spend on different parts of your roles (just the bits that are to do with working together, e.g. how long the teacher spends on writing plans for LSAs, or how long LSAs spend on filling in record sheets).
- Estimate how much time is spent on unplanned activities (e.g. a sick child).
- Estimate how much time LSAs spend not actually supporting anyone (e.g. teacher-led activity when LSAs are listening, but are not actually supporting an individual or a group).
- Estimate how much time LSAs feel that they are 'teaching' (e.g. rephrasing something in the lesson; asking questions to make children think; explaining why they have got something wrong).
- Estimate how much time LSAs are supporting individuals or groups (e.g. keeping a child on task; pointing out the different steps of a task).
- Estimate how much time LSAs are supporting the teacher (e.g. 'controlling' disruptive pupils; conveying to the teacher when pupils don't understand or need a different approach).

Estimating how much time is spent on different aspects of the work of LSAs can help in the joint reflection of how to develop the effectiveness of that work.

You will need to discuss certain basic things with each class teacher with whom you work about the boundaries of your roles in their room [8.1:viii; 22.1:i]. You may be inferior in terms of academic qualifications, although this is not always so. Whatever your and the teacher's backgrounds are, you can contribute to the partnership; it is not a one-way process, and I am not referring to feeding back after lessons. You will have differing life experiences as well as previous or current work experiences. Many newly qualified teachers (NQTs) lean heavily on their TA to find their way around the conventions of a school, which everyone but them seems to know about. You have to be tactful, but that is the essence of promoting good relationships: a sensitivity to know when and where and how to say things so that they help and do not upset [22.1:2 & 22.2:i].

Another useful way of looking at the partnership is that described in the development of mentoring between a more experienced teacher and a trainee. Maynard and Furlong (1995) talk of the transition from 'apprenticeship', or the collaborative model where all you need to do is work alongside an experienced practitioner, through the 'competency model' where you get systematic training, to the 'reflective' where you and the teacher switch from focusing on your or their skills to a focus on the learning of the pupils and what is best for them. You and the teacher become 'co-enquirers'. Clearly, such a partnership is developmental and based on those elements of trust, respect and common aims talked about at the beginning of this chapter [22.1:1].

You have to be reliable in carrying out your part of the partnership; you should be punctual, accurate in relating anything which you have observed or heard, undertaking only those tasks which you understand and can do [22.1:3 & ii]. If you say you will make something, or find something or make contact with others, then you should do it or immediately let the teacher know if circumstances intervene to prevent you. A phrase often used when promising to do things is to remember your 'yes' is only as good as your 'no'; only promise what you can carry out, otherwise refuse.

Your relationships with the teachers with whom you work are not just important for your and their sense of well-being, or even for the direct enhancement of learning strategies for the pupils, but your mutual personalities and compatibility will affect the atmosphere in the room. Make yourself aware of possible signs of tension, particularly when working with a teacher new to you. You are the 'additional adult' and many teachers were trained and became experienced in an era when TAs did not exist. Sometimes teachers feel exposed to view by having another adult in the room, and they can feel their role is threatened if you seem to 'take over' parts of the lesson even with some pupils. Your demeanour – say, a grim face if you have a headache – can influence how the teacher perceives the partnership. They could feel they would be better off without you! Respect and good manners mean you should be quiet and quieten your group if the teacher addresses the class. If you feel there are problems, talk about them.

Think of two partnerships which you know well, one good and one which seems weak. They could be from a marriage, a business, people who enter games together such as tennis or bridge, or who go on holiday together.

- Can you list their characteristics against the list at the beginning of this chapter?
- Does the weakness affect the second partnership's function?
- What could they change to improve the partnership?
- What is stopping them?
- What is it about the first partnership that makes it work so well?
- Do any of these thoughts affect your school working relationships?

Being part of a team

You may be part of a TA team as well as the whole-school team, particularly in a special school or a secondary school, where the numbers are larger. Even in the smallest schools now there are several TAs, so you are likely to be part of such a group. You may be part of an SEN team or a subject team in a secondary school, or even a year group team, such as the Early Years team. This means you can form relationships with people who may have similar problems and joys to yourself and probably similar training needs, at least where supporting your particular school is concerned. You will also be part of a large group called support staff (hopefully not 'non-teaching staff' as you do teach and you are not a non-anything).

Teams are not just groups of people working together; they have common aims and purposes and in schools if the group can meet, communicate and have good relationships they will achieve a consistency of practice [21.2:7]. It means teaching methods and discipline will be consistent and not confusing for pupils. It means individual pupil needs can be shared and problems aired, where all the team members have respect for and trust each other and observe proper codes of confidentiality [21.1:2 & 9]. Teams need members to play an active part, to speak openly and honestly, to know when to put themselves forward for tasks and when to take instructions from others. This takes thought and sometimes patience or initiative. An ideal team person can listen, yet contribute when they have something to say or do, and help others achieve their tasks [13.1:iii; 15.1:iii; 16.1:iii; 16.2:1; 21.1:6; 21.2:v]. Each has their role to play in a team, has individual characteristics and strengths of use to the team purpose [21.1:ii & v; 21.2:ii]. As people are different, from differing backgrounds and experiences, there will be a range of possibilities within the group. If you consider what you can contribute, try to find out what the others can contribute as well, and how this can make things go more smoothly [21.1:iii; 21.2:iii & 6]. In order for the team to work, they do need to meet from time to time, ensure they understand what they are trying to achieve, learning more about the methods needed to achieve it and review the relevance of this to their day-to-day working practices. Lacey (2001: 58) suggests that 'what is needed is a combination of the best long term personal education with the relevance of institution based projects, with particular help for participants in transferring learning to practice'.

Examples of good practice

A team of TAs in a primary school met for half an hour every Wednesday morning during assembly as well as informally in the staffroom. It was they who suggested using a common feedback form in every class for the teacher, as they went into different classes from time to time. The teachers were highly delighted and the ICT literate TA produced the trial templates for the whole school to use.

Another primary school TA team met every half-term with the head, and then had the odd meeting with the SENCO. They so enjoyed these meetings they asked for a regular weekly session. They determined together what the agenda for such a meeting could be and the head allocated financial resources to support these meetings after school. As they had been in the habit of voluntarily helping the teachers clear up at the end of some days, they found they could manage their family circumstances for a short time once a week to ensure they could attend the meetings. The head considered the financial outlay well worth the cost in terms of increased team sprit and professional development.

Learning together had welded the team and enhanced the learning opportunities for the pupils.

TAs in a secondary school had been appointed over the years to address individual pupils' needs. The SENCO had always line-managed the team successfully but began to realise that, as the team grew, so did the expectations of the teachers as to what they could be asked to do. She asked the TAs to discuss the problem. She was prepared to put in some extra training in curriculum areas and was already sounding out the heads of departments with the idea of having their input on the training. The idea came up of having the TAs more team based in subject areas, but she was reluctant to let go the SEN element of the team. The TAs pointed out that there could be up to three of them in one classroom with a teacher if the pupils with SEN happened to be setted together for certain subjects. The SENCO, again with discussion with her line manger, the TAs and the heads of department, decided on a full review of the systems of support. This entailed a review of job descriptions, resource base, training programmes and IEP fulfilment programmes. It took a year to complete, but the end result was a series of TA teams, each based with a subject department or group of them, and each having a team leader who met regularly with the SENCO to ensure individual pupil needs were met. Reviewing the strengths of the team members meant that each TA could be placed where they were most able to contribute, and each teacher got a support system addressing both the needs of the pupils and the classroom or laboratory circumstances. Parents were unhappy at first, because of the break-up of the individual attention for their child, but slowly they realised the benefits of the team approach.

There can be weak or difficult members of the team, and part of the strength of a group is that the stronger ones can support the weaker ones in times of stress. Each member can feed back to another when things have gone well [21.2:3]. It is up to the team leader to see that individuals pull their weight and are not continually carried by the rest. Being part of a team means that, if you are ill, there should be someone who can take over your work at short notice. You should always keep sufficient records, securely, preferably in a way decided by the team so that they can easily be interpreted and your work can be continued in your absence [21.1:4].

Sometimes differing personalities can cause conflict but differing opinions can be healthy, provided discussion is constructive [21.1:vi]. As a team member you need to speak your mind appropriately as well as listen to your colleagues and acknowledge their views [21.1:3]. You can see that, in the example given above, there could easily have been conflict if no one in the TA team wanted to work in a laboratory, or if the review had found some of the TAs were actually redundant, because of the doubling up in some lessons where it was not necessary. Such situations have to be handled sensitively, and within proper personnel guidelines to ensure that people are not hurt unnecessarily by potentially negative situations [21.1:viii]. You will probably have a team leader, and as a more experienced TA you may even become a leader of a small team. If so, this should be written into your job description, paid time given to you to perform what is required and the rate of pay commensurate with the responsibilities required of you. A team leader may have to take decisions and ensure that the rest of the team abide by them, or by decisions made by the team collegially [21.1:1]. The same procedures should apply to teams as to individuals; that is, if there is misunderstanding or even conflict which the group themselves cannot resolve, then the next in the hierarchy should become involved – your line manager if you are individually concerned [21.1:4 & 8]. As in any situation you should be honest and accurate in your dealings with superiors, not stretching the truth because you do not like someone. There will be reviews of the ways in which the team works, because circumstances have changed, the membership of the group or the needs of the pupils have changed, or there are new initiatives coming along. You can use this opportunity to share your ideas; as an experienced person you will have much to contribute and can help the group move forwards constructively [21:2:1 & 2].

Relationships within and between the school teams

The good practice guidance (DfEE 2000a) has a section about teachers and TAs working cooperatively and learning together, which requires meeting together largely outside the classroom and needs joint commitment and partnership. Another section looks at TAs' attendance at functions, the involvement of governors, parents and visiting advisers in liaising and linking with TAs, and liaison within the schools between relevant senior staff and TAs; and yet another is about meetings, liaisons and communication. All of these will require the understanding, funding and action of the senior management team. Although this document is meant for managers it is available free from the DfES and can be downloaded from their website (www.teachernet.gov.uk/teachingassistants).

An example of good practice

Five Trees Primary School has 10 classes and fields a team of 11 TAs. Many of the TAs were appointed for children with specific SEN, but the policy of the school has been for teachers to use them more widely in class, in order to encourage independent learning. In the early days of the Open University STAC course, two TAs undertook the year-long study. Such was the involvement of the teaching staff and the opportunities for communicating the content of the course both to teachers and TAs that each year another TA has been encouraged to undertake the course. The resultant staffroom discussion on academic and children's needs has to be heard to be believed. However, the TAs, now alerted to many different possible ways of working with children, occasionally have concerns. They have different ways to deal with these. Sometimes they go straight to the head, if it is a misunderstanding with the teachers, say, over timetables;

sometimes to the SENCO, if it is about particular children; and sometimes to their line manager, the deputy, if it is about pay and conditions, such as during the recent single status realignment. They discuss everyday matters in the classroom after lessons with the class teachers. While some of these issues are potentially quite divisive, they have always been settled – such is the climate of respect and trust within the school. The staff talk of 'doing things the Five Trees way'; they are quite clear that the pupils' welfare and learning is the reason for the school. The TAs and teachers all feel valued and part of a whole-school team.

One TA, referring to the SENCO, said, 'We can always go to her anyway; if there was anything you weren't quite sure about how to approach, she'd come into the classroom and show you how to do it. If we want more meetings we just say we want a meeting. Everybody's happy with that.' Another TA said, 'I think there is a lot of team spirit, not just the TAs, but the teachers; we all work together as a team. I get a lot of support from everybody really at the school. It's a nice school.'

MacBeath *et al.* (1996: 36) give the five key features of good relationships in schools as:

- There is a shared sense of teamwork among all staff
- Older pupils help younger ones
- Bullying is not tolerated
- Parents and governors feel welcomed and valued in the school
- People address one another in ways which confirm their value as individuals.

These things could all take place if each individual was committed to it, but 'Teamwork leads to better decisions and speedier completion of work through the pooling of expertise and the sharing of tasks' (Hargreaves and Hopkins, 1991: 137).

Questions to ask yourself

- With whom do I come into contact at my workplace?
- Do I need to give more thought to how I get on with the other adults in general?
- Are there any colleagues I need to spend more time with or try to understand better?
- Do I have favourites among the pupils and does it show?
- Do I have any problems with adults or pupils which I should talk over with someone?
- Do I know of any problems with pupils relating to each other that I should report to someone?
- Would I like to specialise in this area and get training in counselling?
- Of which teams am I part?
- Am I playing my part?

Some further reading

DfEE (2000a) *Working with Teaching Assistants: A Good Practice Guide*. London: Department for Education and Employment.

Dunne, E. and Bennett, N. (1994) *Talking and Learning in Groups*. London and New York: Routledge.

Lacey, P. (1999) *On a Wing and a Prayer*. MENCAP.

Lacey, P. (2001) *Support Partnerships*. London: David Fulton Publishers.

Lazear, D. (1994) *Seven Pathways of Learning: Teaching Students and Parents about Multiple Intelligences*. Arizona: Zephyr Press.

Smith, A. (1996) *Accelerated Learning in the Classroom*. Stafford: Network Educational Press.

Williams, T., Wetton, N. and Moon, A. (1989) *Health for Life: Health Education in the Primary School; The Health Education Authority's Primary School Project*. Walton on Thames: Nelson.

Useful website

www.teachernet.gov.uk/teachingassistants

4 Working in the school team

Being part of the whole-school team

As well as being part of the TA and classroom teams, you are a member of the whole-school team. You need to know where you fit into the hierarchy, who does what and when, how the systems and structures of your school work for communication and consultation. Chapter 3 suggested that you put together a school staff structure, so you should know to whom you can go for help in various aspects of your work.

The governors have the responsibility for the standards of the school and the ways in which that is carried out, the budget and the staffing. For the everyday running of the school, they appoint a chief executive, a professionally trained person – the headteacher. The head will be assisted by various deputies or assistant heads depending on the size of the school and will delegate much of the teaching and business side of the school to various staff. There will be a teacher who is head of department or coordinator for each curriculum subject or aspect, such as health education and SEN. There will be someone to whom you can go about health, safety and security matters, equipment repair, ICT support, finance problems or other areas of school work. There may be other posts of responsibility such as inclusion coordinator or head of pastoral care. You must find out to whom you go for what and when [22.2:v & vi]. You must cooperate with them when needed and develop as good a working relationship as you can, always abiding by the policies and procedures within the school [22.1:5; 22.2:3].

Look at this list and check how you feel about it, and then discuss it with your mentor. Is there anything you two together can do to improve any ways of working in your school?

Teams are working well when:

- members are clear what needs to be done, the time-scale involved and who is to do what;
- members feel they have a unique contribution to make to the work of the team;
- mutual respect prevails among members;

- a climate of trust encourages the free expression of ideas, suggestions, doubts, reservations and fears;
- individual talents and skills are used effectively;
- members are able to discuss alternative approaches and solutions before taking decisions;
- there are established ways of working together which are supportive and efficient in the use of time;
- progress is checked regularly and members are clear about who they report to and when.

(Hargreaves and Hopkins, 1991: 137)

Some schools have tried teambuilding techniques, similar to those found in some industries and businesses. Sometimes they can provide a bit of light relief on an otherwise intense in-service education and training (for teachers) (INSET) day and participating in these, or any school based meeting, will help you feel part of the whole school. If there is a consultation of any kind, do make an effort to take part; you should have your say in formulating policy as well as carrying it out. Any kind of working together helps. Balshaw's book (1999) is designed for SENCOs and other TA team leaders and is largely made up of exercises that teachers and TAs can do together to enhance their working relationships. She does give a health warning that schools need to have a collaborative culture before embarking on them; otherwise they could throw up discussions that some people feel uncomfortable with.

Collaboration:
- creates a commitment to a common purpose among governors, head and staff and the school's partners;
- improves communication and reduces misunderstanding;
- fosters creativity in finding solutions when problems are discussed;
- enhances motivation;
- prevents individuals from becoming isolated;
- generates a sense of collective achievement;
- supports teamwork.

(Hopkins and Hargreaves 1991: 137)

Kerry (2001: 60) talks about promoting 'creative dissatisfaction' through what he calls 'superteams'. These are teams who:

- constantly re-visit what they are trying to achieve;
- are persistent;
- set high expectations and standards;
- are highly committed to each other and to the task;
- communicate effectively with others;
- are proactive;
- bring in others to help the work of the team;

- prioritise and hit their targets;
- are never fully satisfied.

Where the school is secure in its aims, and has a positive ethos and collaborative culture, where relationships are good and team members can challenge each other with respect, the systems and procedures will provide the machinery to carry out the aims. Adults and pupils enjoy their time in the school and provide enhanced opportunities for learning.

Working with agencies from outside the school

TAs increasing work directly with advisers and specialists visiting the school, again under the guidance of teachers. This is particularly true if their job is concerned with pupils with SEN. They can be trained by physiotherapists and occupational therapists in the exercises needed daily to maintain flexibility or assist pupils with conditions such as cystic fibrosis. Schools employing special needs support teachers may use them to liaise with TAs or even to train them. Educational psychologists (EPs) or speech therapists find it useful to consult TAs because they have a more intimate knowledge of the pupils [16.2:6]. You need to find out what each of these people does, their role in the care and education of the pupils with whom you are connected. The following descriptions are very general and may vary from school to school and certainly from area to area [22.1:7].

- EPs are experienced ex-teachers who have a first degree in psychology and additional training for their role. If working with the LEA, they will have a patch of schools for which they are responsible. They can give advice, even training, but their role is usually diagnostic and consultative.
- Psychiatrists are medical doctors, working in the health service, and you are unlikely to have contact with them.
- Special needs support teachers are ex-teachers who have considerable SEN experience in mainstream or special schools, and may well have postgraduate SEN qualifications. They usually belong to an LEA team and visit several schools in the course of a week. They can give advice and training and often work directly with pupils or with teams of TAs.
- Therapists will work under the health service, not the education department. The three main ones visiting schools are speech therapists, who can help with language acquisition as well as the actual formation of sounds by pupils; physiotherapists, who help with physical mobility problems; and occupational therapists, who also help with coordination problems, helping pupils access normal life routines.
- Education welfare officers are employed by the LEA and monitor school absences and do home visits to support families with problems. They may also be involved in child protection issues.
- Social workers come from social services and are usually only involved in schools over child protection issues or issues concerned with the operation of the Children Act 1989. They generally only link with senior

managers or the named child protection person in the school with regard to vulnerable children. If you have any dealings with them, you should be fully briefed as to your role in any case conference or meetings.

- The police may visit the school on a community policing/liaison role – a 'meet the local bobby' kind of visit, doing the 'never go with strangers' and similar talks – but this type of work is very patchy and depends on local resources. Some schools in very difficult areas may have a police presence for staff protection from time to time, but this is still rare. Otherwise, police visits will probably be in connection with some incident and they will involve the appropriate senior manager. Again, you will only deal with them under the direction of your managers.
- Other visiting advisers or specialists such as librarians or ICT technicians will usually be dealt with by teachers, only with you by arrangement. They may be from the LEA, working for some private company or freelance.

It is vital that you also have lines of communication with the pupil's tutor or class teacher to ensure that appropriate information from your work with any visiting specialist is regularly passed on, and records are kept up to date [16.2:9; 22.1:1 & 2]. You will have to use your judgement about this. A teacher will not want to know of minor changes to regular routines but must know if there is any deterioration in the condition of the pupil detected by the experts, or any changes to routines that will affect the pupil when they are not with you. You must keep accurate and clear records of any meeting or work with such specialists where the teacher is not also present, and these should be accessible to the teacher or SENCO in the event of your illness or departure. They must also be kept in a secure place, as obviously such records are confidential to the school. As well as leaving records, do ensure someone else knows how to support the particular pupil or resource base about which you have been consulting the outside adviser. This may be in written form or by demonstrating a skill that you have been taught [22.2:5].

Visits of governors, inspectors and assessors

You will find that you are either talking with or being observed by this group of people from time to time. Their purpose will vary to an extent but they are all concerned with your wider accountability. You are directly accountable to your class teacher, line manager or the person who has been appointed your supervisor under the proposed regulations. Your assessor may be an in-school person but is quite likely to be someone from the college or organisation where you are studying if you are aiming for a Level 3 qualification. The governors and inspectors are concerned with the effectiveness of the teaching and learning in the school, of which you are part. All three may directly observe you and record what they see and give comments [22.1:6]. Assessors should share this with you completely; their purpose should be your increasing competence and confidence. Talking with them is part of your training.

Governors will probably talk with you and the class teacher and may write a visit note for the headteacher, of which you could have a copy. Inspectors may observe your work as part of an observation of the teacher. Only very occasionally do they do a direct observation of you. Of course, with revisions of the Framework for Inspection which occur every few years and the continuing spotlight on yourselves, this may increase in frequency. Inspectors will not show you their written record, but should give you feedback if you request it; they do this with teachers. None of these people should be intimidating, and if they are, you should tell your line manager immediately. They should all be working to various codes of practice, which direct them to be properly professional in their approaches to staff. Intimidation does not produce the best results from those being observed and could be detrimental to your work with pupils. If you are able to talk with them, be honest and open and listen to what they have to say; they usually have a lot of experience of various kinds and may have some helpful ideas for you. Keep a dated note of any visits, the occasion, purpose and outcomes, along with a copy of any related paperwork.

Working with parents and carers

In all that you do, you must recognise that you are working with pupils who are someone's children. You may be a member of the school who is *in loco parentis* – acting as a caring parent while the child is with you – but this does not give you 'parental rights'. Home has a significant central role to play in all our lives. School only provides contact for between 25 and 30 hours a week for 38 weeks a year for 10 years of a child's life. Around that time there may well be lengthy periods of care from nurseries, child minders, clubs and friends' homes, but these will all be controlled by the home, not the school, except maybe for nursery classes, breakfast and after-school clubs and games [23.2:ii]. Every family will have different needs and traditions. The vast majority of parents do have the best intentions for their children, even if they sometimes appear misguided. The Children Act 1989 gives parents rights and responsibilities, intending that families are to be respected and given help in coping with the difficulties in bringing up children. The school will deal with matters concerning parental rights and who is eligible for these in the cases of separation and changing of partners in the child's home. You must be guided by more senior school staff if there is any doubt over matters of care. Very occasionally there can be disputes over responsibility which spill over into school, as when acrimonious divorces end up in 'tug of love' problems, court orders and even very rare cases of abduction by one partner of children from the school. It is not your place to try to intervene, but do follow instructions in the rare cases of anxiety. Information and access must only be given to authorised people. Be very clear what can and cannot be communicated and what the school policies are on releasing pupils from the school.

The teacher should have written permission for the child to leave other than at the ends of sessions and at that point there will be clear procedures for pupils leaving, especially the younger ones or where there is transport involved [23.1:iv & v; 23.2:iv & v]. There will be clear policies and procedures within the school for parent–school relationships, some schools even having a formal signed agreement as to the various roles, rights and responsibilities of parents, pupils and the school. Make sure you have a copy of this and understand its significance for your work [23.1:3]. Establish your role and boundaries in dealing with parents as early as possible [23.1:3 & vii]. Always report difficulties and pass on requests to the class teacher or tutor concerned, possibly in writing and dated to ensure that they get the message – Post-its are invaluable for such quick communications [23.1:6 & ix; 23.2:5].

The relationship of parents and carers with TAs varies with the school and the needs of the pupils. Where the pupil has distinct physical needs, it makes sense that the TA liaises directly with the parent or carer to report on any changes in their needs. In some cases of supporting pupils with SEN, it becomes more useful and appropriate for the TA to deal directly with the parents. In other schools, there is little or no direct contact between the TAs and parents. If you are hoping to show your competence in this area for accreditation purposes [Unit 23], you need to be working in a school that recognises the possibilities of TAs liaising directly with parents or carers. Carers may be of different status: they could be daily child minders who bring and collect pupils from the school; they could be foster parents, grandparents or partners of one of the blood parents. It is not your role to sort this out, but it is your role to know with whom you are dealing and what each person's responsibility is before embarking on prolonged conversations. You could be betraying confidences, and putting yourself in a compromising situation. Check with the class teacher your exact role and what information is relevant and allowed for you to pass on to the parents from school [23.1:viii; 23.2:iv]. Also, remember to communicate with the teacher whenever you feel parental information should be passed on to them. This is particularly important when there are changes in parental circumstances, which, however positive, may affect the emotional state of the pupil and thus their capacity to work well at school or maintain their normal relationships [23.2:2]. Do not get into conversations that rightly should be held with the teacher either about a pupil's academic progress or about more domestic matters [23.1:4; 23.2:viii]. It is definitely not your place to make any comment on the home situation to parents, however strongly you feel. If you are worried about the welfare of the pupil, discuss this with the class teacher or tutor, not the parent or carer, and take their advice. Different cultures have differing standards, values and practices [23.2: 1], and you and other school staff must have regard for home background and parents' wishes. For instance, there may be questions of dress, or modes of address and preferred names. You must be guided by the teachers in these matters, and any concerns should go through them [23.1:5; 23.2:4 & vi].

In some schools, communication can be by note, such as with the pupils in a unit for the hearing impaired, who are bussed to school. Here, for instance, notes could accompany the hearing aids if there were problems. Do word any notes carefully, remembering to use the minimum of educational jargon, and having regard for the language needs of the parent concerned [23.1:3 & vi]. Sometimes TAs are closer to the parents in that they often live in the vicinity of the school and may be parents of children in the school themselves. The way in which you talk with pupils and deal with situations that might arise in front of the parents can give positive images of child care and respect for the pupil. Develop positive relationships with parents whenever you can, showing respect and giving reassurance [23.1:1,2,ii & iii; 23.2:3 & iii].

An example of good practice

In Hawthornberry Secondary School, the TAs are part of the SEN support team, and part of their defined role is to liaise with parents regarding day-to-day needs. They sit in on any visit of the parent to the school where logistically possible, although sometimes they may have responsibilities elsewhere in the school. Some do primary school visits with the SENCO, and attend the induction meeting for parents. They have full copies of the IEPs, provide reports for SEN reviews, and attend the review meetings. TAs are present on parents' consultation evenings and are available to liaise directly with parents over the implementation of specific teaching programmes designed for individual pupils. Where the pupil has severe physical needs, requiring intimate help from the TA, the TA completes the home/school diary, as does the parent, monitoring any significant changes in the pupil's condition or circumstances. This same diary is completed where the TAs are providing the physiotherapy assistance in the lunch break, and messages from the physiotherapist are often passed on in this way. Where the parents are in full-time employment and release is difficult for direct parent–therapist communication a TA can act as a useful go-between, without worrying the teachers. The diary also acts as a record in the event of TA illness. In one or two cases, with the knowledge and written permission of both parent and tutor, a TA has accompanied a pupil to an out-of-school appointment such as for an eye test. Some of the TAs have been involved in the parent literacy class run by the school one afternoon a week, which has helped to cement relationships for the future. Two TAs come from the same ethnic group as a large majority of the school population and this has been invaluable for communication with parents whose English is not yet fluent enough to cope with school jargon, and for internal school discussions on the needs of a community with differing cultural backgrounds.

The new Code of Practice (DfES 2001b) suggests that TAs be included in IEP reviews, and the training of TAs for secondary schools promotes this kind of involvement. The chapter on working in partnership with parents (pp. 16–19), while meant for SENCOs and other senior managers, is worth reading to get a flavour of the way in which this should go. It defines parental responsibility and recognises the importance of the partnership of parents and school. It promises positive attitudes, user-friendly information and procedures. For instance, it suggests (p. 17) that:

To make communications effective professionals should:

- Acknowledge and draw on parental knowledge and expertise in relation to their child. Focus on the children's strengths as well as areas of additional need
- Recognise the personal and emotional investment of parents and be aware of their feelings
- Ensure that parents understand procedures, are aware of how to access support in preparing their contributions and are given documents to be discussed well before meetings
- Respect the validity of offering different perspectives and seek constructive ways of reconciling different viewpoints
- Respect the differing needs parents themselves may have, such as a disability or communication or linguistic barriers
- Recognise the need for flexibility in the timing and structure of meetings.

TAs have not voiced problems over themselves being parents of children at the school, although one problem which then faces TAs is how to deal with enquiries from anxious parents who see the TA as a source of information on what goes on in the school. This reinforces the importance of knowing and following the school code of confidentiality.

School policies and procedures

As the whole-school team will consist at the very minimum of about ten people even in the smallest school, and could consist of several hundred people, written policies and guidelines are in place to ensure consistency and compliance with the law. Parental and volunteer involvement in schools, governors' and parents' rights and responsibilities, along with the increasing recognition of the need to take heed of the views of pupils, mean that consultation and paperwork have become a regular part of school life. This means that you, as a member of staff, must make very sure you know your role and responsibilities within the system and take opportunities to participate in debates about any changes. These policies and procedures may seem bureaucracy gone mad, but they do provide the skeleton on which the flesh of the body of the school can fix and so become a working organism. They lay out everything from the common aims and purposes of everyone associated with the school – essential to enable the teams to have their purpose – to the ways in which individual pupils are to be treated in varying circumstances.

The main document determining the work of the school is the School Development Plan (SDP). This is the business plan of the organisation and should be reviewed annually. As part of this review, there should be a cycle of reviews of all the policies in place in the school. The total number of these will be considerable, and you do not need to know the content or have them all. A master copy should be available for anyone to consult when required, but there are some policies which you do need not only to have but also to know and understand. The following is a list of those mentioned somewhere in the standards:

Essential school policies

Health and safety [5.1:iv]
    child protection [1.1:ii; 1.2:i; 9.1:viii; 9.3:vii]
Teaching and learning and learning support [3.1:i]
Inclusion [3.1:iv; 5.1:iii; 8.1:iv]
    SEN and EAL [3.1:v]
Behaviour [1.1:i; 1.2:i; 9.1:vi; 9.3:i]
    dealing with conflict [9.1:vii]
    emotional expression [9.3:vi]
    bullying [1.1:ii]
    recognition of reward and effort, praise and assistance [3.1:viii; 9.2:vii]
Curriculum policies [8.1:v; 20.1:i; 20.2:i]
    ICT [17.2:iii]
    English [18.1:ii; 18.2:ii; 18.3:ii]
    mathematics [19.1:iii; 19.2:i]
Equal opportunities [1.1:ii; 3.1:iv; 8.1:iv; 9.1:ii]
    valuing cultural diversity [9.1:ii]
    non-discriminatory behaviour and anti-racism [2.1:iii; 9.1:ii]
    disability awareness [9.1:ii]
Record keeping and confidentiality [6.1:vii; 9.3:x; 22.2:iii; 23.1:v; 23.2:v]
Dealing with difficulties in working relationships [21.1:viii]
Communication with and providing information for professionals, parents and carers [22.1:iv; 22.2:ii; 23.1:i; 23.2:i]
Enabling parents and carers to have access to teachers [23.2:vii]

Health, safety and security

One of the most useful exercises to do with young pupils, or those who have difficulty in expressing themselves verbally, is to get them to draw pictures. There are some excellent examples of this in *Health for Life* (Williams *et al.* 1989). You might like to try this for yourself.

Can you draw a healthy person? Describe one in words if you prefer.
Now look at your drawing and answer a few questions for yourself.
Does age, gender, ethnic origin or religious belief matter?
Is diet or exercise important? Is being healthy only about visible, physical appearance?

Is mental capacity important? Does one have to be intelligent to be healthy?
Does happiness or sadness affect health? Does state of mind affect health?
What is a healthy mind? Is it part of having a healthy body?
Do attitudes to others and relationships matter?
Is family background, education, financial stability important?
Can a person in a wheelchair be healthy? Can a poor person be healthy?

Now can you define a healthy school?
What are the important factors affecting the all-round health of a school?

Although the following section is about obvious health issues, such as dealing with accidents and first aid, do not forget the importance of relationships which enable the school to function in a healthy way in the broadest terms. Schools should be providing not only an environment which is safe for exploring and growing bodies but also a learning environment for enquiring minds [5.1:vii].

All employees have a duty to observe the in-house organisational requirements in this area [10.1:i; 10.2:6]. There is considerable legislation governing health and safety at work, based on the 1974 Act and subsequent legislation such as the Management of Health and Safety at Work Regulations 1992. These indicate that establishments must have health and safety policies [5.1:iv; 5.3:iii] and carry out risk assessments for people, equipment and off-site activities. It puts the responsibility for health and safety on employers, which in the case of schools may be the LEA, the governing body, trustees or owners, depending on what type of school it is. The Health and Safety Executive produce some useful information leaflets and have local offices. However, all employees have a responsibility to observe local policies and take all reasonable precautions to keep themselves and others using the premises safe. This includes being personally vigilant for potential risks to adults or pupils. It does not mean you necessarily have to mend things or make things safe on your own, but you need to ensure that pupils in your care observe proper procedures [5.1:v]. Your responsibilities regarding health and safety may be spelt out in your job description. The requirements for all staff in the areas of health, safety, security and supervision will be in writing somewhere; you need to find these [5.1:viii].

All schools will have an appointed health and safety officer among the staff, usually a teacher, often linked with union affiliation. They will advise you if you have queries, or take concerns to the appropriate quarter if you have any [5.1:ii,iii & 3; 5.3:vi]. The standards provide useful checklists of areas which you must attend to and find out about in your particular school. For instance, the scope of safety equipment indicates that you should know about the location of first aid boxes, how to protect children and adults against accidents and how to use different equipment in emergencies (LGNTO 2001: 5). The standards apply to all pupils whatever their special needs, to all colleagues and other adults or children who may be in the building, and to all areas of the school: in and out of the classroom, outside the school buildings and in places you might visit with pupils on an educational trip.

Even if you are not undertaking these units for accreditation purposes you should read the following and undertake some of the tasks [10.1:1]. These items are required of all employees either by law [10.1:ii] or for the protection of all the people within the organisation.

Emergency and accident procedures

Before you even go to a classroom, you should know about fire alarms and procedures [10.1:x]. This includes how to evacuate the building, what to do if there is a bomb scare or an intruder. As a visitor to the school, you are usually asked to sign in so that the responsible people know who is in the building if there is an emergency. As a member of staff, it is assumed that you are on the premises if the timetable indicates so. You need to familiarise yourself with the fire alarm points, the whereabouts of extinguishers and fire blankets and their use. Remember, if you are in laboratories or wherever hazardous liquids are about, there may be different kinds of extinguisher to use [10.1:xi]. Water should not be put on oil or electrical fires; it can make matters far worse. Carbon dioxide extinguishers or fire blankets will be available in vulnerable situations; check out how and when they should be used [5.1:2 & viii].

Usually the fire alarm is the signal for any evacuation of the building, whatever the cause. You need to ensure any pupils in your charge behave appropriately at such times, 'silence' and 'walking only' usually being paramount. Both of these reduce panic as well as being something positive to maintain. All rooms should have evacuation instructions. If they do not, tell someone in the office [5.3:vi].

If you are appointed to support a pupil with special physical needs, make sure you know where all their equipment is, and what you do with it in emergencies. This could be personal to them or arise in an evacuation procedure. A wheelchair may need a special route out of some areas, such as by a lift. Alert the SENCO if you have any worries [5.1:vi; 5.3:v].

First aid

All schools will have at least one appointed person responsible for ensuring correct procedures are followed and probably a trained first-aider. You need to find out who these people are and where they may be found at different times of the day. Cover of some kind should be available at all times when people are on the school premises. You do not need to have first aid training but it helps, and schools usually have sessions every so often which deal with resuscitation, choking and bleeding and other simple procedures. Be wary of getting information from the Internet or books on home medicine unless you are sure of their validity, as some methods are not helpful. The Red Cross and St. John Ambulance run courses in any community and usually will come to a specific venue to run a course if sufficient people are interested. These associations also publish useful manuals about first aid, at work and at home, for adults or children, some of which are available as CD-ROMs. The details can be found on the Red Cross website. The school will have a designated first-aider who will at least have some of this training, and you will be told when and how you should use them [10.2:iii]. Common sense and experience, particularly of bringing up a family, can help you, but you must know your limitations both personally and within the procedures of the school [10.2:vi].

There may be a school nurse visiting on occasion or very rarely nowadays a school doctor. Visiting therapists such as occupational therapists, speech therapists and physiotherapists can be very helpful in giving information on how to cope with pupils with particular needs. There may also be religious or cultural 'dos and don'ts' with some pupils or staff, such as problems with removing certain items of clothing, and you need to be aware of these [10.2:v]. The important thing is not to panic, but to make a quick assessment of the situation. Usually your first port of call in any emergency will be the class teacher, but you may find yourself in a learning area out of sight of such a person. You need to know who can help and how to summon assistance [5.1:3; 10.2:1]. Find out where the trained first-aiders are situated, where people who deal with sick pupils are located, where first aid materials are kept and who has access to them [11.3:iv].

You should ensure you can recognise all the following emergencies, and know what to do, and what not to do [10.2:iv]:

a. severe bleeding
b. cardiac arrest
c. shock
d. fainting or loss of consciousness
e. epileptic seizure
f. choking and difficulty with breathing
g. falls – potential and actual fracture
h. burns and scalds
i. poisoning
j. electrocution
k. substance abuse

(LGNTO 2001 Level 3: 46)

- Look for danger: you may have to deal with this.
- Remove any danger: only move the casualty if absolutely necessary.
- Assess the casualty: check for consciousness, open the airway, and check for breathing and pulse.
- Get help as soon as you can.

You should know what to do if a pupil has an accident, or if you have an accident [5.1:ix], and you should know the procedures for dealing with the results of illness as well as the sick pupils [5.1:v]. Remember that simple things such as reassurance and maintaining some privacy and calmness will help, whatever the situation. Afterwards, you may need to clear up vomit, urine, faeces or blood and you should find out about protective clothing for yourself, such as surgical gloves, whether to use sand, sawdust, disinfectant or not, and where to locate a site manager or other help. Sickness or accidents to one person can be a health risk to others [10.2:4 & viii].

Checklist

- Do you know your own limitations in first aid skills?
- Do you know what is expected of you by the school?
- Are there any cultural or religious limitations to your possible actions of which you should be aware?
- Do you know to whom to turn for help?
- Where is the first aid box kept?
- Should you use it?
- What do you do when you have finished using it – whom do you tell about replacing items [5.3:vi]?
- What would you do if any of the above list happened to you? Or happened to a pupil in your care?

All incidents and accidents should be recorded somewhere in the school, along with the action taken, the time and cause, so be sure you ask about this as well when informing yourself about your appropriate action. The reporting of major incidents can then be dealt with by the appropriate person. You should record incidents in which you are involved; check the requirements for your school [5.2:iv & 6; 5.3:vi; 10.1:x]. Most schools have notes which can be sent home, signed by someone in authority, to tell parents or carers of incidents in school. It may or may not be your responsibility to inform parents directly; it will depend on the pupil and the nature of the incident [11.2:v]. For instance, bumped heads are always considered important, as symptoms of concussion can develop many hours after the incident, so the parents or carers need to be on the lookout for any problem, but the note may need to be signed by a senior member of staff, not you.

Some chemicals and medical materials are not allowed in school, and all medicines should be properly secure [11.2:viii & 3:vi]. Do not administer medicines or apply ointments or plasters unless you are sure that it is all right. Never use your own creams or lotions on a pupil. Always record your actions.

Equipment, materials and buildings

Prevention is better than cure and it is part of your responsibility as a member of staff, particularly one dealing closely with children and young people, to ensure your surroundings are hygienic and safe [10.1:2 & 4]. You will need to get to know the routines for keeping the place tidy and clean [10.1:5] as well as who is responsible for the environment, probably the site manager or caretaker [5.1:ii], the equipment and materials including stock control [5.2:iii], and allowing access to the premises and store rooms [5.1:viii]. Be firm about school routines, but be careful. It is not your place to criticise or denigrate family customs, but to carry out the procedures recommended for your school. Gentle reminders can help; some pupils appear to have got used to people clearing up for them – that is not your job, but the safety of others is! [11.2:1,2]. You need to be a good role model where tidiness is concerned.

You may have to visit toilet areas to ensure they are being used properly; you may need to ensure young pupils wash their hands after using the toilet or before handling food. Make sure you know the appropriate places for you and your pupils to eat or drink in your school. Remember families differ in their standards of tidiness and hygiene at home. Some religious groups have strict rules about eating particular foods, so be careful when commenting on the content of lunch bags [11.2:iii]. Some schools have strict rules about handling soil or animals, most leave it to common sense; that is, wash your hands well after handling either. Fewer schools actually keep animals these days but many still do. Do familiarise yourself with their care in case your particular pupils are interested. The RSPCA has a lot of information about the proper care of animals in schools as well as at home. This includes aquaria and ponds, as well as the more obvious things such as mammals [10.1:vii]. The World Wildlife Fund has some good information on developing wildlife areas in schools, as do Learning Through Landscapes. Some people are allergic to animal fur and even caterpillar hairs so *always* ask before bringing any animals to school yourself.

There may be occasions when gender is important; for instance, you may have care of a female pupil who begins to menstruate yet has not got any protection with them at school, or even to whom the event comes as a surprise. This can occur as young as eight years of age. Whatever gender you are, make sure you know the school's arrangements for accessing emergency supplies of protective clothing and disposal of soiled materials, and, if you are male, identify whom to go to for help should this condition become apparent to you. Some physically disabled girls may need intimate help at this time. Seek clear advice before undertaking this.

Make sure you report any problems with pupils carrying out your hygiene rules or creating unsafe situations to a teacher or your line manager, as well as any hazard which you find while using any of the school's facilities [11.2:6]. The named health and safety officer may need to be informed [10.1:vi].

It is your responsibility to ensure that where you work with pupils is safe – you could be asked to take a group in the grounds where there is a pond, for instance – and that any tools you work with are used safely. You should follow all manufacturers' instructions and school health and safely regulations concerning equipment and materials [5.2:2]. Pupils using tools, equipment and materials should be taught how to use them and how to put them away appropriately. This goes for cutlery and pencil sharpeners as well as craft knives and complicated apparatus. There may be special rules and regulations, even risk assessments, associated with particular things, especially if you are helping in science, design and technology (DT), ICT or art areas [5.3:i]. Part of safety routines will be the proper use of tools and equipment, including care and storage. It will be up to you to ensure there is a minimal risk in using such apparatus. All electrical equipment should be used appropriately and safely [17.1:3–7]. You may need to be trained to use specialist equipment and that may include specialist safety equipment on lathes or other power tools. If in doubt about the use of any tools or equipment, ask and take note. Clearing up afterwards may also include disposing of materials. Does your school separate waste paper for recycling? Know where and how to dispose of broken glass, chemicals and other possibly toxic materials. Be a good role model in the way you use tools and materials, the way in which you organise your own belongings.

Health and safety procedures also include ensuring security procedures are observed, being alert for strangers and keeping locked areas or equipment that should be away from general use. Schools now contain much expensive equipment such as ICT and laboratory equipment, some of which is highly portable and desirable to thieves. Secondary schools probably have some dangerous chemicals and even radioactive materials in various stores. All of us have heard of the thankfully very rare but devastating acts of aggressive visitors to schools.

A phrase that is often used in schools is 'risk assessment' [10.1:2 & v]. This is not necessarily a complicated paper-based task for using dangerous chemicals or machinery but can become part of your everyday thinking. A simple example is teaching children to cross the road safely. You can teach them the Green Cross Code, but as they get older they will want to cross on their own, where it is not 'safe to cross', say from between parked cars. To do this they need to make a mental assessment of how dangerous the place is, how far they need to go out between the cars after stepping off the kerb to see adequately, whether they have the right footwear on to run, and so on. We take this kind of assessment for granted, but when in school we need to be alert for possible dangers, mentally assessing the risk of certain procedures. This does not mean not doing certain procedures which may be interesting or fun, but being sure before you undertake them that you have thought the process through [10.1:7]. Some activities need formal risk assessments before they are undertaken, such as visits off site or use of certain chemicals. Risk assessments are routine procedures in science laboratories and DT areas.

- Keep a diary for a week of where you are working with pupils.
- Note any incidents that did happen – what did you do? Could these incidents have been prevented by any action you could have taken?
- Think of all the potential hazards that could have occurred during that week, e.g. spillages, falls, conflicts, injuries, breakages.
- How did you avoid them happening?
- Can you avoid more incidents in future by taking more care?

Questions to ask yourself

- Do you have copies of the policies that concern you?
- Have you read them? Do you understand your role in them?
- Have you identified the lead person for each of these policies?
- Do you need any training in first aid?
- Do you know what to do in an emergency wherever you are in the building, whatever pupils you are with, whatever you are doing?

Essential reading

LGNTO (2001) *Teaching/Classroom Assistants National Occupational Standards.* London: Local Government National Training Organisation.

Some further reading

Balshaw, M. (1999) *Help in the Classroom*, 2nd edn. London: David Fulton Publishers.

Balshaw, M. and Farrell, P. (2002) *Teaching Assistants: Practical Strategies for Effective Classroom Support.* London: David Fulton Publishers. (Especially Chapters 10 and 11.)

Bastiani, J. (1989) *Working with Parents: A Whole-school Approach.* London: Routledge and NFER-Nelson.

Blamires, M., Robertson, C. and Blamires, J. (1997) *Parent–Teacher Partnership.* London: David Fulton Publishers.

Bruce, T. and Meggitt, C. (1996) *Child Care and Education.* London: Hodder and Stoughton. (Especially Chapter 10.)

DfES (2001b) *Special Educational Needs Code of Practice.* London: Department for Education and Skills.

Hargreaves, D. H. and Hopkins, D. (1991) *The Empowered School.* London: Cassell Education Limited.

Kerry, T. (2001) *Working with Support Staff: Their Roles and Effective Management in Schools.* London: Pearson Education.

Williams, T., Wetton, N. and Moon, A. (1989) *Health for Life: Health Education in the Primary School; The Health Education Authority's Primary School Project.* Walton on Thames: Nelson.

Useful websites

www.ltl.org.uk
www.redcross.org.uk
www.rspca.org.uk
www.wwf.org.uk

5 Understanding pupils' physical and intellectual development

The importance of studying how children grow and learn

Child development has been a neglected area of study for those in teaching in recent years. The emphasis has been on curriculum delivery rather than how pupils learn. While it is clearly important that the teachers and TAs should know what they are teaching in terms of subject content, and that they should be both as accurate and as up to date as possible, there are two other factors always to be borne in mind; the way in which the subject matter is 'delivered'

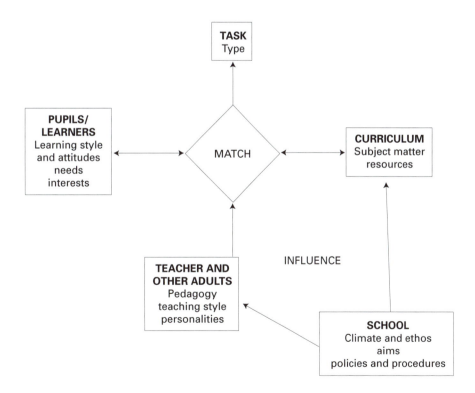

Figure 5.1 The interaction of curriculum, adults and learners in the classroom

– the teaching methods, background and personality of the teacher (or TA, using 'teacher' in the widest sense) – and the characteristics of the learner – the one on the receiving end of the delivery.

This and the following chapters will look at various aspects of this matching process and how your understanding of these aspects will help you enhance the learning of the pupils with whom you work, starting with the learners themselves.

Child development is much more widely used in considering the teaching and learning of pupils in the early years, and the very term has connotations of childhood and primary schools. It is, however, the term used to cover the area of study from birth to adulthood, whenever that it supposed to be. When working in secondary schools or even tertiary colleges an understanding of how the growth processes influence the way in which the pupils learn is important. Indeed, most of us regress at times to methods learnt in childhood when undertaking new fields of study. The need to 'play around' with a new television, or 'fiddle about' with a new tool, is part of all our experience. Play is not confined to the early years, but is an essential part of learning.

Nor can we study the learning process in isolation; not only does the physical and emotional state of our bodies influence the way we learn and efficacy of our learning, but much of our intellectual development has a physical and emotional basis. Our social, cultural and spiritual selves also develop as we become adult, and continue to do so throughout our lives. We are made up of all these facets, each influencing the other to produce a whole person. We have to try to see our pupils as whole human beings, yet in order to study the complexity which makes up the whole, we have to look at each facet separately. If these facets get out of balance, one develops but another does not, then the pupil, or adult, becomes frustrated, even disturbed. This can be seen sometimes in very bright children who are emotionally their chronological age, but socially immature. They can throw tantrums. Most children develop and grow normally and do so in a recognisable sequence which can be studied and forms the basis of designing schools, equipment, teaching methods and curriculum. Thus in studying development you will understand the rationale behind most of the things we do, not only in school but in all our lives as shoppers, parents or home builders. Also, a study of what are called 'norms', the stages that researchers, medical practitioners and teachers have identified over the years, enables practitioners to understand better when things are not developing as they should. Many of you will be helping pupils with developmental delay in one area or another, and it will help if you learn more about normal development [7.1:i]. The most obvious area to start with is that of physical development.

Physical development

A family photograph album will give you material to identify some of the norms of physical development [7.1:i; 7.2:i]. In Great Britain we are relatively well fed and clothed, with a modern medical service, and so most of us have the privilege of growing to adulthood normally. Many of you have children of your own, and have kept that height chart on the kitchen or bathroom walls and entered your family heights on each birthday. Some of you may even have kept up entries in your baby books, recording weight, first teeth, first walking and talking, toilet training milestones and so forth. Doctors and nurses have tables of norms and will check development at certain critical intervals, particularly when children are in infancy. The milestones of puberty are also marked by bodily changes. Physically, we are able to procreate in our early teens, yet we are not fully mature until our early twenties. Some might say it is 'downhill' after that; certainly we become less fertile. Mothers may have more complications in childbirth after 30 years of age, and menstruation ceases in the forties or fifties; sperm counts tend to drop with age. Boys tend to mature later than girls in many aspects of physical and intellectual development [2.1:vii].

However, we all know that diet, exercise and environmental factors affect that growth pattern. In the so-called western world, people are living longer overall as well as being inches taller than their grandparents' generation. Understanding of disease, its causes and many cures have contributed to this longevity.

Looking at physical norms

Get out your family albums with photographs of either yourself and your family or your children. If you have them, find your children's 'baby books'. Ask other members of your family for some remembrances. Can you identify at what age the following happened? Try following the development of one child at a time. When did they:

- Sit up on their own
- Turn over
- Crawl
- Stand up unaided
- Walk unaided
- Kick a ball
- Ride a bicycle
- Hold a pencil
- Draw a shape
- Draw a recognisable person
- Write their name
- Catch a ball with one hand
- Skip with a skipping rope
- Tie their own shoelaces?

As you do this with several family members you will begin to see a pattern emerging. Did the boys develop later than the girls in any of these respects?

Early years practitioners will divide the abilities mentioned above into two types – gross and fine motor skills. The fine motor skills – those using just the hands – are the ones that schools usually identify as important, except in PE.

If you are particularly interested in physical development, either because the pupils you help have some physical impairment or you wish to specialise in an area of physical education, you might like to ask a friendly nurse or doctor to let you have a look at their more specialised charts. The work of Mary Sheridan was invaluable in establishing some of the schedules which were used as paediatric tools in clinics and hospitals in studying children from birth to five years. A simplified version from birth to eight years can be found in *Child Care and Education* (Bruce and Meggitt 1996: 33–5). You need to recognise the important stages in physical development, as they may impinge upon your work. For instance, girls can start to menstruate while at primary school. Tall pupils will need larger furniture to enable them to work in comfort. Many of you will be working with children with particular physical needs for which you need to understand how best to help them. So-called clumsy children may need more help in concentrating, others may need special furniture or equipment [5.1:vi].

Genetic and environmental factors

There has long been a debate as to the source of differences from the norms. The main contenders have been inherited characteristics and environmental factors. The real answer is that both are responsible in closely linked ways. Our physical characteristics are dependent on our genes, the DNA which provides the code for cell development and distribution. But various things can intervene, either in the very protein which makes up the DNA or in the cells to influence the way in which the genes can operate. Irradiation from atomic bombs dropped in Japan at the end of the Second World War caused mutations of human genetic material which resulted in anything from death to minor physical deformity. Diet and environmental factors such as water or air pollution, housing, exercise or lack of it all have their effect. The environmental factors do not necessarily have a lifelong effect; sometimes reversal of circumstance can allow the body to catch up. You may be helping pupils who have come from countries where malnutrition was endemic; they may seem small for their age, listless and slow in learning. With proper diet and medical aid to rid the body of possible infection incurred through dirty water or bad housing, the pupil may grow and regain some of their lost ground.

There are also best times for certain development. Language acquisition appears to be easiest in the pre-school years, when children seem not only able to learn their mother tongue but also to become bilingual or multilingual with more ease. Some of the muscles of the palate used or unused in that period can make it difficult in later life to articulate certain sounds; for instance, people who have been brought up speaking in a Chinese dialect find it hard in adult life to articulate all the sounds that we use in the English language. Children seem able to learn to read most quickly between five and seven years of age. It does not mean they cannot learn to read at other ages, but the effort both they and the teacher have to exert will be greater. Some of this will be due to the maturation of the brain itself.

Intellectual development

The brain

Intellectual development or cognitive (knowing) development and the development of learning are dependent, just like the rest of the body, on genetic and environmental factors. Learning takes place in the brain. The physical development of the brain is going to influence what learning can take place, just as physical development of the limbs influences whether walking can take place. However, there is one major difference in the cellular structure of the brain from that of the rest of the body. With some exceptions and within some limitations, the number of brain cells does not increase as the brain grows but each cell will grow. There is also very limited regeneration of the cells if they are damaged. There have been some great advances in the treatment of stroke victims in recent years, with recovery of speech and movement previously thought impossible. The changes brought about by constant appropriate exercise are not due to new brain cells growing to replace those lost, as when skin heals or bone knits after a break has been mended, but to the ability of the brain messages to find alternative pathways.

There are many billions of brain cells, each with many connections to other brain cells. Electrical and chemical messages are transmitted at enormous speeds when we think or do anything. While we are alive, all the body systems are maintained in balance by the various parts of the brain, enabling us to breathe while we sleep, our blood to be pumped without our conscious intervention and our senses, such as hearing, to be alerted in emergencies. In order for this to happen, the blood has to pump oxygen and nutrients to the cells of the brain, which die in a matter of minutes if starved of them. Recent developments in scanning techniques have enabled doctors and scientists to study the physical basis of brain functioning while people are still alive. Previously, it was only possible to track some of the electrical impulses while people were alive and then study brain tissue after death. It is research such as this that suggests that we should keep up our intake of water between meals, to reduce the risk of dehydration and thus enhance brain function. Some schools have encouraged their pupils to carry water in bottles around with them.

If the brain cells are not increasing in number, and may well be decreasing in number as we get older, how do we go on learning? There have been many theories, and some of these have determined the way in which we teach and what we teach over the past century. As is the case with most research, the more we know the more we find we do not know, and currently we recognise the complexity of what goes on in the brain; no one theory fits all cases and we need to look at the variety of theories, and recognise some of the strategies that have developed from them. Different pupils, different subjects and different

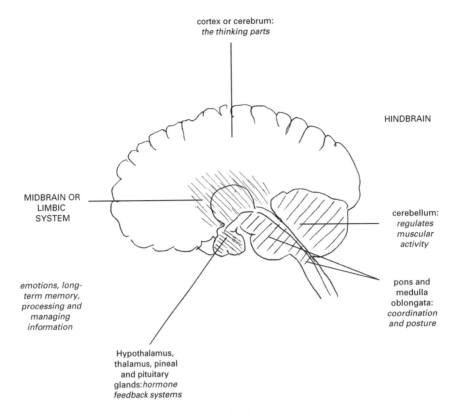

cortex or cerebrum:
the thinking parts

HINDBRAIN

MIDBRAIN OR
LIMBIC
SYSTEM

cerebellum:
*regulates
muscular
activity*

*emotions, long-
term memory,
processing and
managing
information*

pons and
medulla
oblongata:
*coordination
and posture*

Hypothalamus,
thalamus, pineal
and pituitary
glands:*hormone
feedback systems*

Figure 5.2   Diagrammatic drawing of a brain

situations call for different strategies and using different parts of the brain. You will soon get to recognise the characteristics of the pupils with whom you work closely and adapt your techniques to fit them – things such as how long a pupil can concentrate without taking a break [3.1:vii].

The brain is not one entity; the hindbrain is more like a swollen end to the top of the spinal cord. It regulates your heartbeat and breathing, the activities which go on even if you are unconscious. Part of the hindbrain controls your movements, coordination and balance, so important in learning to walk and talk. The middle part of the brain is responsible for memory, emotions and processing and managing information. The upper part of the brain, the cortex, the bit that looks like an outsize walnut without its shell, has the main thinking parts and personality. The right and left parts of the cortex do different things and there are pathways between the two sides. Buried inside the midbrain are some important glands whose hormones determine things such as our bodily clock, which triggers off hormones such as the sex hormones or thyroxine controlling our daily metabolism. So you can see how closely thinking and our emotions are to controlling other functions of our body.

What is more, the cell structure of the brain is distinct. Each cell in the cortex has many branches like a tree, and each of the branches ends in a join to a branch of another tree-like cell. It is estimated you may have 100 billion of these cells in your cortex. It is the connections between the branches which

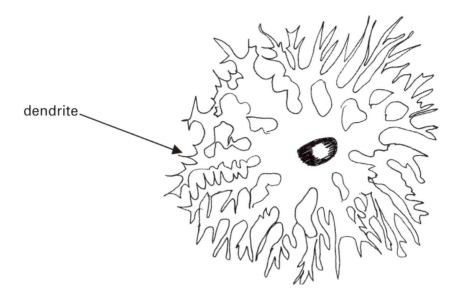

dendrite

Figure 5.3 A diagrammatic drawing of a cell in the grey matter of the brain cortex

make the complexity of the brain, enable the memory to increase, enable us to learn skills and even, with thought, change our habits and behaviour. It operates with the mediation of minute electrical impulses and complex chemicals, rather like a massive computer. There are some more lengthy descriptions of the brain function and its relationship to learning in *Accelerated Learning* (Smith 1996: 13–23) and *The Learning Revolution* (Dryden and Vos 1994: 109–37). You can see that, with such a complex network, if some cells die or are damaged through an accident or a stroke, it is possible that alternative pathways can be found, provided the owner of the brain continues to exercise it. Obviously, it depends on the extent of the damage and the location. If it is possible to relocate pathways, it is also possible to establish new ones – the process of learning.

While an understanding of the biology and biochemistry of the brain is helping us establish the best physical conditions for learning, it still does not address the psychological aspects. Doctors treating people with personality disorders or mental illness use a combination of drugs, psychotherapy and even at times electrical stimulation, although the last is used much less frequently than, say, fifty years ago, when there were few drugs available other than those inducing sleep or hallucinations. Modern therapies take a much more holistic approach to mental illness, recognising that we are complex beings with body, mind and spirit, all of which can become unbalanced in different ways and all of which affect the function of each other. We all live in different social contexts, with different backgrounds, talents and needs.

Luckily, most of the pupils and parents with whom we work are not suffering from mental illness, but the principle is the same. Enhancing learning is not just a matter of having the right breakfast and drinking water, but these do make a difference. As with the whole body, exercise is important, not just indicating elderly folk should go on trying to do their daily crossword or whatever, but there are ways of practising thinking. Some schools do 'brain gym', as a sort of club for certain pupils, and others introduce specific techniques such as those developed by Edward de Bono. He has published widely, with many ideas for lessons and games, and is responsible for phrases such as 'lateral thinking'. Unfortunately, thinking – activities like brainstorming, pupils offering differing opinions, discussion, challenge – takes time, when there is a mountain of curriculum facts to be delivered to pupils. However, without time for these activities, the pupils will not develop their own understanding of the facts being put forward and will not be creative, be problem solvers and grow in their learning capacity. It is a dilemma which all those working within the constraints of a set curriculum have to solve for themselves.

Getting pupils thinking

Discuss with your mentor or a friendly class teacher how they solve the dilemma of balancing telling time with thinking time for pupils.

If they are willing (do not do this without discussing it with them first, and see Chapter 11 for observation techniques) observe some lessons and note how long the teacher spends telling the class things, how long the pupils are allowed to offer their opinions on the subject of the lesson and how long the teacher allows for silent thought before a task is undertaken.

Jot down any questions asked by the teacher.

After the lesson go through these questions and sort them.

Which ones wanted factual answers (sometimes called closed questions)?

Which ones were asking for ideas or opinions (sometimes called open questions)?

Discuss your findings with the teacher you observed.

Current theories of learning

One definition of learning is 'that reflective activity which enables the learner to draw upon previous experience, to understand and evaluate the present, so as to shape future action and formulate new knowledge' (Abbott 1996: 1). The Office for Standards in Education tried to define good and less than satisfactory learning in terms of observable behaviour in the 1993 *Handbook for the Inspection of Schools* (Ofsted 1993: 9):

> Where learning is good, most pupils respond readily to the challenge of the tasks set, show a willingness to concentrate on them, and make good progress. They adjust well to the demands of working in different contexts, selecting appropriate methods and organising effectively the resources they need. Work is sustained with a sense of commitment and enjoyment. Pupils

are sufficiently confident and alert to raise questions and to persevere with their work when answers are not readily available. They evaluate their own work and come to realistic judgements about it. Where appropriate, pupils readily help one another.

Where learning is unsatisfactory, pupils are either insufficiently engaged in their work, or demonstrate undue dependence on the teacher or uncritical use of resources. They are reluctant to take initiatives or accept responsibility. They find it difficult to sustain concentration for more than short periods of time. They are unable to apply their learning in new context.

This definition was dropped in the 1995 handbook and replaced by definitions of pupils' responses, attainment and progress. The latest handbook (Ofsted 1999) concentrates on standards and attainment, referring to the learning of pupils within the section on teaching. The problem is that learning itself cannot be seen, only the behaviour which shows itself during and after it has taken place. There are the heart-stopping moments of seeing 'the penny drop', but these do not constitute all that is going on; most is unseen.

Learning is a process of change taking place in the brain. The brain's basic structure will be determined by genetic factors, but the capacity to learn, or intelligence, is not fixed. People used to believe that this power of thinking was finite, fixed and measurable, hence the development of intelligence quotient (IQ) tests such as the Standford-Binet test favoured in the middle of the twentieth century. There are some inherited parameters, as can be observed in the inheritance of aptitudes or talents, say, in music or dexterity for a craft, but such traits can be encouraged (or discouraged) by the environment in which children are brought up. Identical twins inherit many similar characteristics but can have quite different personalities, which affect their performance.

Recent ideas on learning have been influenced by the theory of **Gardner** who suggests that there is not just one intelligence, but multiple strands or aspects or dimensions or domains. There are different intelligences for different things, and you can be clever in one area only or several:

- *verbal/linguistic*: enables individuals to communicate and make sense of the world through language (e.g. as journalists, novelists and lawyers)
- *logical/mathematical*: allows individuals to use and appreciate abstract relations (e.g. scientists, accountants, philosophers)
- *visual/spatial*: makes it possible for people to visualise, transform and use spatial information (e.g. architects, sculptors and mechanics)
- *bodily/kinaesthetic*: enables people to use high levels of physical movement, control and expression (e.g. athletes, dancers and actors)
- *musical/rhythmic*: allows people to create, communicate and understand meanings made from sound (e.g. composers, singers, musicians)
- *interpersonal*: helps people to recognise and make distinctions about others' feelings and intentions and respond accordingly (e.g. teachers, politicians and sales people)

- *intrapersonal*: enables a capacity for a reflective understanding of others and oneself (e.g. therapists and some types of artist and religious leader)
- *naturalist*: allows people to understand and develop the environment (e.g. farmers, gardeners and geologists).

(Pollard 2002: 150)

Smith (1996: 60, 61) has some useful checklists for doing this sort of analysis and has designed them for children of different ages to complete themselves, using smiley faces for the younger ones. His book is full of little exercises and explanations of these various intelligences. The idea is that if we know what our own best way of thinking is, we can use it to help our own learning, and if we know how the pupils we work with are operating we can support them better [2.1:5]. Another suggestion is that we may need rather to work on the areas we or the pupils function in less well, in order to develop pathways of thinking that are currently underdeveloped. Say, if we are not good at intrapersonal skills (working with others), maybe we should spend some time on developing them; or vice versa, if we always need to operate in a group, maybe we need to develop our ways of working on our own. Some people find aspects of one mode in which they are comfortable help them operate in another; for example, having music on while you learn something off by heart, even singing straight prose or lists of things [2.1:vi].

Physical factors affect learning, just as they do any other activity. If we are tired or ill we do not learn as well as normal. Children and young people with a physical disability are liable to have to spend effort and time in dealing with the disability that more able-bodied people can put into intellectual activity. Visual or hearing impairment will impede or prevent access to written or spoken communication [18.3:vi]. The list is endless and those of you who work with pupils with special educational needs of a physical origin will know the kinds of effect these disabilities can have. For these children and young people, the role of a TA is to provide the support that takes away some of the hassle their physical condition causes to enable them to use their mental powers to the full. However, in some children the very lack of physical development of the brain in the womb may have resulted in a reduced number of brain cells, which may prevent full intellectual development [3.1:iii; 14.2:ii].

The world around us – people, social interaction, rewards, as well as the physical conditions – can influence how we learn, and the world inside us – our physical status, personality, motivation and learning style – can also affect the process. We learn facts (knowledge), how to do things (skills), ideas (concepts), and about ourselves (attitudes). Learning together can result in greater achievements than learning in isolation. What we have learnt can lead to thinking and creating new ideas or solving problems [3.1:iii].

Learning about our own way of learning can help us to improve, and assisting pupils to look at their own processes will help them to improve. Abbott (1997) explores the theories of intelligence and the building up of network pathways which enable memory to be accessed. 'All brain activity occurs spontaneously, automatically in response to challenge. The brain does not have to be taught how to learn. To thrive it needs plenty of stimulation, and it needs suitable feedback systems' (p. 4). 'The ability to think about your own thinking (metacognition) is essential in a world of continuous change. Through metacognition, we can develop skills that are genuinely transferable. These skills are linked to reflective intelligence, or wits' (p. 5).

Behaviourism

The hindbrain which controls the more reflex behaviour is the area that is susceptible to the so-called Pavlovian, behaviourist training. **Pavlov** lived in Russia in the late nineteenth century and worked with dogs. He found hungry dogs would salivate at the sound or smells associated with food. We all know how we experience this if friends describe a new restaurant or recipe for our favourite food. We do it without thinking, without using the higher order part of the brain; it is a mechanistic thing.

Thorndike, in America about the same time, trained cats to use levers to get at their food. We train ourselves to use the clutch and brake to bring a car to an emergency stop when learning to drive. We are at first using our higher order brain, to think about what we are doing, but practising makes it become a more reflex activity. **Skinner** worked with pigeons, and recognised that repeating the stimulus strengthened or *reinforced* the connections. The mind, or the thinking part of the brain, is significant, but skills and memory pathways need this kind of reinforcement, and some school learning needs this kind of behaviourist approach – lots of praise and repetition [3.1:9].

Constructivism

Piaget worked in the 1930s and 1940s. He was a biologist by training but was fascinated by his own children, whom he observed intensely, recording and commenting in depth on what he found. His work has come under criticism because of his limited area of study, just a few children, but his influence has been profound. Being a biologist, he took a biological, developmental view of how thinking develops. Piaget became interested in thinking or *intellectual* or *cognitive* development. He recognised that thinking develops just like any other physical part of the body and goes through stages [7.1:i; 7.2:i]. However he was dogmatic about the stages, saw only one type of development and considered that there was linear progression through the stages. We now appreciate different aspects of learning and thinking develop differently, and the stages are not fixed or as age-related as Piaget proposed. Because of his more fixed ideas on the process of cognitive development, people thought that children had to go through the stages, and one had to wait for the right stage to teach certain things. This went along with theories that all one had to do in educating children was to wait and see, offer a rich learning environment and the child's exploration would do all that was necessary.

His developmental stages of concept development were as follows:

- Up to about 18 months old the infant is involved in developing skills of mobility and sensing his/her environment – the 'sensori-motor stage'.
- From 2 to 4 years is the 'pre-operational' stage – the child is only concerned with themselves (egocentric).
- By about 4 years they are 'intuitive' – thinking logically but unaware of what they are doing.
- From 7 to 11 years old, the child can operate logically, but still needs to see and work with real objects to learn and understand – the 'concrete stage'.
- Then the child is capable of 'formal' thinking about things without the 'props' – the 'abstract' stage.

This is why younger children need 'props' for their learning, things like blocks for counting, or artefacts and films about days gone by. Yet we know that even small children can have amazing imagination. Piaget ignored the context of learning, and did not ask how to facilitate or accelerate cognitive development. Very young children have all the parts of the brain functioning, formal thinking is possible for them, but often the more sensori-motor needs dominate.

Piaget also believed that learning was similar to digestion. We take in food, and digest it to make it part of ourselves. He spoke of 'assimilating' ideas and 'accommodating' them; they then become part of our own mental make-up. He also spoke of 'conservation', the ability to 'operate' internally with 'schemes'. This is how we carry out mental operations. He believed that children are born without substantive knowledge but have the definite means of coming to know the world. We construct miniature theories of how the world works; we may be problem solvers – testing strategies or 'schemes'. This all makes a lot of sense, in that we need to present children with ideas and facts in stages, give them props and practical experiences – the 'play' of children – and allow them time to assimilate.

There are some classic experiments regarding the conservation ideas of Piaget that we can do with children and which are fun.

Conservation of number

With a three-year-old who is just learning to count:
Ask them to count the fingers on your hand.
Do they match a number to a finger or do they count several numbers while resting on one finger?
With a five-year-old:
Try lining up two rows of 10 counters, one equally spaced and the other spread out.
Ask which row has more in.

Conservation of length

Take two pieces of tape, each about 20 cm long.
Put them together in parallel on the table in front of you, with the ends together.
Now pull one away to the left or right.
Ask if they are still the same length.

Conservation of weight or volume

Take a ball of plasticene or dough.
Carefully cut it in half, flatten one piece.
Ask if they are still the same size.
Or balance two pieces of plasticene on a pair of scales, demonstrating they are
  the same weight, and then flatten one piece.
Ask if they are the same size.

Much of the development of the science curriculum has been based on Piaget's ideas of the development of understanding, but teachers recognise that this development is not directly related to age. Intervening can change the way in which pupils look at their own thinking. This gives what are called 'higher order skills' with which they can tackle the ordinary curriculum and look at ideas. Researchers have found that these pupils can get better results, particularly in the secondary school [3.1:iii].

If you are interested in the details of Piaget's work and can cope with the jargon, the appendix of *Children's Minds* (Donaldson 1984: 129–46) is useful. This book, which constructively criticised his work, was first published in 1978, before other theories came to the fore, particularly those connecting language and thought development and recognising the importance of the context of learning.

Language and background – social constructivism

Chomsky, an American linguist, wrote in the 1950s of the connection between language and thought. He believed that language development was special and not explained as part of general knowledge acquisition. Language and communication is needed in literacy and numeracy as a vehicle for development. **Bernstein** argued that the differences in children from different backgrounds were due to the differing ways different groups of people used language – that people of a lower class or income group had a restricted vocabulary and grammar structure and could be inhibiting the mental development of their children. There are still arguments about which comes first, the restricted code of language or the mental capacity to use language. There are powerful non-verbal ways of communicating, such as a hand gesture or a smile. Body language can create discomfort or raise expectations. We should also recognise that changes of background, language or culture can create barriers to learning [3.1:iii]. And it is important not to talk down to children, thinking you are using the appropriate language for their age or stage of development. You must recognise that they need to increase their vocabulary, and can take part in quite sophisticated conversations and arguments, given the opportunity. Listen, observe and discuss any findings with your class teacher.

The social environment

Vygotsky, working in the 1970s and 1980s, believed that the tools or symbols of language enable people to act outside as well as within their environment, broadening their horizons, and this gives added possibilities to their development. While studying children's development like Piaget, he felt we should be considering potential, not what has already occurred. Development, he said, lagged behind learning. He also thought that others could assist us in achieving our potential more effectively by working with us than if we worked alone. Social interaction is part of learning. He described higher mental functions as 'internalised social relationships', and said you could see this in the influence of parents on learning to talk.

We learn a lot from each other and our surroundings in ways that do not use words. Offices and hotels can give 'messages' about the kind of places they are from the décor of their reception areas and the body language of their receptionists. Schools have a 'hidden curriculum'; we receive motivation and encouragement in our learning from other people.

He particularly developed the concept of a 'zone of proximal development' (ZPD) and emphasised the importance of guidance or collaboration in learning. If we can see the potential learning of pupils we can put in place stepping stones or 'scaffolding' to bring them to the next stage of development – a clear role for a perceptive TA. As the pupils develop 'mastery', external guidance or scaffolding can be reduced. The important thing for the pupil is that the TAs provide the scaffolding, not build the complete tower.

Bruner also used the idea of scaffolding, but added that we can help this process by searching out the patterns and putting the right pieces in place at the right time. As with language, it is important to use the appropriate equipment for the development levels of the pupils with whom you work [17.2:vi]. By inventing codes and rules, seeking out the regularity and predictability of patterns in knowledge or skills, the teacher–pupil interaction can be speeded up. Bruner emphasised the importance of culture and social interaction but he also acknowledged the constraints of our genetic make-up.

The cyclical nature of learning

One way of looking at the learning process is that of a cycle of activity, first proposed by **Kolb**.

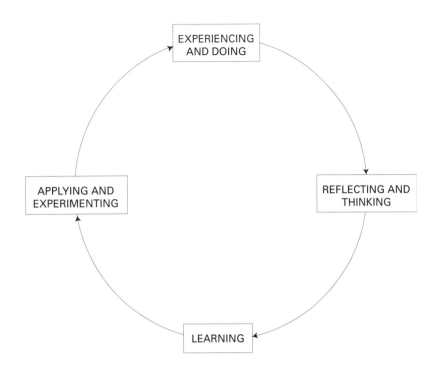

Figure 5.4 A learning cycle

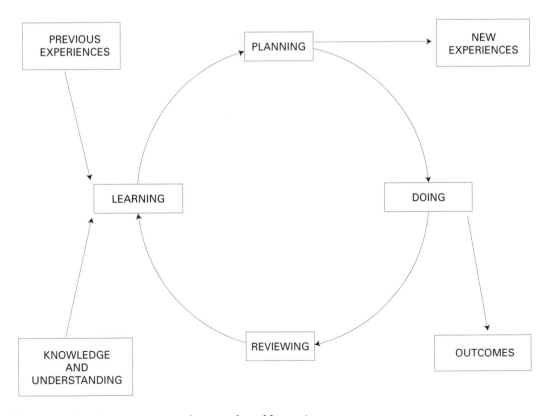

Figure 5.5 A more complex cycle of learning

Learning is not as straightforward as these cycles try to depict; it will be spiral because of the effect of maturation, interventions and the social context of the learning, which will influence how it is repeated [3.1:iii].

Outcomes of learning

As learning is so difficult to see and assess in process, the emphasis has been put on the outcomes of learning – the results of assignments, tests and examinations. We count the number of right answers to our questions and believe this relates to how much the pupil knows. Such is the number-crunching facility of computers, and the related ability of communicating the numeric results in written and electronic forms, that a whole industry of league tables and target setting has grown up around the results of such tests. The arguments about selection are always interesting, whether it is for a place in a school, university or football team or for a job. Are the results of competitive examinations or tests reliable indicators of potential? Many other kinds of test have been devised, such as assessing competence by watching, or psychometric tests designed to find out hidden thoughts, but still the humble interview, talking face to face with the candidate, has a place. A teacher's assessment of pupils will include things such as attitude to learning and progress made over time as well as test results [8.1:iv].

Unfortunately, this emphasis on outcomes has resulted in publicity and even rewards. People move to live in the catchment areas of schools with high places in the league tables, resulting in more pupils going to those schools and thus more funding for them. Within some schools it has resulted in a dispro-portionate amount of time being spent on revision and rote fact learning and inappropriate booster classes. There are good things to come out of the publicity. It has increased the debate about the purpose of education; it has made some so-called 'coasting schools' recognise that their pupils could do better, and some inner-city schools realise that other similar schools enable their pupils to achieve higher standards. Do talk with your mentor or class teacher about their feelings about these matters, recognising the very real tensions that all schools and teachers are under.

Another thing to bear in mind is that we learn by making mistakes, not just by being able to produce right answers. All pupils like to see a page of sums with ticks, yet this can indicate they are not being stretched enough by the questions. Many pupils, when asked to guess or estimate a quantity, will feel good if they are right or near in their guess, and even alter their incorrect guess to match the correct quantity, rather than recognise the process of estimating is the important learning point, not the answer.

Some outcomes of learning that are very difficult to quantify are in the areas of creativity and problem solving. With the emphasis on easily assessible outcomes and formal examinations such as the GCSE and 'A' level, the creative arts and vocational skills have had to struggle for recognition. It is this debate which underlies the apparent muddle that 14 to 19 years education sometimes seems to have become. It must be difficult to be a student or pupil within that age group, or a parent of such a person, but the proposals for a baccalaureate and the recognition of vocational qualifications will mean more pupils have their talents and potential recognised.

It is important that you consider not just what you are learning but how you learn, and to continue that process for the pupils with whom you work. There is more about observing pupils, planning work for them and helping with assessment in Chapter 11 [8.1:v].

Questions to ask yourself

Look again at the factors which have affected a recent learning experience of your own.

- Why did you start it?
- What did you need to help you – books, an instructor, discussion with other people, time on your own, the right tools or machine, practice?
- What facts did you learn? What skills?
- How has your understanding of the matter increased?
- What mistakes did you make?
- What went wrong? Why?
- What went well? Why?
- Did a certificate at the end help?
- Did other people's views matter?
- Can you still improve?
- Would you do it again?

Now consider a recent topic you have been following with a pupil or group of pupils.

- Can you answer the same questions about their learning?
- Can they answer the questions?
- Do you or the pupils need to make any changes in the way you work together?
- Can you help your pupils understand their own learning styles better?

Some further reading

Bruce, T. and Meggitt, C. (1996) *Child Care and Education*. London: Hodder and Stoughton. (Especially Chapters 6 and 9.)

Bruner, J. S. (1966) *Towards a Theory of Instruction*. Cambridge, Mass. and London: The Belknap Press of Harvard University Press.

Donaldson, M. (1984) *Children's Minds*. London: Fontana Paperbacks.

Dryden, G. and Vos, J. (1994) *The Learning Revolution*. Aylesbury: Accelerated Learning Systems.

Lazear, D. (1994) *Seven Pathways of Learning: Teaching Students and Parents about Multiple Intelligences*. Arizona: Zephyr Press.

Lee, V. (1990) *Children's Learning in School*. London: Hodder and Stoughton for the Open University. (Especially Part 1 Learning theories.)

Pollard, A. (2002) *Reflective Teaching: Effective and Evidence-informed Professional Practice*. London and New York: Continuum. (Especially Chapter 7.)

Smith, A. (1996) *Accelerated Learning in the Classroom*. Stafford: Network Educational Press.

Wood, D. (1988) *How Children Think and Learn*. Oxford: Blackwell. (Especially Chapters 1 and 2.)

6 Understanding other aspects of pupils' development

The Education Reform Act (ERA) of 1988, which brought in the National Curriculum (NC), set it in the context of spiritual, moral and cultural development as well as the physical and mental development which appears to be emphasised by the NC itself.

Emotional development

Sometimes computers are held up to be analogous with the brain function. Certainly, there are definite similarities, and many things the computer can do better than a single brain, such as multiple calculations. But computers cannot feel in the way humans do, and this characteristic, that of having emotions, is a major difference.

If you think back to that learning experience you have had as an adult, you will recognise that however bright you are and however good the supporting environment, including the teacher, if you are preoccupied by other problems, bored or insecure, your feelings get in the way [3.1:iii]. Emotional development and condition affects learning; this is sometimes called the *affective* domain of our brains. Part of growing up is to become able to put some of our emotions on hold when having to do other things. Younger children are less able to control their emotions and teenagers' hormones play havoc with their control systems. TAs can be of great help to the learning situation by providing an understanding ear to pupils in distress. There must be a warning attached to this about dealing with confidences, and this is dealt with in greater depth in the next chapter.

A relatively new concept that has been proposed is that of 'emotional intelligence'. This follows the ideas about multiple intelligences, but really indicates that our emotional state is part and parcel of the way we think and act.

Motivation

This is one of the greatest influences on learning. The will to achieve can overcome many physical and social handicaps. When one becomes bored, or other interests take over, it is difficult to concentrate or persevere. Even easier tasks become a chore. Setting up a home of one's own can make do-it-yourself experts of even the most impractical people. Learning to read for some is a matter of accessing information about football, keeping a pet or using a computer. One of the skills TAs develop is finding out what interests a reluctant pupil and building upon that: finding the book about football, or advertisements for guinea pig food or an Internet guide [3.2:iii]. Another skill is being able to repeat a task but change it slightly to create interest, while retaining the learning objective. Keep a note of changes you make and share them with the teacher; these make a useful assessment tool for them [3.1:9].

Self-confidence and self-esteem

This was sometimes overlooked in the past [15.3:xi]. We all have stories of the teacher who was demeaning of our efforts. Sometimes the put-down can motivate a person to achieve despite the comments, but even then the memory stays of the sense of discomfort [2.1:2]. Failure or even perceived failure can prevent us all from trying a second time. An interesting and readable couple of books are those by John Holt, *How Children Fail* (1964) and *How Children Learn* (1967), where he emphasises the impact of feelings on our capacity to learn, and the blow to our progress that failure or even apparent failure can be [15.3:v]. Fox (2001: 19–31) devotes a whole chapter to the importance of self-esteem, with many ideas on how an assistant can encourage this [15.3:ii]. Another useful book for those who work in primary schools is *Feeling Good* (Whetton and Cansell 1993) [12.1:x].

Small children normally come to recognise their own identity in their first year; they understand that there are other people, some who love them particularly and others who are on the periphery of their lives. These early relationships are crucial in helping the child form a concept of themselves – a self-image. They know they are valued and develop the self-confidence to walk and talk, which later on gives them the self-confidence to accept challenges. Adults who have good self-images will be a good role model for children. Confident, encouraging parents and teachers (even though they may be acting) will support younger learners [18.3:9].

Sometimes adults underestimate or overestimate a child's emotional maturity. Small children can be very sensitive to atmosphere and recognise when adults are very distressed, yet nobody talks to them about what might have happened in the family circumstances to cause the distress. Conversely, an adult can sometimes assume that the child can cope with difficult happenings without problems. The increased recognition of the need for pupils to talk to someone after traumatic events has meant an increased emphasis on the work of counsellors. Children often regress in terms of physical development when they are under emotional stress: toddlers can revert to soiling, primary age children can become bedwetters, and children who were apparently more detached show the need for more comforting and cuddles. Some children may stop eating properly or talking [18.3:vi]. Elective mutes are children who appear not to be able to speak yet clearly understand all that is spoken, and have no physical disability preventing them. They can talk but choose not to in particular circumstances, such as with people they do not know.

You need to think about what causes emotional distress, things such as changed circumstances or instability at home, changing boundaries, people or places. Pupils with SEN or EAL may find it more difficult to understand what is happening and therefore find it more difficult to adjust to such changes [12.1:vii].

Small children without words to express their feelings will show their distress or temper in tantrums and their joy or excitement by running around. By the time they are of school age, able to voice their feelings and to understand circumstances, tantrums are usually under control. Communication is important as a means of self-expression and developing self-esteem [18.3:ix]. By seven or eight years of age they have a concept of the passage of time and the excitement of anticipation of things such as parties and holidays becomes more manageable. By ten and eleven they are competent to deal with more complex situations without panicking, such as finding themselves lost in a shopping centre or falling off their bicycle in a strange place [9.2:vi; 9.3:ii].

The body's hormones – the chemical messengers – can disrupt emotional stability in puberty, creating frustrations, mood swings, even tantrums again. An apparently stable child becomes a stranger at times, yet this is the time when crucial life choices have to be made and the main external examinations are held. It is important that you recognise such changes for what they are, and know how to manage them. Do seek help if you feel an emotional outburst calls for intervention, and tell someone what has happened even if you have dealt with it appropriately. It may happen again, and parents might need to be told [9.3:iii]. Emotional distress may not just be signalled by tantrums. Moody or withdrawn behaviour can signify that something is wrong. Some cases of the teenage eating disorders of anorexia (not eating enough) and bulimia (eating but then inducing vomiting to stop the food being digested) may be due to emotions being unbalanced. As you will be closer to some of the pupils than many of the teachers, you will notice such changes and you will be able to alert them to a possible problem.

Adults, too, have problems in this area, particularly, it seems, if you are in the caring professions. If you are a social worker or a doctor or working in schools, there will be times when you are 'at work' and times when you are with your family or doing other things. You never have enough time to do all that you want to do, so you experience a sense of failure. This can colour your way of dealing with the next problem – 'I can't do it' may be the thought. Feeling good about what you can do is a necessary part of the job. In teaching you cannot 'win them all' and this has to be faced, but you can do some things well. TAs have suffered quite significantly from lack of self-confidence in the past, because of your comparative invisibility in the school system and your low pay. Where you are valued by the school and your colleagues, and they make you know this, you feel good about the job. It is a job with great job satisfaction – a reason most TAs give for remaining. You are doing a most worthwhile thing – remind yourself about this when you feel low.

Then, consider how the pupils you work with feel – probably singled out for their lack of achieving what the others in the class can do. Be an active listener, don't feel you have to 'do' anything; understanding the problem is half way to solving it [9.2:1]. Communicating feelings can help, letting the pupils express themselves in words, spoken or written, or drawings or even music or some kind of supervised physical activity. Giving them time for this may enable them to control what would otherwise be an uncontrolled and possibly dangerous outburst and to maintain their self-esteem [13.2:viii; 18.3:7]. Let the pupil talk; sometimes getting them to keep a diary will help them to express their needs and ideas [9.2:1]. Do make sure that anything you do is within the school guidelines for dealing with emotional problems [9.2:4].

Often smaller children can draw their feelings rather than write. They can make lists or flowcharts which can be positive or negative. If they are negative, try to get them to work also on the opposite:

- What I did wrong – what went well today.
- What I hate about school – what I like about school.
- What makes me sad – what makes me happy.

Older pupils may be able to think of positive things about other people, e.g. 'What I like about Miss Smith, Jane or Ahmed'.

Some pupils may need some help with describing words, so you could make a collection of these in case you need them [9.2:1 & 5].

The main theme is to look for strengths in the pupil – what they can do, not what they cannot – and build on them, and to provide the pupils with a positive role model in yourself. Appropriate praise is important, phrases like 'well tried' rather than 'well done' if the work is still not up to the standard it should be [3.1:viii; 9.2:4; 13.2:ix; 14.2:6; 15.3:x]. Encourage pupils to look for the positive in situations, in adults and in their peers [13.1:8; 16.2:7,8]. Discourage them from 'putting down' their fellow pupils, particularly when they resort to stereotypes such as 'he can't play in the team, he's too young', 'she's stupid, she's just a girl', 'he's thick because he's in a wheelchair' or 'black people smell' [9.2:v; 12.2:8]). Remember, 'there are many kinds of abilities and one challenge for teachers is to enrich their pupils' lives by identifying, developing and celebrating the diverse attributes of each child' (Pollard 2002: 151).

When pupils are more able to cope with expressing their feelings you can move on to more constructive ideas to help them prepare for such feelings and deal with them [9.2:2,3,iii & iv]. Use the language of choice – 'you can either accept a situation and move on or make yourself even more miserable', 'I can help you with your reading/writing if you put in your bit of effort.' Make sure they have telephone numbers of friends or even helplines. In the end, you cannot live the pupils' lives for them; you can only give them the tools and strategies to make the best of what they have got.

Some schools are particularly good at what they call 'life skills', enabling all their pupils to cope with the challenges that life outside school might bring. These may just be about doing basic things such as shopping, handling money, contacting emergency services or cooking, but most programmes will include dealing with relationships, becoming independent from the family home and living with oneself as a person. Talk to the person in your school who is responsible for PSHE about what strategies they use, and whether they have any books you can read or any simple tips for dealing with pupils about whom you may be concerned [15.3:iii & iv]. Always tell the class teacher what you are doing and keep them informed of your progress (or lack of it).

Social, cultural and spiritual development

Social development

Some of the discussion about the development of good relationships in Chapter 3 is relevant to this aspect of development. Children need to develop good relationships with those around them, or life will become unbearable for them. Children learn about relationships from watching and imitating people around them. The bonding between parents and babies is considered crucial and mothers are encouraged to hold new-born babies from the word 'go'. Fathers are encouraged to be present at the baby's birth.

If you do not work with very young children, it is very interesting to spend time in a nursery or playgroup just watching the children in the role-play areas. Children will act out what they have seen at home or sometimes on television screens. They will cook and look after other children if that is what happens in their home, or shout at the other children and send one out for a takeaway if that is what they are used to. You need to be careful when interpreting role-play, as sometimes children act out their fears as well as reality, so always discuss what you see with the staff in the group. Father figures or male role models in the home are still considered significant whether the children are male or female, even in this era of successful one-parent families. Educationalists are concerned that schools, particularly primary schools, are becoming increasingly female domains. Toys such as teddy bears and for the very young even a piece of blanket can become a surrogate friend. Many of us have had imaginary friends when little. **Bowlby** was a significant influence on childcare strategies in early childhood, believing that the mother – or mother figure – was the significant central person in a baby's life. However, while there is a lot of truth in this, it is not only relationships with parents that are important, but also having grandparents, carers, brothers and sisters. It is the quality of the care and of people that determines their significance and influence. Many babies attend day nurseries successfully from a very early age, but a key worker is usually assigned to them in these stages to ensure that the right sort of bonding and relationships develop [15.3:ix].

By about three years of age, the toddler is able to leave their mother or influential carer or the close caring of a day nursery for a while and this has become the general entry age for playgroups and nursery schools. Here, children are encouraged to play with other children whom they will only see in those surroundings. By five they are happy to spend the day at school sharing the teacher with up to thirty other children, although if you work in these classes you will understand the importance of the settling routines. You may have seen the way in which some children still find it difficult to adjust to not being able to demand the teacher's attention without waiting their turn. During the primary years children develop firm friendships, occasionally forming small gangs or clubs for different activities. They join organisations such as Brownies or judo clubs, and can operate in teams, collaborating and sharing. All the time, they try out their boundaries, and experiment with situations. They see what happens when they do things that are not allowed, and can have several ways of operating depending on differing circumstances. They also influence how other children and adults behave to them by the way they behave. Often parents will say to teachers, when their child's behaviour at school is described on an open evening, 'But he's not like that at home' or 'She's never done that before.'

When children change schools, either because their family has moved house or they are of the age for the next kind of school, they have to re-form friendships and teacher–pupil relationships, as well as find their way about a strange building and adjust to different timetables and subjects. All sorts of things affect a child's ability to settle in a new environment [11.1:iii]. Generally, an unsettled child will be fearful and tearful, but such feelings could show themselves in angry or even aggressive behaviour as the pupil is cross at being put in this strange situation [11.1:iv]. Pupils with learning problems, a disability or with little ability to communicate, either because of home language being different or through speech problems, have a higher risk of unease with new situations, as they find it more difficult to understand what is happening. But beware of misinterpreting the reasons for difficult behaviour; always talk matters through with the teacher if you have concerns, and respond as he or she directs [11.1:4 & 5]. It is important that you are aware of the pupils' need to make relationships as well as just get on with the task in hand. You cannot make people get on with each other but you can help them see the point of doing so [1.1:vii]. The language of choice is helpful: 'Shall we do something together or can you do it on your own?' Children choose whom they want to be with and do things with; social relationships are a two-way process.

As children get older, they become much more influenced by the children around them, particularly so in the teenage years, when peer pressure can induce long-lasting changes in lifestyle and attitude. Strong friendships formed in the late teens, in the last few years at school, at college or university, or in a first job tend to be friendships for life [9.1.i]. Hopefully by the time the pupils reach this stage they can both recognise and control their own behaviour to fit in with the society in which they live.

While you may have your ideas of what is antisocial behaviour, you must determine the school's policy for what is acceptable in the various situations. Classrooms, playground, lunch hall, laboratories, toilet areas will all have their limits of acceptability. Different cultures will have their own rules or customs of behaviour towards others, and even their own ways of being abusive [9.1:iv]. Not only will differing languages have different words which are considered offensive, but gestures which are ordinary to some are obscene to others. Even within our own culture things change. For instance, it would have been wholly unacceptable in my own childhood to have received an invitation or posted present and not to reply with thanks in writing, but now the use of telephone and e-mail mean that such a practice is much rarer.

More can be found about dealing with antisocial behaviour in the section on behaviour management in the next chapter. The principles of positive strategies, reinforcing and rewarding the good and providing choice and sanctions for the less acceptable hold good [9.2:viii].

Cultural development

It can be seen from much of the above that language and culture are going to influence social and emotional development as well as intellectual development. The power of being able to express feelings in discussion, or even confession, and being able to share ideas is enormous. The way in which different cultures have differing methods of child care – whether boys and girls are educated together, or whether girls are educated at all – clearly makes a difference to other development [18.3:9]. The kind of clothing, food, art and music which surround a child from the early years will influence development and growth; they are part of the environmental influences on inherited characteristics mentioned in the previous chapter. The rituals and customs of daily life or religious festivals become part of our lives but also influence the kind of person we grow up to be. You must guard against forming stereotypical assumptions that, because of a person's gender or apparent ethnic origin, they will behave in a certain way or hold certain opinions [15.3:viii].

Your main objective when working with pupils whose cultural background, dialect or home language is different from your own is to appreciate the additional richness that they bring to school life [12.1:10 & vii; 18.3:9]. It is about reinforcing their self-image. Their knowledge and understanding of ways different to yours, their food, clothing, art, music and traditions add a diversity and interest. Multilingual pupils have a skill that many of us do not have [12.1:xi]. There will be school policies about such celebration of cultural diversity, about how various different religious festivals might be observed, how dress codes might be modified and where additional resources might be found [2.1:iii; 2.2:iv].

Variations in family values and practices may make pupils' responses to school work differ [15.3:vii]. For instance, it may be traditional within a family or group that females never answer before males have had their turn, or that it is not done to contradict a teacher. Thus a pupil may be reluctant to challenge ideas or comments. Homes where books are rare and conversation is limited may encourage children to feel that all books are pointless and words are not helpful to express feelings. For them the motivation to learn from the printed word is minimal and problems may be resolved by violence rather than open discussion [2.1:vii]. Understanding the background from which its pupils come obviously helps the school, and it may be your role to act as an intermediary between the parents or carers, as you know them from where you live in the vicinity of the school, and the teachers [12.2:iv & v; 23.1:ii].

Spiritual and moral development

These aspects of development are often ignored. Moral development appears to come about as part of social and cultural development. Even small children, where boundaries are clear, whether they are strict or lenient, know when they are doing 'wrong'. It seems to be natural to challenge boundaries, and if these are flexible or ever-moving, the children may experience problems. The child knows they have overstepped the boundary by the reaction of the one setting the boundary. Too great a reaction can result in rebellion.

Spiritual development is not confined to the development of religious belief or participation in the practice of a particular faith. Young children experience wonder and joy, they accept mystery, they are curious, creative and imaginative, and suppression of such feelings in infancy or the early years of school can inhibit their expression for many years to come. Eight to ten-year-olds begin to seek the meaning of things, want a purpose for doing things, and even for their own existence, and are beginning to recognise their own and others' identities as people. They get a very strong sense of injustice, and often start small action groups to raise money for worthy causes, or argue strongly for fairness in a game. It is at this age they will start asking abstract questions about beliefs, such as 'Do you believe in a life after death?' Primary age children can face death in others, in their pets and even in themselves, as terminally ill children do. They can appreciate straight but sensitive talking from adults, although many adults will feel that they need help in talking with children about such matters. They begin to sort out legends and myths from factual evidence; for instance, recognising the myth behind the tradition of 'Father Christmas' delivering presents.

Many teenagers will fight shy of discussing their deep feelings about spiritual matters; peer pressure and fashion may dictate that such things are cissy. Yet most of them will be trying out their own beliefs in practice, and will still feel strongly about the beauty of the world around them or the expression of joy or sadness in poetry, music, art or drama. They can get emotionally involved with the more extreme versions of religious belief or practice, as their instinct for trying new ways and rebellion comes to the fore, but most young people come through such experiences. They develop a greater understanding of the variety of human nature, the reality of the consequences of their actions, their place in the world and their interdependence with their family and the community around them. You can be an active listener at all these stages of development but as in all such matters, ensure you know what the school policy is before you contribute too much of your own beliefs. You may be working in a faith school, or where some parents hold firm views such as those of Jehovah's Witnesses. It is not your place to uphold or change any particular belief. The school will be inspected on how well pupils 'respect other people's differences, particularly their feelings, values and beliefs . . . [and] how well the school provides opportunities for pupils' spiritual, moral, social and cultural development' (Ofsted 1999: 38, 39).

Schools need to help children and young people retain 'a capacity for reflection, curiosity, and a sense of awe and wonder as well as an ability to discuss beliefs and understand how they contribute to individual and group identity' (Ofsted 1993: 15) at the world about them, as well as encouraging the sense of fair play. A few moments spent in looking at some new flowers growing in the school grounds, or pointing out a rainbow formed by the edge of bevelled glass in the sunshine, the growth of the class pet, or the colours of a visiting bird or butterfly can all help spiritual growth. The intensity of the curriculum and the constraints of a timetable have tended to squeeze out not only thinking time but also reflecting time. This is not part of religious worship, although of course it can be, but is part of feeding an aspect of life that can so easily be lost. For some, poetry or music may trigger such a moment, and it is always worth trying to include something that has moved you when planning work. Different people are moved by different things, but you never know when such moments might happen.

The individual and independence

Personality

While in a school, pupils have to conform to certain rules and boundaries, so that they are safe and their activity is purposeful, but they are all individuals, and will grow into separate adults responsible not only for their own lives, but probably those of their children or colleagues at work or fellow members of a team. Any of you who are parents or managers will understand the dilemmas that face adults working in schools. You always have to maintain a balance between encouraging or allowing individual wishes against the needs of the family or organisation or your perception of the future. Where there is mutual respect for the role and needs of the other members, such a balance is easier. Even very small children will show their personality in many ways. Your personality will affect the way you work with both the adults and the pupils in your school and it is worth spending time reflecting on facets of your own personality and the kind of contribution you will make to the life of the school. Pollard (2002) has quite a powerful section on knowing oneself as a teacher (pp. 90–6), and an equally useful section on understanding individual children (pp. 96–108). In completing the first few sections of your personal/professional portfolio you will have identified many of the contributions you can make in terms of experience and qualifications, but it is also useful to reflect on your own personality. As with your self-review of your job, your self-analysis is something that is ongoing throughout your life. Knowing yourself as a person and a learner helps you have an insight into the ways of pupils, to establish a rapport with them and empathise with their efforts to learn. For many managers, the personality of a TA is a strong contributor to acceptability for the job.

Promoting independent learning

One of the problems you will encounter is that it is very likely that you have been appointed to help those who need assistance, and this very assistance labels the pupils as being disadvantaged in some way. It is a fine balance, and a continually changing one, between helping appropriately and enabling the pupils to achieve more of their potential and feel a sense of their own achievement [15.3:5; 16.1:8]. Somehow, the pupil has to maintain their own self-esteem and self-confidence and become increasingly independent of you [3.2:4; 13.1:7]. It is important that pupils do not become dependent on their helpers whatever the nature of the SEN [3.2:i; 14.2:7,8 & 9; 15.1:xi; 15.3:6 & vi]. This can have two effects: first, the pupil does not try for themselves, and will not be able to repeat the exercise without you being present; and secondly, the situation could label the pupil in the eyes of the rest of the class. Some TAs have even described 'doing myself out of a job' as part of their role.

Discuss with the teacher the sort of strategies they use and would like you to use to promote independence, to encourage and support pupils, to enable them to make their own decisions [3.2:1]. It is about getting pupils organised into a system so that they can operate without you; for example, with ICT equipment [17.2:ix]. It is also about helping pupils with SEN to learn and operate with minimum support [16.2:xi]. It is about showing them how to do a task but not doing it for them, working alongside on a separate sheet of paper but ensuring they do not copy your work directly. If they ask for a spelling get them to try first, sound out the word, and praise them for how close they have got; or send them to a dictionary or show them how to use the spellchecker on their word processor; do not just give them the spelling of the word [16.1:xiii]. Watch out for those 'zones of proximal development' where you can put in 'scaffolding' to support the crucial next step [14.2:5]. Tell pupils to remember what the teacher said on a previous occasion, to jog their memory; do not let them rely on yours. Sometimes aids to independence cost money, but schools have ways and means of getting assistance for those with SEN. Items such as laptops, for those with a physical impairment which makes writing difficult, mean that a pupil can write independently of a scribe. Even simple tools such as left-handed scissors can mean the difference between the pupil doing it for themselves and you having to do it for them. Sometimes it is a question of time, to allow for a slower way of doing things or a thought process [3.2:ii]. Remember, praise for trying is as important, if not more so, than praise for succeeding. Part of all children's growth and development into adulthood is the increasing acceptance of responsibility for their own actions and their own learning [3.2:2 & 7].

This and the previous chapter have looked at the many facets of the learning process. Sometimes the theories and ideas seem in conflict:

- Inherited characteristics versus the influence of the environment
- Maturity versus accelerating learning
- Stages in development versus intuitive jumps of reasoning
- The biological function of the brain, the computer-type action of the brain, versus the more ephemeral things such as emotions and spirituality
- The importance of social and cultural context versus 'scientifically proven' facts
- Valuing diversity versus the need for school conformity
- Collaborative learning versus independent learning.

All these go to make up a complex process of development which result in a person being like the facets of a well-cut gemstone. Different surfaces catch the light at different times and turns of the stone. Different stones need different cutting techniques to bring out their particular brightness. It is part of your job to be alert to the nature of the learning, personality and context of the pupil you are working with; listen to them, watch them at work and encourage them to talk about their own feelings and learning [3.2:6]. You can then assist the teacher in utilising the best learning strategy for each one and planning for their future development [3.2:8].

Questions to ask yourself

- If you are now part of the way through reading this book or your course, have your feelings about learning changed since you started?
- Do your feelings or beliefs influence how you behave?
- Are you clear about the ethos and values which your school stands for and your role within them?
- Is there any conflict between your belief systems and that promoted by the school? What can you do about this?
- What do you do when pupils ask you about your feelings or beliefs?
- Do you know about the cultural backgrounds and sensitivities of the families whose children come to your school?
- What does the religious education policy for your school contain? Or the policy for collective worship?
- To whom can you go in the school to discuss any problems which may arise when dealing with pupils?

Some further reading

Bruce, T. and Meggitt, C. (1996) *Child Care and Education*. London: Hodder and Stoughton. (Especially Chapter 7.)

Holt, J. (1964) *How Children Fail*. London: Penguin Books.

Holt, J. (1967) *How Children Learn*. London: Penguin Books.

Hook, P. and Vass, A. (2000a) *Confident Classroom Leadership*. London: David Fulton Publishers. (Especially Chapter 2.)

Hook, P. and Vass, A. (2000b) *Creating Winning Classrooms*. London: David Fulton Publishers. (Especially Chapters 2 and 3.)

Lovey, J. (2002) *Supporting Special Educational Needs in Secondary School Classrooms*, 2nd edn. London: David Fulton Publishers. (Especially Chapter 3.)

Ofsted (1999) *Handbook for Inspecting Primary and Nursery Schools*. London: Ofsted. (Especially pp. 70–3.)

O'Hagan, M. and Smith, M. (1993) *Special Issues in Child Care*. London: Baillière Tindall. (Especially pp. 21–40.)

Pollard, A. (2002) *Reflective Teaching: Effective and Evidence-informed Professional Practice*. London and New York: Continuum. (Especially Chapter 5.)

SCAA (1996) *Education for Adult Life: The Spiritual and Moral Development of Young People* (Discussion papers: No 6). London: School Curriculum and Assessment Authority.

Whetton, N. and Cansell, P. (1993) *Feeling Good: Raising Self-esteem in the Primary School Classroom*. London: Forbes Publications.

7 Supporting pupils throughout the school

Most of this chapter is an edited version of material from *The Essential Guide for Competent Teaching Assistants* (Watkinson 2003) as Standards 3–1, 3–10 and 3–11 were optional Level 2 units. It is included for those of you who have not read the other book. Unit 3–1 is now a compulsory unit and I believe that all TAs should be able to cope with health and safety issues and all staff working in a school should know and understand the aspects of child protection dealt with in this chapter.

Supporting physical health

You must remember that

> Teachers and other school staff have a common law duty to act as any proud parent would to make sure that pupils are healthy and safe on school premises and this might, in exceptional circumstances, extend to administering medicine and/or taking action in an emergency.
>
> (DfEE 1996: 3)

There will be school policies for all health, hygiene and medical matters; you must make sure you have a copy of all the relevant ones and that you read them, understand them and follow the guidelines set out in them [11.2:i & vii]. Sick children or adults will not work well, and may be infectious to others. If you see anything which concerns you, always tell the class teacher [11.3:3].

Always reassure an ill pupil, and comfort an unhappy one, but only verbally unless they seek physical comfort from you. Comforting must be done in an appropriate manner and place. A hug returned in a public place to a small child missing a parent is one thing, but the same action in a quiet corner can be misconstrued [11.3:5]. Younger children need more physical support than older ones and are less likely to be able to tell you what is wrong if they are miserable. Be sure to read the notes on child protection below. You may need to summon help [10.2:ii]. It may be important to help pupils not directly involved in an incident; they can suffer shock, particularly if the incident is severe. This is the kind of role you can play if you have to summon expert help;

you can support the onlookers. This may just be reassurance or removing them from the incident site [10.2:2,3,4 and ix].

You need to be able to recognise if a pupil is just 'under the weather' or is really feeling ill [11.3:1 & i]. The important thing is to get to know the pupils with whom you are working closely, what is their normal range of behaviour and appearance, then you will recognise significant changes should they occur. As you are likely to be working more closely with the pupils than any other member of staff, you may be the first to notice [10.2; i; 11.2:3].

The sort of things you may notice are:

- becoming very red or pale in the face, becoming very hot or cold, becoming clammy or shivering – fever usually means some kind of infection;
- changes in behaviour, such as not wanting to go out at break-time when they usually want to be first out;
- general distress;
- reduced concentration, even to the point of falling asleep at their desk;
- scratching more than usual – ask about the school policy regarding head lice – you should not examine a head unless it is appropriate in your school;
- complaining of pain which persists, including headaches and stomach pain, particularly if they are not easily distracted from mentioning it;
- rashes – these can develop rapidly and may be associated with fever in the case of infection or could be an allergic reaction;
- coughing and sneezing excessively;
- diarrhoea or vomiting – these you will have to deal with as emergencies.

[11.3:1]

You should not try to diagnose from these conditions, but always note any unusual circumstances that you see or the pupil mentions. Make sure you know where to send sick pupils, and to whom to report the symptoms you have noticed. You may need to summon help rather than leave a sick pupil [11.3:4].

Remember that changes in mental and emotional state can also occur, particularly if something traumatic or dramatic has happened at home, which can show itself in unhappiness, mood swings, lack of concentration and attention seeking or withdrawal from activities [11.3:6 & ii]. Some cultures and religions have different ways of dealing with illness, so, if in doubt, ask [11.3:ii]. The age of the pupil will affect how well they can tell you what is wrong; once you know the pupil well, you will be able to tell how reliable any information from them might be and the circumstances of the incident. Some pupils can fake illness if they do not like sports or the weather is inclement. There may be changes in patterns of behaviour. A small child who has always come to chat stands alone, or a usually friendly teenager is moody or withdrawn, or a usually quiet but confident pupil follows you around. It could be just growing up, the hormones of puberty taking over, or it could indicate something more significant. Either way, you need mentally to register the changes, keep an eye on the pupil over a period of time and, if really concerned, talk to the pupil's teacher or tutor. Such changes could indicate problems at home, even abuse of some kind – self-inflicted substance abuse or bullying within or outside the school [1.1:ix]. If the pupil will talk to you, follow the guidelines set out below regarding child protection – never promise confidentiality, always tell someone of the conversation and make a simple record of it.

Many TAs are appointed to help a child with special learning or physical needs [11.3:2]. You must ensure you know the full extent of your role and responsibilities with any pupil, and all the appropriate ways to support them; there is more about these topics in the following chapter.

- Ask your line manager for the four most common ailments of pupils within the school.
- See what more you can find out about these ailments.
- Find out whether these ailments are treated the same way in all countries.
- Does your school have any pupils from the countries where customs are different?
- Find out more about any conditions which apply to pupils you are working with closely.
- Does the school have any written guidelines in any of these areas?
- If so, do you have a copy?

Whatever the problem, make sure you know where and when to seek help, what kind of written records are needed and to whom you should report any concerns, including whether you contact parents directly or notify someone else to do this [10.2:6 & x; 11.3:7 & iii].

Health education [11.2:vi]

The school will have a policy on health education of the pupils. It is usually part of the PSHE policy. A healthy school is not only hygienic and physically safe but a welcoming and secure place with good relationships between all who work there. The way you listen, or are prepared to follow up problems, get help, even remember names shows that you care and are prepared to bother about others. If you are willing to assist with preparation of resources for teachers or get someone a cup of tea when they are fed up or overstretched, it shows you can think about them and do something practical to assist [11.2:1,2 & ii]. If all staff had such an attitude, the school would be good place to work, and pupils would soon recognise it as a good place to learn.

It is highly likely that you will be asked personal questions by pupils [11.2:4], as they get to know you and you work in close proximity to a small group or individuals. Note that primary schools only have to have a sex education policy – that policy does not have to ensure sex education is done by the school; it may indicate that it should be done at home.

Find out

- Should you listen to the exploits of teenagers without comment, such as
    - smoking on the school premises?
    - substance abuse?
    - getting drunk at the weekend?
    - declaring their sexual habits or preferences or that they are pregnant?
- What do you do if you are told of incidents of bullying, or disastrous friendships?
- Can you talk about HIV and AIDS if they ask the questions?
- What should you do if they show you pornography?
- Should you comment on a pupil's diet or exercise level to them if they seem excessively thin or obese?
- Whom do you tell if they are so upset about something it is affecting the way they behave?
- Simple ways to boost pupils' self-esteem.

Settling pupils

One area where you are likely to be involved, particularly if you are working with children in the early years class (sometimes called the reception or foundation class), or with Year 7s in a secondary school (Year 5s or 9s if your area has a middle school system) is with pupils who are new to the school [11.1]. The school is likely to have well-thought-out procedures, some of which will have taken place before you meet the pupils. The teachers may have visited their previous school or playgroup, or even their homes, and pupils are most likely to have had at least one visit to the school before their first 'real' day. You need to find out what these procedures are and may even accompany members of the teaching staff on their visits [11.1:ii].

Remember

- How you felt like when you started school.
- How you felt when you transferred schools.
- How you felt when you started this new job.
- How you felt if you went to a new school when you moved house as a child.
- What helped you to settle.
- Who helped you to settle.
- How long it took.

So – what can you do to help newcomers to your school?

As a TA, you can be invaluable in settling pupils in. It may be a good idea to negotiate with the teachers for you just to be available for this task at the beginning of a new school year. In this way the pupils will get down to the school work much more quickly and satisfactorily. It may even be important to change your timetable for a couple of weeks to spend more time at the beginning and end of the day ensuring the new ones know where they are going and get there happily. The teacher may ask you to liaise directly with the parents and stagger entry and exit times for the new pupils. In this way an easier transition can take place, especially if a large number are starting together. Changing classrooms or teachers can unsettle pupils; a constant change of teacher when supply teachers are standing in for a teacher on sick leave can also be a problem. In these situations you may be the one constant person in their school lives. Talk to the class teacher if you continue to notice signs of distress after a week or so, or to a more senior teacher if the class teacher's absence is the problem [11.1:5].

Strategies which may help to settle pupils [11.1:1 & i]

- Be warm and welcoming.
- Learn to recognise distressed pupils.
- Learn their names as soon as possible.
- Make sure they know the names of their class teacher or tutor and encourage the other pupils with you to befriend and help the newcomer.
- Make sure they know where they are going in the building, where their next classroom is, where their cloakroom and the toilets are, and to whom they can go if they are worried.
- Smile at them when you see them in the building but are not directly working with them.
- Allow them to talk about their previous school or playschool.
- Allow them to work a little more slowly at first.
- Have patience, listen and possibly talk about your own experiences if appropriate.
- Keep to classroom routines and, where possible, the same layout.
- Make sure you know whether they have special educational needs or speak a different language.
- Try wording your sentences more simply if that is a problem.
- Try to learn a few words of their language, as they begin to learn ours – their words for mum and dad, for home and toilet, bag, book and table would do for a start.
- Carry the tissue box with you in case of tears.
- Ensure you tell their class teacher or tutor if they have problems after the first week.

[11.1:1,2,3 & i]

Behaviour management

It is possible that you have been appointed to assist in the support of a pupil who has problems with conforming to the expected behaviour patterns of the school, thus disrupting the work of other pupils and not learning well themselves. But, whatever the reason for your appointment, and at whatever level you are studying or working, you must become part of the whole school's system for behaviour management [15.1:8]. While all of you need to know about your own general situation, as detailed in Unit 3–1, Unit 3–15 contains more specific details for those of you undertaking special support. You must be aware that this optional unit demands a high level of skill and understanding in order to deal with some of the problems associated with behaviour management. This book can only give you the essentials, and you *must* get both training and more specialised information for dealing with specific situations and specific pupils. For general use you will find Fox (2001) helpful. Senior members of staff will always be available for you if a situation becomes more than you should deal with, either to refer matters to at the time or later for advice. Schools also have access to specialist teams and psychologists to whom you may be able to talk. There will be courses available both within the school INSET programme and externally delivered. Discuss with your mentor at an early stage what would be most suitable for your needs [1.2:ix].

All schools have policies and procedures which all staff must follow, the important factor being consistency of approach whatever the incident [1.1:i; 2.2:iii; 15.1:2]. Some of the policies that do not directly give guidance about behaviour management are also important in this area [1.1:ii; 1.2:i; 15.1:i]. For instance, if you withdraw a pupil from class because he or she is behaving badly, you are depriving him or her of that part of the curriculum but sometimes it has to be done; restraining a pupil could be construed as child abuse; dealing with bullying may be in a separate policy. You must know the limits of your authority, when and to whom you refer incidents outside that authority, your particular role within the school and the roles of others [1.1:iii; 1.2:iii; 15.1:iii]. As you become more experienced you may see situations or learn of strategies which could be introduced into your school. Again, talk with your mentor or line manager about them, and feed them back in any in-house training sessions for discussion [1.2:7].

Rogers (1991: 43) has some useful things to say about discipline and behaviour: decisive discipline is marked by these characteristics:

- a focus on the due rights of all
- an assertive stance (Assertion is distinguished from aggression and hostility on the one hand, and passivity or capitulating to student demands on the other. Essentially, assertion communicates one's own need and due rights without trampling on the other parties' rights.)
- refusal to rely on power or role-status to gain respect
- speaking and acting respectfully even when frustrated or angry

- choosing to respond to discipline incidents (from prior reflection and planning) rather than reacting to incidents as they arise
- preparing for discipline as rigorously as for any aspect of the curriculum.

When actually disciplining, a decisive approach engages the student by

- establishing eye contact
- speaking clearly with appropriate firmness
- speaking briefly, addressing primary behaviour and ignoring as much of the secondary behaviour as possible
- distinguishing between the child and his or her behaviour
- expecting compliance rather than demanding or merely hoping for it
- re-establishing working relationships as soon as possible.

You must quickly learn what is acceptable behaviour in the various areas of the school and what is not, how to identify pupils in difficulties and what is normal [1.1:4]. Negative behaviour may be verbally or physically abusive or offensive. Racial or sexist actions or language should not be tolerated. Bullying needs to be recognised and dealt with. Try to spot signs of potential conflict – it is more easily dealt with in the early stages – then monitor developments. You must also recognise that sometimes circumstances change, both for pupils and the school, and be alert to these changes [1.1:vi]. Changing rooms or buildings or going from inside the school to the playground or sports field can alter behaviour. In order to learn all this you will need to understand the limits of normal behaviour and have copies of the policies and procedures for your school on dealing with what, for the school, is inappropriate behaviour [15.1:xiii]. Go through them with a mentor or line manager to identify your role and appropriate strategies [1.2:1; 15.1:1].

Behaviour patterns develop as do other aspects of physical and mental development. Emotional and social development also take place, so expectations of behaviour will vary with the age of the pupils. Physical changes such as those experienced by pupils going through puberty can alter their behaviour radically, as any parent of this age child will know. Peer pressure can make an otherwise well-behaved child do something out of character, such as play truant or cheek a teacher [1.1:7; 15.2:i]. In some cultures, certain behaviour is acceptable for boys but not girls. This can sometimes be seen in early years settings where rough play might be acceptable for boys, but girls will be admonished for similar behaviour. We all have assumptions of what is appropriate, depending on our own upbringing. For instance, many people still have the idea that young people with severe learning problems do not have sexual urges; they do, and can fall in love just like more able youngsters. The paraplegic athletes have challenged our ideas of physical capacity in recent years [1.1:viii]. What is age-appropriate in an infant school pupil may be considered inappropriate in a secondary school pupil yet some secondary pupils may behave in an infantile way, expressing their feelings or emotions in coping with a problem [15.2:ii]. While you will aim to respond to the older pupil hoping they will respond in a more mature way, in responding to their behaviour rather than them personally you may need to modify your actions. You need to observe carefully and make allowances for the pupil according to his/her level of development and be able to recognise uncharacteristic behaviour. You need to report this and your actions to the relevant teacher and find out more about the pupil [15.1:7].

It is also important to recognise that behaviour management takes place all the time, not just when things go wrong. Thanking, smiling, praising appropriately all contribute to positive attitudes in relationships [1.1:1 & v; 1.2:vii]. Encouragement is very important for all children, and adults too. Think back to that personal learning experience suggested in Chapter 5, and your own relationships. How much easier it is to work with people who recognise your effort, even if the actual achievement is small. Many of those with learning problems have poor self-esteem and this can be a real drawback when learning, although low self-esteem can affect a pupil of any ability [1.1:vii]. Let them know when they are doing well and show them how close they are to getting the desired outcome. Ask the teacher whether you can write on pupil's work and what kind of comment is acceptable. Specific remarks are much more useful: 'completed quickly' and 'clearer handwriting' say more than 'well done'. Be careful not to do too much for them (no matter how much they wheedle). One of the real problems is that children with poor learning skills can develop a kind of learnt helplessness.

Being pleasant whenever possible means that when you have to correct inappropriate behaviour it has more effect. Role model how you wish children to behave; modulate your voice; walk, don't run; be punctual and polite [1.1:2 & iv;15.1:3,i & x; 15.2:vii]. Keep calm (whatever you are feeling inside), listen and be consistent [1.1:6; 1.2:2]. Respect breeds respect. We all need boundaries, so rules are developed [1.2:vi]. We all have rights, but we also have responsibilities. This includes access to school facilities, equipment and materials for staff and pupils, and developing responsibility in pupils. The aim is to make pupils take responsibility for their own behaviour [1.1:3;15.1:xi]. The behaviour management training (DfEE 2000c) talks of the 4Rs approach: Rules, Routines, Rights and Responsibilities, leading to choices which have consequences.

Your school may have a systematic reward system, with stickers and certificates for achievements. If so, you will need to know whether you can operate this and what for, and, if not, how you can best bring achievements to the attention of someone who can do the rewarding [15.1:xii]. Similarly, there may be sanctions which you can use, such as giving a pupil 'time out' for misbehaving in the playground, or ensuring a particular item gets mentioned in a home dialogue or report book [1.1:x]. Usually you are there on the spot to see to the immediate situation, but a more senior member of staff will carry out a punishment such as detention or informing parents [1.1:8]. If the situation occurs in the classroom in a lesson, you need to know what to refer to the teacher and what you can deal with [1.2:x & 4; 15.1:xvi]. Once you know the ways of the school, you are in a strong position to say to a pupil who might argue with you, 'You have a choice – you can do what you know is right or . . .' whatever the consequence is for that misbehaviour in your school [15.2:6; 15.3:3].

Using the language of choice

- gives children confidence by giving them responsibility
- regards mistakes as a normal part of learning
- removes the struggle for power
- has a positive emphasis
- is an overt link between principles and strategy.

(DfEE 2000b: 17)

Deal with matters immediately you see inappropriate behaviour [1.1:5]. The secret is to be assertive without being aggressive or confrontational and to ensure that you are separating any inappropriate behaviour from the pupil. This enables the pupil to save face and maintain their self-esteem, which is probably low. Keep the focus on the primary behaviour, the thing that drew your attention in the first place, and actively try to build up your relationship with the pupil concerned [15.2:4]. Always follow up on things that count: if you have said you will refer the matter to someone else, or you will talk to the pupil again the next day, then be sure you do it. Always seek help if you need it [2.1:7; 15.2:5]. Try not to get yourself into a situation where you are alone with very challenging pupils [15.1:9]. If you see a potential problem situation, make someone else aware and attempt to defuse it [1.2:3; 15.1:10]. Such a situation can occur with an individual if there is a shortage of equipment or a challenging piece of work; or with a group, for instance, in a slow lunch queue. Typical positive strategies include appropriate praise and encouragement. Pupils who are motivated and interested are less likely to misbehave. Do not touch or restrain a pupil in a conflict situation unless you have been specially taught the procedure for your school [1.2:ii].

Counselling is a skill. Before you embark on any in-depth work of this kind with pupils, do take advice and, if possible, training to ensure you know what you are doing.

You need to find out

what is appropriate for

- classrooms (different teacher's classrooms will vary slightly)
- other areas of the school (laboratories or technical areas will have different rules or codes of practice)
- outside the school premises
- individuals
- groups
- whole classes

what are
- the rules [1.2:vi]
- the rewards and sanctions that can be applied [15.3:5]
  - by you
  - by others [1.2:v]

---

what strategies are available for you to use in managing inappropriate behaviour [1.2:viii]

- time-out places
- sources of help and referral at different times of the day
- report forms or notes
- withdrawal of privileges

how you
- report incidents
- develop your skills of behaviour management
- seek advice.

Individual pupils may have individual targets, plans and performance indicators, similar to those of a pupil with learning difficulties, called Behaviour Support Plans (BSP) [1.2:iv; 15.1:vi]. If you are likely to come into contact with such a pupil, you must acquaint yourself with these. The targets will be small, such as to keep the pupil on task for ten minutes. Your aim will not be to take responsibility for or independently change the pupil's behaviour, but to encourage pupils to take responsibility for their own behaviour [15.1:5]. There will be the equivalent of an IEP for behaviour, showing what you are to do, and usually any paperwork of which you have copies will have a space for you to comment on progress [1.2:5,6]. As the pupil will know their targets, any comments about progress that you might make to the pupil can also relate to the target, such as: 'You didn't interrupt the lesson today, well done, let's see if you can do it again tomorrow.' You may be asked to monitor behaviour of pupils with or without a BSP [15.1:6].

An example of good behaviour management

An infant school in a very poor social area, where few children received pre-school education apart from the school nursery class, had had low expectations of behaviour and academic standards in the past. Over some years, the new head established a positive behaviour management regime which enabled the whole school to become a happy learning establishment. It took time to establish the ethos and train all sectors of the staff to understand the detailed approach. Each teacher and their own TA became a small team, and the teaching staff had away-days, sometimes incorporating teambuilding exercises. Over several years teaching staff went to summer schools in their own time to undertake specific training in positive techniques which were incorporated in their classroom practice with their TAs. This even included practice sessions, with agreed prompt phrases pinned inside cupboard doors. Later, as classroom support staff became converted to the particular way of dealing with all the children, office, caretaking and midday staff were trained. Money was put into resource organisation such as shelves, labelled boxes, sufficient quality tools, materials and equipment to enable children to organise themselves and take responsibility for their own learning. Playground equipment and activities were organised; joint curriculum planning reflected the whole-school ethos. Even the youngest pupils had to plan some of their own work, and all children helped in cleaning up. Children were thanked for walking; assemblies were quiet, disciplined affairs. Parents became aware of the calm and even started to emulate the staff's attitudes and phrases while on the school site. Test results began to climb as the philosophy of high expectations permeated the formal curriculum.

Bullying

This is a particular concern of many pupils and parents. No school is without its bullies and the nature of bullying is that it will take place away from adult sight, so may be hard to detect. 'Bullying is forcing others to do, act and feel the very things a bully would never want done to him. Bullying is not accidental, it is learned.' Schools have policies for dealing with bullying issues, as there need to be 'clear, school-wide consequences' (Rogers 1994: 101). There should be strategies not only for dealing with the bully, but also for helping the victim, both in the short term and in the long term, to become more assertive. It is likely that pupils will debate the issue in class and strategies such as circle time are available to help. These are probably run by the teachers, but you may be asked to undertake training in this area to run such sessions as well as participate in discussions.

Conflict resolution

Relationships do not always go well. Sometimes there is a competitive element which gets out of hand and becomes conflict [9.1:ix]. You need to be able to recognise when the competitive element is constructive to the relationship and also understand some of the principles of conflict resolution. This will help you both in enabling pupils' relationships to be positive and in your work with colleagues. Competition often enhances team spirit in a group of people; for instance, sporting teams in training need to have a purpose: leagues, cups and matches of all kinds create a rationale for developing the team. But, as football hooliganism shows only too clearly, it can get out of hand. Patriotism can become ethnic cleansing. House points in schools can spur pupils on to greater effort, but can also create for some a sense of being bottom of the pile. Where there are winners, there are always losers, and it is a skill to lose gracefully. Conflict is usually the result of some other incident or issue intruding into the relationship, causing the participants to get out of control. When people are stressed or unsupported they get aggressive for less reason than normal. This can be caused by low morale, an ambiguity over the allocation of roles, or timing of events. Factors that prevent good relationships, such as poor communication, over-assertive colleagues, lack of sensitivity to feelings, misunderstandings and distrust, create the climate for conflict. Physical tiredness or emotional exhaustion from the job or home circumstances, illness, anxiety or a sense of personal inadequacy can all contribute. Continually dealing with pupils or parents who are challenging or have difficulties can drain you and make you less able to cope with situations you would normally take in your stride. These are things to look out for in yourself, to try to prevent or understand, and to make allowances for in your colleagues. Conflict resolution is about trying to unravel the causes of the breakdown in normal relationships and then attempting to deal with the causes as swiftly, safely and considerately as possible [3.1:7; 9.1:4].

If you are placed in a situation where you are the mediator, you may need to seek the help of a trained counsellor. Many conflicts can be helped by enabling the participants to explain their point of view separately to a mediator, and then feeding both points of view back to both parties to help them see what is going wrong. Looking for some jointly acceptable resolution together is then needed. Simple versions of this will work even with small children, who given time and understanding should be able to make more constructive relationships. Time-out places in playgrounds provide a thinking time for pupils as well as taking the heat out of the situation for the others using the space [15.2:xii].

Some basic principles of conflict resolution are given by Rogers (1991):

1. Address the situation – the problem not the people involved.
2. Avoid put-downs and criticism of the person – getting uptight yourself will not help, explain if it happens.
3. Acknowledge the emotional climate – recognise feelings and state them, including your own; respect is important.
4. Keep the heat down and avoid a power struggle – try to remain calm, assertive without being aggressive.
5. Call in a third party – get help.
6. Follow up conflict situations – use trained mediators if necessary; look towards future situations and their resolution.

Pupil conflict resolution
It is important that you are well-versed in the school policies for behaviour management and child protection, the limits of acceptable behaviour for your school, the reward and sanctions systems for your school and your limitations in being able to enforce any of them [9.1:vi,vii,viii & x; 15,2:x]. It is also important that you get special advice and training in this area to protect yourself.

Be on the look out for potential situations such as two pupils getting together who you know are trouble when they are together. Windy days make little ones restless; parties or matches taking place in the locality may create excitement, or the arrival in town of a popular group or film. A new face in the class or playground may change the dynamics, or September can bring a new year group who are feeling their feet by upsetting established ways of working. You should be able to recognise signs of anxiety and distress [9.3:v]. Changes in personality can be cause for concern: do watch out for possible bullying, although it tends to take place away from adult eyes. Recognise that there could be problems due to a breakdown in relationships between you and the pupils. Do tell a teacher of your concerns and if necessary make a private note of time and place and concern [2.1:8; 9.3:ix].

In a playground situation, you may find you are able to interact with a group of pupils and help them deal with disagreements, or give individuals an opportunity to tell you of their problems or anxieties. You may see pupils reacting to other pupils in an aggressive way, a potential situation for a fight; facial expressions give away a lot [9.3:viii]. Swearing, tantrums and emotional outbursts, irritating and annoying mannerisms can all be indicators of possible trouble spots [15.1:7]. Have some strategies for diverting or diffusing potential situations, such as sending a participant on an errand, engaging them in conversation, or offering to start a game or activity [9.1:ix]. Keep calm, reassure, give time out for each to think things through, and an opportunity for rethinking [9.3:3]. Again, you should be a good listener, hear all sides and offer choices not solutions. This allows potential situations to be defused without anyone losing face [9.3:1]. Use those protocols mentioned above; remember the language of choice, reminding pupils of their rights *and* responsibilities [1.9:5; 15.2:6]. Rogers (1991) also talks of stages in conflict, both in the classroom and in the playground:

1. Antecedent conditions: environmental factors
2. Parties feeling or recognising the situation
3. A conflict situation: arguing, yelling, screaming, fighting, etc.
4. Resolution: communication, mediation, withdrawal and intervention
5. Aftermath: maintained hostility, revenge or genuine resolution – needs discussed, negotiated and resolved.

Do not use physical restraint unless you have been specifically trained in this area [15.1:xv]. You should always know where to get help, whether during a situation or afterwards, both for yourself and the participants [15.1:9]. You must also recognise your own emotions when dealing with these kinds of situation. You may well get angry and frustrated. Do discuss how you feel with a mentor in the school, don't just bottle it up till you get home and then take it out on your own children or partner. Go through what you did with your mentor, and whether it could have been handled differently and whether anything could have been done to prevent the situation developing [15.1:4]. There are some very useful contributions about understanding behaviour during school break-time in Blatchford and Sharp (1994: 13–76); discuss the content with your mentor.

Child protection

It is essential to know about this, although it is a sensitive area [10.1:iv; 11.3:vii]. Some of you may have had close personal involvement with family or friends where problems have arisen, or feel that these matters are better not dealt with until an incident arises. You will all have been checked by the police through the Criminal Records Bureau before you took up your post. However, there are a few things that, as a member of staff likely to come into close physical and pastoral contact with pupils, you need to be aware of. It is hoped that all schools these days have written policies in this area and make sure all staff are trained together, but it does not always happen. If it does not happen in your school, then suggest it.

There are legal and organisational requirements and implications for you when you work with other people's children [11.2:ix]. Teachers and other school staff act *in loco parentis*. The Children Act 1989 applies to schools as well as the general population. The school policy should lay out clear guidelines for *all* staff on what to do if there is a suspicion of abuse and how to prevent allegations against staff themselves. There should be a designated child protection person whose name is known by all staff and who is trained in what to do and where to go if help is needed.

There are two main areas of sensitivity, one in recognising the signs of abuse and the other in behaving appropriately as a member of staff. The possible signs of abuse are not always physical. They can also be mental, emotional or the result of neglect. While some of these signs can be listed, they must be considered only indicators. All sorts of personal or family events can cause changes in behaviour. The important thing is to tell someone senior to yourself of your concern, as patterns may emerge when several people's evidence is collated or several different signs appear in the same pupil [1.1:ix].

Signs and symptoms of abuse

Possible signs of physical abuse
- Unexplained injuries or burns, particularly if they are recurrent
- Refusal to discuss injuries
- Improbable explanations for injuries
- Untreated injuries or lingering illness not attended to
- Admission of punishment which appears excessive
- Shrinking from physical contact
- Fear of returning home or of parents being contacted
- Fear of undressing
- Fear of medical help
- Aggression or bullying
- Over-compliant behaviour or a 'watchful attitude'
- Running away
- Significant changes in behaviour without explanation
- Deterioration in work

- Unexplained pattern of absences which may serve to hide bruises or other physical injuries

Possible signs of emotional abuse
- Continual self-deprecation
- Fear of new situations
- Inappropriate emotional responses to painful situations
- Self-harm or mutilation
- Compulsive stealing or scrounging
- Drug or solvent abuse
- 'Neurotic' behaviour – obsessive rocking, thumb-sucking, and so on
- Air of detachment – 'don't care' attitude
- Social isolation – does not join in and has few friends
- Desperate attention-seeking behaviour
- Eating problems, including overeating and lack of appetite
- Depression, withdrawal

Possible signs of neglect
- Constant hunger
- Poor personal hygiene
- Inappropriate clothing
- Frequent lateness or non-attendance at school
- Untreated medical problems
- Low self-esteem
- Poor social relationships
- Compulsive stealing or scrounging
- Constant tiredness

Possible signs of sexual abuse
- Bruises, scratches, burns or bite marks on the body
- Scratches, abrasions or persistent infections in the anal or genital region
- Pregnancy, particularly in the case of young adolescents who are evasive concerning the identity of the father
- Sexual awareness inappropriate to the child's age – shown, for example, in drawings, vocabulary and games
- Frequent public masturbation
- Attempts to teach other children about sexual activity
- Refusing to stay with certain people or go to certain places
- Aggressiveness, anger, anxiety, tearfulness
- Withdrawal from friends

Possible signs in older children
- Promiscuity, prostitution, provocative sexual behaviour
- Self-injury, self-destructive behaviour, suicide attempts
- Eating disorders
- Tiredness, lethargy, listlessness

- Over-compliant behaviour
- Sleep disturbances
- Unexplained gifts of money
- Depression
- Changes in behaviour.

(Schonveld 1995: 18–19)

Do not regard this list as definitive; you need proper training from the LEA Child Protection Officer or whoever does it in your area. All children can have bruises from accidents or playing roughly. It is the type of bruise and where it is on the body that can be important. Do not be obsessive or inquisitive, but just be vigilant; for instance, when children change for PE or are talking informally.

Revealing

A child may reveal to you what has happened to them. You are particularly well placed for children to feel secure with you. No school staff are trained to deal with children or families in detail in child protection matters, but you all have a responsibility to report to people who are. You should not question a child in these circumstances, as you may ask leading questions. You should never promise not to tell anyone. Listen carefully, sensitively, caringly, inwardly note what they say, and then tell the designated member of staff as soon as possible. Make a short written record afterwards, date it, and give it to the named member of staff. It is that person's responsibility to deal with it by informing social services or the police, who have trained personnel for helping the children and their families and for dealing with any matters that arise.

It is difficult, because you make assumptions or have memories which could prevent you from listening properly, but it is a responsibility that you take on when working in a school. If you have any doubts about what you have heard or seen, and these incidents are rarely clear cut, discuss it with the class teacher, your teacher mentor, the designated teacher or the head. If you are involved further, be guided by the named person in the school. These people will understand about case conferences, child protection registers, and agencies who can support vulnerable children and their families. Of course, you must maintain confidentiality with the staff concerned in all these proceedings.

Intimate situations

Another area where you can be involved in these issues is when you are dealing with children in intimate situations. This often happens when TAs have been appointed to deal with pupils with physical disabilities, or very young children who have toileting accidents. Usually the parents know what the policy is as well: whether school staff can clean children up after toilet accidents or change underclothes. TAs are sometimes asked to work in pairs when these events occur. Always comfort unhappy children, but do it in public not privately. Pupils need sometimes to see school as a haven, a place of safety and security which they may not otherwise have, but do not put yourself into a situation which could lead to unjustified accusation. Always be aware of, and respond to, troubled children, but do this appropriately. Do not single them out for attention; it is better for them to come to you.

Contact

When dealing with difficult pupils the proper procedures cannot be taught to you in a book. Touching pupils, let alone restraining pupils, can get you into difficulties with parents and even the law. The pupils concerned are usually particularly volatile, liable to act up, or react unnecessarily to being told how to behave. So, do make sure you know the school policy on restraint, and if possible get appropriate training in this area. The policies and procedures in health and safety issues may seem irksome but they are written to protect the pupils and you. Ensure you know what liaison there is with parents over various incidents and what records the school requires to be kept, and maintain confidentiality appropriately at all times [11.3:v, vi, ix].

Implications for your role

Dealing with other people's children can put you in a vulnerable position, open to allegations of abuse, sometimes made by quite small children. Such is the publicity given to child protection matters these days, and the angry, emotional responses of some people to any suspicion of abuse, that children in households where such matters are discussed in this manner may see an opportunity for some meddling or for attention. In order to prevent false allegations, you are advised to ensure that you do not put yourself in a position where it is only the pupil's word against yours. Follow strictly any guidance given to you by the school. Try to deal with toileting accidents with a colleague; do not stay alone in classrooms with only one or two pupils late in the day; do not put a child on your lap, particularly if your are male, unless it is essential to their well-being and you are in an open situation. Discuss this issue with your mentor at an early stage.

Questions to ask yourself

- What health problems do I have? Do these affect my performance at school?
- Should I discuss these with anyone in the school? Will that be difficult?
- What can I bring from my own experience to any discussion which is part of the school health education programme? Is this important?
- Do I know the expectations of behaviour for my school and what to do in any circumstances? (Try out some 'what if' situations in your mind and the actions you hope you would take.)
- To whom do I turn in a difficult situation?

Essential reading

The local LEA guidance on child protection.

Some further reading

Baginsky, M. (2000) *Child Protection and Education*. London: NSPCC.

Blatchford, P. and Sharp, S. (1994) *Breaktime and the School: Understanding and Changing Playground Behaviour*. London and New York: Routledge.

Bruce, T. and Meggitt, C. (1996) *Child Care and Education*. London: Hodder and Stoughton. (Especially Chapter 14.)

DfEE (2000c) *Behaviour Management Module: Induction Training for Teaching Assistants*. London: DfEE.

Fox, G. (2001) *Supporting Children with Behaviour Difficulties*. London: David Fulton Publishers.

Hook, P. and Vass, A. (2000a) *Confident Classroom Leadership*. London: David Fulton Publishers.

O'Hagan, M. and Smith, M. (1993) *Special Issues in Child Care*. London: Baillière Tindall. (Especially Chapter 7.)

Rogers, B. (1991) *'You Know the Fair Rule'*. Harlow: Longman.

Rogers, B. (1994) *Behaviour Recovery*. Harlow: Longman.

Rogers, B. (2000) *Classroom Behaviour*. London: Paul Chapman Publishing (Sage).

Schonveld, A. (1998) *Child Protection and School Support Staff*. Coventry: Community Education Development Centre.

Watkinson, A. (2002) *Assisting Learning and Supporting Teaching*. London: David Fulton Publishers.

Watkinson, A. (2003) *The Essential Guide for Competent Teaching Assistants: Meeting the National Occupational Standards at Level 2*. London: David Fulton Publishers.

Williams, T., Wetton, N. and Moon, A. (1989) *Health for Life: Health Education in the Primary School; The Health Education Authority's Primary School Project*. Walton on Thames: Nelson.

8 Supporting pupils with individual needs

Equal opportunities and individual needs

One of the difficulties of teaching, maybe the main one, is that we are all different and all pupils are different. The expression 'delivering' the curriculum is largely inappropriate when you think of the learners who are 'receiving' the curriculum. Teaching pupils in classes depends on there being more similarities than differences and provides a cost-effective and efficient way of assisting learning, particularly when imparting information is required. As pointed out in the previous chapter, learning also has a social context; groups and classes provide the way to do this. The size of the group or class will depend on the age of the pupils, the subject being taught and sometimes the size of room available. Students in university can be taught in a lecture hall of 500, seminars of 15 and tutorials of two people. Assemblies can similarly have several hundred present, classes can be 20–30, and groups from two to eight. All pre-school provision has to have a ratio of at least one adult to 13 children.

Schools in the United Kingdom usually organise their classes in year groups. With the demands of the NC, annual assessments and the suggestions of nationally published schemes of work, fewer and fewer mixed-age groups are now found. Other countries are more flexible in some ways. If a pupil 'fails' to make the grade one year, they stay on and go through that year's work again, so the teacher is more likely to have a mixed-age similar-ability class than a teacher is in the United Kingdom. Secondary schools, and more frequently primary schools, have recognised that teaching a 'mixed-ability' class is not as easy as taking classes where pupils have similar ability. In the middle of the twentieth century, in the state system there were selective grammar schools and secondary modern schools. Streaming was widespread, pupils were in classes and schools supposedly suitable for their perceived ability. Primary classrooms were organised hierarchically on ability with the 'bright' children at the back of the set of desks and the slower ones at the front. Special schools were those where children went who were deemed unable to cope with ordinary or 'mainstream' schools, and some children never went to school at all. Research found that this kind of extreme segregation labelled pupils, and many pupils lived up to the predictions that others had made on their behalf. The system meant that pupils who were late developers, or 'handicapped', or even just lacking in self-esteem or self-confidence, never got the opportunities offered to others. Much talent and potential was missed.

The comprehensive system of schools, totally mixed-ability classes, and the increasing integration of those with special needs into mainstream school were moves to try to redress the balance and be more in keeping with the increased emphasis on equal opportunities for all. But organisation or reorganisation of systems was not enough to enable all children to progress according to their ability and needs. Teaching tended to aim at the middle of the ability range and those with higher or lower abilities were neglected. It was hoped that those with higher abilities would be able to fend for themselves, but those with physical or learning problems needed support, hence the emphasis on what is now called SEN. The increased use of testing and the published league tables have highlighted discrepancies in the higher-ability range, hence the increased emphasis on specialist schools and the pinpointing of the gifted and able in all schools. Many schools, including primary schools, 'set' pupils as a way of organising them in ability groups for some subjects, but retain the mixed social grouping of ordinary classes for all the other subjects. Some gifted and able children are offered special classes or activities particularly designed to stretch their ability. Some of these children have emotional or social problems because they are thinking so differently from their peers, and need special help in dealing with these problems. You may be working with such pupils, and sometimes TAs are asked to work with the more able children who need encouragement or adult support for an activity. Traditionally, however, your role has been to support those who are less able.

Until fairly recently pupils with learning difficulties or disabilities that impeded their access to teaching in a mainstream school were described as educationally handicapped. As such they were considered to require education in special schools that offered a curriculum different from that taught in mainstream school, or that had specialist staff and equipment. The two kinds of school co-existed in most education authorities: mainstream schools, which the majority attended, and special schools, which catered for a minority of pupils with learning difficulties or physical and sensory disabilities.

Since the implementation of the Education Act 1981 this picture has been changing gradually. Although special schools continue to provide for a section of the school population, an increasing number of pupils with significant learning difficulties or physical and sensory disabilities are being educated in mainstream schools. This is described as *inclusion*.

Integration and inclusion

Until 1990 the term 'inclusion' had not been in common use in education. 'Integration' was more commonly used to express the alternative to education that segregated a section of children from the mainstream. Segregation was seen to be undesirable for social reasons as well as for educational reasons. If one group is segregated from the rest of society there is a tendency for them to become second class or low priority even if that was not the original intention. Special educational needs became low status within the education system and the poor quality of education in many special schools went unnoticed. Dessent (1987: 14) summed up the general picture with 'There are no votes in children with special educational needs.'

The contemporary picture has changed. However, the integration of increasing numbers of pupils with special educational needs into mainstream schools and classrooms is insufficient if it means simply placing them in situations with learners who do not have special needs. A deeper level of integration is needed. This is expressed as 'inclusion' or 'belonging'. The inclusive classroom is not one where, for example, the child with Down's Syndrome sits with a TA engaged in learning tasks that bear no relationship to the curriculum followed by the rest of the class. Inclusive classrooms should be communities that accommodate and value every member. Thus one of the teacher's primary goals is to make sure that all children are able to participate as fully as possible in the routines and rituals of the classroom culture.

While inclusive education of children with special educational needs is now an objective of public policy in the United Kingdom, it remains the subject of debate. Change brings with it uncertainty and anxiety. It may also require an adjustment of values and a reframing of formerly held beliefs. The appointment of TAs in a school may be part of a strategy to increase the inclusive nature of a school. If so, your contribution to the strategy will be enhanced by an understanding of the theory of inclusive education. You need to find your school's policy on inclusion, equal opportunities, SEN and behaviour when looking at standards 3–13, 3–14, 3–15 and 3–16.

Participation in the routines and rituals of the classroom culture includes sharing in the curriculum and learning experiences of the class. It includes working collaboratively with other children and learning from them as well as with them. Learning in school is a social activity and it is important that the pupil with SEN is fully engaged in the social dimension of learning in the classroom and in the social life of the school as a whole. If the school is trying to support fully the theory of inclusion, you will be there, not to take the child aside while the teacher enables the other children to move on, but to work with the teacher to intervene sensitively where support is required to enable the child to engage in learning as an equal participant with his or her class peers.

It is not only pupils who need to feel included. The most effective TAs are those who perceive themselves to be an integral and recognised part of the whole-school team and approach their role as such, hence the emphasis in this book on relationships and teamwork. Included TAs will not underestimate the value of their contribution to the ethos of the school: 'Where the assistants feel as included as these, the likelihood is that pupils they support will also feel they are fully included in the classroom and school learning environment' (Balshaw and Farrell 2002: 140).

Special educational needs

Pupils are no longer described as educationally handicapped but rather as having special educational needs. Many TAs are employed specifically to assist one or more pupils with SEN. All of you will come across pupils with SEN in your work in mainstream classrooms. The Education Act 1996, which revised the original Act, contained a clear expectation that pupils with SEN will be included in mainstream schools. The Act requires education services to do everything possible to provide a mainstream place for a pupil with special educational needs if their parents want it. Schools cannot refuse to admit a pupil on the grounds that they cannot cater for their special educational needs. Even if you have not been employed specifically to support such pupils and are working in a mainstream school, an understanding of SEN is necessary to the effectiveness of your role. It will also help you understand that the principles of support for pupils with SEN are not significantly different from those applied to supporting pupils generally.

The concept of special educational needs

The formal definition can be found in the Education Act 1996, which is cited in *Special Educational Needs Code of Practice* (DfES, 2001b: 6):

> Children have special educational needs if they have a *learning difficulty* which calls for *special educational provision* to be made for them. Children have a *learning difficulty* if they:
>
> (a) have a significantly greater difficulty in learning than the majority of children of the same age; or
> (b) have a disability which prevents or hinders them from making use of educational facilities of a kind generally provided for children of the same age in schools within the area of the local education authority;
> (c) are under compulsory school age and fall within the definition at (a) or (b) above or would so do if special educational provision was not made for them.
>
> Children must not be regarded as having a learning difficulty solely because the language or form of language of their home is different from the language in which they will be taught. *Special educational provision* means:
>
> (a) for children of two or over, educational provision which is additional to, or otherwise different from, the educational provision made generally for children of their age in schools maintained by the LEA, other than special schools, in the area;
> (b) for children under two, educational provision of any kind.

The Code (p. 7) goes on to define disability:

> A child is disabled if he is blind, deaf or dumb or suffers from a mental disorder of any kind or is substantially and permanently handicapped by illness, injury or congenital deformity or such other disability as may be prescribed.
>
> (Section 17 (11), Children Act 1989)

> A person has a disability for the purposes of this Act if he has a physical or mental impairment which has a substantial and long-term adverse effect on his ability to carry out normal day-to day activities.
>
> (Section 1 (1), Disability Discrimination Act 1995)

The term special educational needs was intended to facilitate a move away from determining a pupil's education by reference to a handicap or label towards educating them according to their individual needs. It shifts the focus from deficiencies in the pupil to deficiencies in the resources and environment in which they are to be educated. As an example, it is not because of their physical limitations that a physically disabled child with no learning difficulties may have special educational needs but rather because they may need resources to overcome barriers to accessing normal class teaching that their physical disability causes. A child with a learning difficulty has special educational needs only if that difficulty is greater than the norm *and* resources that are not normally available are needed to overcome their difficulties.

The statutory definition of special educational needs is a relative one. A child with special needs in one context or environment may not be considered to have special educational needs in another. The presence of a special need depends upon the interaction of deficiencies within the pupil with deficiencies of the environment. This relativistic notion of special educational needs has been described as follows:

> The problems of the handicap are the result of the **interaction** between the nature of their deficiencies and the nature of their environment. The needs of the handicapped are therefore seen to be relative **both** to the deficiencies 'within' the child **and** to the deficiencies of the environment.
>
> (Weddell 1983: 100)

The task of meeting the pupil's SEN in the classroom therefore requires not only an understanding of what the child's strengths and weaknesses are but also an assessment of the learning situation and what adaptations to it are needed to enable the pupil to learn effectively. There will be circumstances in which your role is an integral part of making the learning environment more 'user-friendly' to the pupil with difficulties. Your time and skilled support is a resource that augments the work of the teacher in a number of ways and increases the chance that a pupil with SEN will be successfully integrated in the class. For example, you can meet a pupil's need for more frequent adult–pupil contact to cope with set tasks or problems. You therefore not only add to the resource of available adult time in the classroom but also to the quality of teaching and learning.

It is frequently said that a school with good provision for pupils with SEN will be a school that makes good provision for all its pupils. Such a maxim recognises that special educational needs exist along a continuum from children who need a very small amount of support in their learning to those who require a considerable degree of help. The pupil who is on the register of pupils with SEN might sometimes differ in only a small degree from other pupils in a class. The division between SEN and the general needs of pupils in a class can therefore be an arbitrary one [13.1:iv; 14.1:iv]. While much of your attention will be focused on the needs of a particular child or group, the effective TA will make themselves aware of the needs of the whole class and offer support at a range of levels. The experienced assistant will be proactive in identifying where this support is needed at any one time.

Statements of special educational need and the Individual Education Plan

As indicated earlier, a pupil may have a statement of special educational need because they have a learning difficulty that is significantly greater than that of other pupils, or they have a disability that impedes their access to the curriculum and requires resources that are not generally available. An allocation of support time may be provided for in the statement and your primary task may be to give that support.

A well-written statement of special educational need should give a clear description of the pupil's strengths and weaknesses. It should indicate the areas of weakness that are interfering with the child's progress, or the disabilities that impede the child's access to the normal curriculum. It should specify a set of aims and objectives for the child's education provision [13.1:v; 13.2:iv; 14.1:vii; 15.1vi]. If the LEA is fully committed to the principle of inclusive education, one aim should be to give the pupil full access to a broad and balanced curriculum appropriate to their age. Some objectives will be very specific and measurable; for example, *to achieve a reading age of x years in y time.* Others may be less exact but nevertheless observable; for example, *Oliver's listening skills will improve.*

Such objectives should be part of the Individual Education Plan (IEP) that follows the statement. The plan will specify short-term targets towards the achievement of objectives set out in the statement [20.1:v; 20.2:v]. For example, a short-term target might be: *By the next review Olivia will be able to recognise the ten most frequently used words by sight.* The plan will outline proposed activities and strategies for meeting such targets, including how the assistant is to be employed. It should also describe arrangements for assessing and reviewing the pupil's progress and achievement of the targets. The school's special needs coordinator (SENCO) will have responsibility for the preparation and management of an IEP but implementation of some or all of its parts will take place in classrooms managed by other teachers. In such circumstances you, charged with supporting the pupil, may be the only person with a direct day-to-day overview of the child's response to the plan. This is particularly true in the secondary school [20.1:x].

You need several things if you are to be effective in such situations. In particular, you should know what the IEP is and keep its objectives in mind at all times. You should also keep a record of your observations and the pupil's progress towards the objectives in the IEP. Where your role is to assist with the delivery of an individual learning programme you should feel well briefed by the SENCO and the class teacher on how the programme fits in with IEP objectives [16.2:2]. You should also be told whether the pupil is on medication and how this might affect their performance and behaviour [14.1:ix; 15.1:iv; 15.2:vi; 16.1:xi; 16.2:vi]. Many SENCOs now hold regular meetings for the TAs not only to brief them on individual pupils but also to keep them up to date with ideas, resources and moves the school may be making to increase inclusion or organise the work of all the TAs. You should be able to report back progress and problems to the SENCO, suggest what works and what is not working and contribute to the general discussion.

When you are supporting a child in the general class lesson you must be aware of the overall aim of the lesson [13.1:1; 14.1:1 & iii; 16.1:1,2 & 3;16.2:1,2 & 3]. You should intervene to support the pupil sensitively and at the minimum

Photograph 2   Supporting a child with cerebral palsy as part of a group

level required [13.1:vi; 14.2:1 & 2]. Do not feel that your task is to follow the pupil and stick by them regardless, sometimes referred to as the 'Velcro' approach.

If an important part of your role is to facilitate inclusivity in the classroom, it should be perceived by all pupils to be a normal part of what goes on there. Offering support at the minimum level required, rather than seeming to impose it on the pupil, is more likely to promote independent learning. The willingness to take risks is important for effective learning. Encouragement in the face of difficult tasks is more likely to promote the child's learning than protection from difficulty, provided that the tasks are achievable. When supporting a pupil in the subject lesson you should have in mind objectives in the IEP relating to the improvement of basic skills as well as the pupil's need for help with the content of the lesson or subject-related tasks. The subject lesson can be seen as providing a context for learning or practising basic literacy or numeracy skills as well as for acquiring subject knowledge and related skills [20.1:x].

School Action and School Action Plus

Not all pupils with learning difficulties have statements of special educational need. However, most will have IEPs that are part of a School Action. The current Special Educational Needs Code of Practice (DfES 2001b) requires schools to identify pupils with learning difficulties and to decide whether action needs to be taken in addition to the normal provision for pupils in the school. The School Action records the nature of the pupil's difficulties and the action the school proposes to take in response to them, including an IEP of the kind described above.

If upon review after a suitable period of time the pupil continues to have significant difficulties resulting in lack of progress in the curriculum, the school might seek expert advice from an advisory teacher or an educational psychologist. Such advice will be incorporated in a School Action Plus. It is only when the school has taken all relevant steps available to it and a pupil is still not making the progress expected of them that the LEA would usually consider starting a statutory assessment of their learning difficulties. The assessment might lead to a statement of special educational needs, or a note in lieu of a statement if the assessment indicates that continued support at the Action Plus stage is appropriate.

The Code requires the parents to be involved at every stage of the process of preparing and reviewing a School Action. The pupil's views must also be taken into account. If you have established a good working relationship with the pupils whom you are supporting, you can make a significant contribution to the process of pupil and parent involvement. Systematic recording of the pupil's approach to learning, their motivation and attitude to support is as important to the evaluation of the School Action as measurement of their progress in a particular skill, such as reading. The Code of Practice requires schools to involve pupils in decision making by ensuring that the pupil understands the purpose of support and is actively involved in monitoring and developing their learning targets. The nature of your role often enables you to get closer to the pupils to whom you are assigned than a teacher can. As a consequence pupils often feel more confident or encouraged to express their view to you and it is not unusual for the TA to be given the task of helping the pupil to record their contribution to a review.

You may also have contact with parents, either at reviews or informally at other times. In general, you should keep in mind when working with parents that your role is a supportive one. The ability to listen is an important skill in the process of building a supportive relationship. When talking with parents you should be aware of how to respond if issues arise that are outside your responsibility or beyond the scope of your role. You should know whom to turn to for advice and to whom to direct the parent, usually the SENCO.

The four areas of special educational needs

While it has been a long-established principle that labelling children with SEN is undesirable, in practice it has proved difficult to avoid describing categories of pupils with SEN. One viewpoint is that labels or categories are needed for purely administrative purposes. Determining the number of pupils in each category helps with the rational distribution of finite resources. On the downside, even the new categories may facilitate the exclusion of some groups of pupils. The current Special Educational Needs Code of Practice describes four areas of need:

- Communication and interaction
- Cognition (understanding and reasoning) and learning
- Behaviour, emotional and social development
- Sensory and/or physical

It would not be difficult for you to identify which category of pupils is most likely to be at risk of exclusion. However, you will undoubtedly meet many pupils whose special needs do not fit readily in any single category. Indeed, the Code of Practice recognises that that SEN are inter-related 'although there are specific needs that usually relate directly to particular types of impairment' (DfES 2001b: 85). The Code refers to some learning difficulties in descriptions of more than one category (e.g. dyslexia). While the focus of an assistant's support may be presumed to be upon a particular type of 'impairment' or learning difficulty, in reality your support for any individual is likely to demand understanding and skill in dealing with any combination of the four areas of need.

It is well known that pupils with SEN often have multiple needs. For example, many pupils with learning difficulties have accompanying problems of behaviour, poor social skills or low self-esteem. The majority of pupils who are singled out on account of primary behavioural or emotional problems also underachieve in basic literacy and number skills. To be effective, you need to recognise that the support you give is not necessarily confined to a specific category of need but that such support may be the context for contributing to the promotion of the child's wider development. For example, if you are assigned to help a child with their reading difficulty, you will need to develop a relationship of trust with them and work on building their self-esteem and confidence before they can make progress with reading.

If you are working towards the NOS in any of the four areas of need or with a pupil with any particular need, you will need more information than this book can provide. Some further reading is suggested at the end of the chapter and SENCOs will guide your study and suggest possible courses or contacts for you.

Communication and interaction

The description of this area of special needs in the Code of Practice covers a wide spectrum of difficulties. The Code acknowledges that most children with SEN have strengths and difficulties in one, some or all of the areas of speech, language and communication. Access to and progress within the curriculum depend upon the ability to understand and communicate through language. By definition, therefore, the child with learning difficulties will have more weaknesses than strengths in their language development [18.3:vii].

The purpose of intervention and support is usually two-fold:

- Facilitating access to the curriculum by helping the child overcome barriers to effective communication in the classroom.
- The development of specific skills.

In the first instance you might be in the classroom to ensure that the child has understood instructions, has the support needed to read texts, or is able to express themselves effectively in written tasks [13.2:x]. In the second instance, your support might focus on developing specific handwriting and spelling skills, or reading fluency and comprehension. In more complex cases where, for example, the pupil has a severe speech and language delay or a hearing impairment, your role might be to focus on broader language and communication skills. It might focus on the development of expressive skills, such as the ability to talk clearly and fluently in age-appropriate sentences; or on the development of receptive skills, such as the ability to listen and to act upon instructions of increasing complexity [13.1:5,6, ix & x; 13.2:v, vi & vii; 18.3:vi; 20.1:x].

Children with severe developmental language delay might benefit from learning a sign language. Signing is often employed in special nursery classes. An assistant working in such a class should be prepared to learn and use sign language with the children, just as in other situations they would expect to interact with children and model proper forms of speech and language. Sign language is not intended to be a long-term substitute for speech in children with developmental delay. However, it is a means by which central processes upon which language development depends can operate. A child who is able to communicate by signing has the basis for later communication by speech. Signing may be the long-term means of communication for profoundly deaf children and for some partially hearing children. Historically, signing has been a subject of dispute amongst educators of the deaf and partially hearing.

The Code lists what a pupil with communication and interaction difficulties might require to meet their special needs (DfES 2001b: 86, para 7: 56). However, if you are helping the pupil in one or more of those areas, you need to be aware that the pupil's needs will often extend beyond the limits of help in articulation, acquiring, comprehending and using language, or any other of the requirements listed.

Language is important to the development of thought and self-regulated behaviour [18.3:ix]. It is the medium by which we relate to and interact with others and as such is important to social development [13.2:1–7]. The child with limited or delayed language skills may therefore be expected to show immature or poorly developed social behaviour. Young children with delayed speech and language skills are likely to be more impulsive and lacking in concentration than expected for their age. Pupils with dyspraxia and those with characteristics within the autistic spectrum have problems of social communication and understanding that are directly caused by deficits in their understanding of the practical effects of language in social situations. They have difficulty in understanding another's point of view. The child with dyspraxia often appears to be rude and provocative in their manner towards other people and this can frequently lead to problems. Supporting a child or young person described as having problems of communication and interaction may therefore demand a high level of professional tolerance on the part of the assistant, as well as good skills of behaviour management [13.1:vii & viii].

English as an additional language
The Code makes special mention of children whose first language is not English [13.2:xi]. Some children may first come to school lacking competence in English not because they have special educational needs but simply because English has not been the preferred language in their home culture and community. The Code states that lack of competence in such circumstances must not be equated with learning difficulties as understood in the Code. In other words, while the child needs assistance to develop fluency in English to access the curriculum in school, it should not be assumed that they have a learning difficulty. There is a separate section at the end of this chapter about supporting EAL pupils.

On the other hand where a child is making slow progress, it should not be assumed that it is because of their language status. Careful assessment is important is such cases. It should include consideration of their background, and their fluency in their first language as reported by parents. It should also include observation of their performance in a range of situations in school.

The observations of an experienced assistant can be a significant contribution to the assessment. How much use the child makes of their own language, how actively they try to make themselves understood in play or group activity with other children, and the skills and competencies they show in activities such as drawing, construction or number can all be indicators of the child's learning capacity. You could report on how quickly the child appears to pick up and use words and phrases from other children. Indeed, the learning of language can be viewed as a social activity and an assistant does as much for developing a child's English language skills by setting up situations for active social learning as by direct instruction.

At the same time, you should take cultural factors into account when observing a child's behaviour in different situations. The social norms that are accepted in nursery class learning might be significantly different from a child's home experience and difficult for the child to interpret and understand. Assumptions about the child's learning abilities cannot be based solely on apparent differences from the norm in the child's social behaviour in the classroom or small group. You and the teacher should always carefully and critically examine the content of the curriculum, and the nature of the learning situation for young children who are at the early stages of learning English, before looking for 'within child' special educational needs to explain a child's progress [18.3:9, vi & vii].

Cognition and learning

The Code of Practice says that children who demonstrate features of moderate, severe or profound learning difficulties, or specific difficulties such as dyspraxia or dyslexia, require specific programmes to aid progress in cognition and learning. Children with physical or sensory impairments may also need help in this area, as will children with conditions on the autistic spectrum [14.1:v].

The overlap between difficulties of cognition (or knowing) and learning and communication and language difficulties is considerable [14.2:v]. Many items on the lists of their requirements in the Code of Practice apply to the needs of both groups. However, the special emphasis given to cognition and learning is an attempt to distinguish between pupils who have an underlying potential for effective learning and those whose general ability is below average and who are likely to progress relatively slowly [14.2:ii & iii].

These are children who need time to take in and grasp ideas. They do not learn as quickly as the average child and need a slower pace of teaching. They need more repetition and practice to learn basic skills. They do not have good memories. Working memory in particular is essential for learning. It is the ability to take in information, hold it in the memory in the short term while organising it mentally. Take a mental arithmetic problem such as

Jean had four sweets; she ate one and gave one to Sally. How many did she have left?

To solve it the child has to take in several pieces of information and keep them in mind while using them in two number operations. To solve the problem therefore requires an efficient working memory. So does the ability to follow instructions and solve problems in any area of the curriculum.

Cognition also refers to the child's level of awareness and understanding of the world around them. It involves being able to see relationships, similarities and differences in things and to solve problems. The type of support that a classroom assistant will be asked to give a child will depend upon the child's age and severity of need [14.1:4]. For children with the most profound learning difficulties it may involve helping to stimulate their senses of sight and touch and helping them develop their ability to respond and interact with their environment [14.1:vi; 14.2:3 & iv]. Support for the pupil with moderate learning difficulties might involve breaking down problems or classroom tasks into manageable steps, checking the child's understanding of the content of the lesson and what is required, and helping with reading, spelling and recording. The intensity of involvement will depend on the severity of the child's difficulties and the degree to which you judge the child to be able to cope independently at any stage [14.1:viii & x; 14.2:4].

Behaviour, emotional and social development

Pupils with emotional and behaviour difficulties may also have general or specific learning difficulties or they may be pupils with normal or good potential. However, it is their emotional and behaviour difficulties that are the main barrier to their learning and access to the curriculum. Sometimes a child's challenging behaviour is a feature of a complex learning or developmental disorder [15.2:v]. Some autistic children, for example, have extreme characteristics of challenging behaviour. In other cases a pupil's emotional and behavioural problems in school are symptomatic of traumas and difficulties in the home or social environment outside the school [15.1:v]. A primary aim of the School Action for a child with these difficulties will be to reduce or eliminate the incidence of behaviours that are interfering with the child's ability to learn and to replace them with more appropriate patterns of behaviour.

The School Action should include a behaviour plan that is known to the child's teachers and you. As with an IEP it should contain clear targets [15.1:vi]. Clear targets mean that the classroom assistant knows exactly what is being focused upon. For example, *John will become less disruptive in class* is a 'fuzzy' or unclear target. A 'fuzzy' is a description of performance that is unclear or ambiguous. It is better to describe problem behaviour in clear, observable terms. Precisely what does John do? He may 'frequently leave his seat without asking permission' or 'shout across the classroom'. These are descriptions of 'disruptive' behaviour that give a clear idea of precisely which behaviour is to be reduced if John is to be less disruptive. Thinking of behaviour in this way will help you by clarifying what you can focus on in your support role.

It is also important to observe the circumstances in which inappropriate or undesirable behaviour occurs and to ask what changes can prevent the behaviour happening in the first place [15.1:6 & 7]. This is like putting a gate at the top of the stairs to protect a child from falling. A child who constantly interferes and disrupts others in their class may have less opportunity if they have their own ruler and rubber and do not have to reach across or leave their seat to 'borrow' one from another child. If you are being observant and react in such small ways you can sometimes pre-empt behaviour which otherwise might escalate into major disruption.

It is not necessary for a classroom assistant who is appointed specifically as a consequence of a statement of special educational need to be allocated exclusively to one child. The assistant's role might be to give general support to the class teacher so that more of their time is available to deal with the child in question [15.1:1 & 2]. You need the general skills of assisting with classroom organisation and management in this case. On the other hand, whether or not your job is related to the needs of a particular child, you will all meet pupils with emotional, social and behavioural problems and will need to have the skills to relate to them. The level of understanding and expertise expected by the NOS 3–15 is very specialised, so do ensure you get specific training if you undertake this unit as part of an NVQ or other award [15.1:viii, ix, xiv & especially xv].

First and foremost you must be able to stand back from any situation and deal with it objectively. This is not always easy but it helps if you have an understanding of what motivates the child to behave in a particular way. The origins may be in their upbringing or disturbing experiences at home [15.1:v; 15.2:iii & iv]. The purpose of all behaviour is to satisfy a need [15.2:ii & iii]. Undesirable or problem behaviour of children in school or at home frequently occurs to satisfy the child's need for one or more of the following:

- attention
- affection
- protection
- power.

Thinking of behaviour in such terms offers clues as to how to respond appropriately to it. For example, frequent reprimands may reward rather than punish the child who is desperate for attention and increase their attention seeking. The child who needs to dominate and exert power over adults does so by refusing to respond to reasonable requests, provoking conflict and anger in adults. Recognising this possibility enables the adult to maintain control by anticipating potential conflict and avoiding confrontation [15.2:viii & x].

Confrontation and conflict often arise in response to secondary behaviours rather than primary behaviours. For example,

Teacher: Jane, put your mobile away, please (*primary behaviour*).
Jane puts mobile away but scowls at teachers and mutters something under breath.
Teacher: Don't look at me in that way and don't be so rude (*secondary behaviour*).
Jane: No I wasn't. Why pick on me? I wasn't the only one.
Teacher: Calm down or you will have to leave the room.

Jane is now in danger of being excluded from class not because she was playing with her mobile but because of her secondary behaviour. It is frequently better to ignore secondary behaviours if the child has responded to your attempt to deal with the initial behaviour. The questions of respect and responding to reasonable requests do not have to be ignored but in cases like Jane's they can be addressed later. You will undoubtedly be faced with many similar situations or observe them in pupil–teacher confrontations.

If you are aware that a child is behaving inappropriately, you should try to respond in the least intrusive or confrontational manner [15.3:5]. Depending on the circumstance, a non-verbal message such as a look, a shake of the head or a gesture might be enough. This keeps the message personal and private between the pupil and you. If it is necessary to speak to the child it is always easier to direct them to what they should be doing than to what they should not [15.2:viii]. Offer simple choices, and establish that they are responsible for the consequences of their behaviour. Reminding the pupil of a class rule may be sufficient [15.2:6]. A casual statement or question can be enough to redirect a pupil's attention to a task. For example, asking the distractible child where they have got up to, or what they are going to write next, can be more effective than drawing attention to the distractible behaviour.

Sensory and/or physical needs

The Code of Practice refers to a 'wide spectrum of sensory, multi-sensory and physical difficulties' (DfES 2001b: 88) affecting children's ability to profit from the curriculum at school [16.1:x & xii]. Special educational provision is usually available to children with the most severe difficulties from an early age. It is possible therefore to find the expertise of TAs deployed in all phases of education from nursery classes to secondary schools.

Your role could be wide-ranging in some contexts, especially at the early years stage or where the individual child's needs are complex. For example, pupils with complex needs require support for their physical management and welfare as well as help in learning tasks. You will need to be aware of the nature of the child's disabilities and how they affect their learning [16.2:i,v & vii]. For example, it is not enough to know that a child is visually impaired and conclude that they will respond to large print. Visual impairment takes different forms and each affects the child's access to print in a different way. If you are aware of the particular form of impairment, you can adjust your approach to helping that child accordingly [16.1:v]. Similarly, a child with a hearing impairment is not hearing 'normally' just because they are wearing an aid. The fact that a child has partial hearing does not mean that their language development will be that of a child with normal hearing [16.1:4]. You will need special advice and training if you are to use equipment designed to support pupils with many of these needs, such as hearing aids, computer-assisted devices, hoists and other supports.

Whatever the impairment, if you are aware of its potential effects on the child's overall functioning, you will be better able to help them in the classroom [16.1:iv]. The fact that you work under the direction of the teacher does not stop you observing the pupil's response to the task or materials and asking questions: can he/she see this properly? is it in the right place, at the right angle, in the right light? has he heard all the parts of the question? is this too difficult or too easy for her?

You also need to be aware of the effects of any medication on the pupil's functioning at any time [16.2:vi]. Some children will be on drugs that suppress their activity levels and responses to stimulation. They may appear at times to be fractious or just plain tired as a result. Your demands for them to take part in activities will need to be adapted accordingly. The school day of children with significant physical and/or neurological disabilities can often be interrupted for therapeutic or medical treatments [16.2:4]. Again, you must be sensitive to the mood and motivation of the pupil on return to the classroom and adapt your work accordingly [16.2:5].

Support for the child in the classroom and wider school will in some circumstances require you to help with physical aspects of the child's needs. At the simplest level this could mean helping to transfer the child from a wheelchair to a special standing frame. You should receive some guidance and training before taking on tasks where correct physical management of the child is necessary, both for the welfare of the child and for your safety. You must not hesitate to ask physiotherapists or experienced teachers for guidance on how to lift the child or use any specialist equipment [16.1:vi & vii; 16.2:iii].

While some children are likely to require care throughout their lives, the development of maximum independence and self-sufficiency should remain a key objective of any long-term plan for them. You should be sensitive to the pupil's age and developmental needs when offering support. Some children seek independence and disabled young students can become resentful of over-intrusive efforts to help them [16.1:viii & ix]. Remember, if you are aware that a teenaged student with physical disabilities is likely to have the same emotional needs for independence as your own teenaged child at home, you will manage them with the same sensitivity and respect. You might also recognise 'learned dependence' in another pupil, in which case your role will be to draw back from giving the child assistance in areas where they are able to cope independently. Here the task might be to encourage the child to take the next step on the path to self-sufficiency rather than giving way to your natural impulse to help. Increasing independence may also form part of the IEP [16.1:xv].

Motor education

A detailed explanation of the principles and practice of motor education is beyond the scope of this chapter. However, a summary of what motor education is will enable you to decide whether you want or need to pursue the subject in more detail.

'Motor education' is a term that includes teaching methods for the physically disabled and neurologically impaired based upon the principles of Conductive Education pioneered at the Peto Institute in Hungary. The method is based upon the theory that physical and some cognitive difficulties, caused by damaged or disorganised nerve pathways in children with congenital conditions such as cerebral palsy, can be reduced through a systematic programme of physical and sensory exercises. The theory suggests that the sensory experiences produced by systematic physical activities develop or activate new neural pathways and enable the child to develop functions that they previously lacked.

For example, normal development involves the gradual integration of senses and the development of structures in the brain that enable the child to respond to their environment in a meaningful way. Thus an infant learns to integrate sight and arm movement to reach and explore an object. They become increasingly aware of the relationship of body parts and learn to use them in a coordinated way to stand and walk. The neurologically impaired child is prevented from developing in this way spontaneously. They therefore need systematic help. Initially they need someone to move their limbs for them so that the relevant sensory messages can establish new pathways in the nervous system that eventually allow the child to move autonomously in a purposeful, coordinated way. If you are a TA working in a special school or unit, you could be involved in programmes of this kind.

Questions to ask yourself

- Do you know where the most recent copy of the Code of Practice is in the school?
- Do you have and have you read and understood the school SEN policy?
- Have you seen the IEP format for the school? Have you seen the IEPs of the pupils with whom you work closely? Have you discussed the content with the SENCO?
- Are there any national associations supporting the pupils with SEN with whom you work closely and their families? Can you make contact with them?

Essential reading

DfEE (1998b) *Excellence for All Children: Meeting Special Educational Needs* (Green paper) London: Department for Education and Employment.

DfEE (1998d) *Meeting Special Educational Needs: A Programme for Action* (MSENPAS). London: Department for Education and Employment.

DfES (2001b) *Special Educational Needs Code of Practice*. London: Department for Education and Skills.

Some further reading

Balshaw, M., and Farrell, P. (2002) *Teaching Assistants: Practical Strategies for Effective Classroom Support*. London: David Fulton Publishers.

Cottam, P. and Sutton, A. (1985) *Conductive Education: A System for Overcoming Motor Disorders*. London: Croom Helm.

Dessent, T. (1987) *Making the Ordinary School Special*. London: The Falmer Press.

East, V. and Evans, L. (2001) *At a Glance: A Quick Guide to Children's Special Needs*. Birmingham: The Questions Publishing Company.

Fox, G. (1998) *A Handbook for Learning Support Assistants*. London: David Fulton Publishers.

Leung, C. and Cable, C. (1997) *English as an Additional Language: Changing Perspectives*. Watford: NALDIC.

Lovey, J. (2002) *Supporting Special Educational Needs in Secondary School Classrooms*, 2nd edn. London: David Fulton Publishers.

Thomas, G., Walker, D. and Webb, J. (1998) *The Making of the Inclusive School*. London and New York: Routledge.

The David Fulton Publishers list for SEN with specific titles, e.g. Dyslexia, Dyspraxia, Asbergers.

9 Supporting bilingual and multilingual pupils

English as an additional language

In schools throughout England and Wales, you will come across pupils who have English as an additional language (EAL). They make up about 9 per cent of the total school population and have origins all over the world, from Colombia to Afghanistan and from Sri Lanka to Lithuania. Pupils with EAL tend to be found in schools in urban areas such as London and Birmingham, with some boroughs having more than 50 per cent of pupils with EAL, such as in Tower Hamlets and Hackney. Schools in rural areas, however, often have EAL pupils too and LEAs such as Devon and Norfolk provide support to these pupils. They provide a cultural and linguistic richness to schools and are sometimes our highest achievers. EAL pupils are referred to in most DfES and Ofsted publications and EAL provision is inspected by Ofsted.

It is useful to be clear about some terminology used concerning EAL pupils. You may have come across the term ESL or English as a second language. This was dropped some years ago because many EAL pupils speak more than two languages. For example, a child from Kenya may speak Swahili and Panjabi and be learning English as a third language. The term EFL (English as a foreign language) should not be used as this usually refers either to students learning English in countries where English is not the mother-tongue, or to students coming to England to study English for short periods of time. The term 'bilingual' is often defined as living in two languages or having access to two languages but not necessarily being fluent in them.

Who are our EAL pupils?

EAL pupils come from a diverse range of backgrounds throughout the world. Not all, however, are born overseas and indeed many have been born here to families whose first language is not English. These pupils may enter school not speaking English as they have grown up in communities in England where English is not the first language. Their television programmes may also not be in English, so little English may be used in the family home.

Of course, not all EAL pupils are beginners in English. LEAs usually have their own system for grading pupils from beginners to fully fluent bilingual pupils. Some LEAs use stages of language learning with between four and seven levels, while others have moved over to additional National Curriculum step levels as recommended by the Qualifications and Curriculum Authority (QCA). You can find out about these through the EAL teacher in your school or through your LEA [12.1:1; 12.2:1]. It is currently thought that it takes children between five and seven years to achieve full fluency in English, although there can be considerable variation depending on the pupil. Remember, full fluency in terms of schooling does not just mean being able to use conversational English but to have knowledge of academic language and the literacy and oracy skills that go with this [12.1:vii].

EAL pupils are not a homogenous group of learners and can be put into three general groups:

1. Some children come into school with little or no spoken English but with strong literacy skills in another language, particularly if they are older. They may have received a good education in their home country and already be competent in many National Curriculum subject areas. These pupils are sometimes referred to as 'elite bilinguals' and often come from middle-class homes where there are considerable expectations and knowledge of the education system. These children may come from families who have chosen to travel abroad for business, academic or diplomatic reasons or may be from educated refugee families, forced to flee their home country.

2. A further group of children are those who enter school with limited spoken English and little or no reading or writing skills in their first language. The child's home language may have low status in wider society yet there will be strong pressure from the local community to maintain the first language and culture. The family may value education highly but not understand what is specifically needed to support a child's academic learning. These pupils are sometimes termed as coming from 'linguistic minorities'.

3. Some children come from homes where another language is spoken by one parent and the child grows up with two languages in a bilingual family. Quite often the language of the host country (English) will predominate as the child gets older.

When working with EAL pupils, it is important to find out as much as you can about their backgrounds to inform your expectations [12.1:vi & vii; 12.2:1,v,vi & iv]. For example, if you are working with an 11-year-old child who is at an early stage of writing development, this may be because the child has had a disrupted education because of war or lack of access to schooling rather than having a special educational need. Other children may have had an excellent education in their home country and may be very good, for example, at maths – you may find the work you have been given to do with them is not at the right level and needs to be more challenging. Do give the teacher you work with any information which you gain about problems and progress and also any background information about the pupils [12.1:11; 12.2:11,12 & 13].

As well as policies, the school may well have protocols about finding out information about pupils and it is important to follow these [12.1:ii; 12.2:ii]. There may be an EAL or Ethnic Minority Achievement (EMA) teacher or department in your school or the class teacher themselves may know a lot about the pupils concerned. The school office should hold much useful information in the pupil files on the languages children speak, their previous educational experience and their ethnicity and religion. Remember that some of the information may be confidential, so please check either with the office or with a senior member of staff that it is all right for you to see this [12.2:1].

Factors affecting pupils' learning of English

Apart from the aspects of a child's background which may affect progress in learning English to do with class, social background and educational experience, and the quality of teaching and support children receive, there are some other factors. These include:

Age

It is often assumed that it is easier for younger children to learn languages than older children. This is not necessarily the case. Some children who arrive at nursery school speaking little English can find it quite a stressful situation and can take some time to start learning English [12.1:iii; 12.2:v]. On the other hand, older secondary age children may well already have considerable language skills in their first language, which they do not have to relearn when learning English. These skills can be transferred to English and this partly explains how some EAL pupils can achieve high GCSE grades within two or three years of arriving at a school in this country.

Immersion

It is often assumed, too, that the best way of learning English is to be thrown in at the deep end: to be immersed in it totally. It seems logical that if the language is all around you, you must learn and learn quickly. However, many high-achieving children, for example from Chinese or Indian backgrounds, speak more than two languages regularly. They may speak English at school in lessons, Chinese and English at home with their parents and watch some Chinese television. There is no evidence of a correlation between time spent in an English-speaking environment and learning English. Indeed the evidence suggests that it is critical to have a well-developed first language and that this is a key factor in learning English. Furthermore in lessons, if you can provide a quick translation of a key word, this can help understanding of a concept and support a child's learning.

Character and emotional factors

Inevitably, a child's character is important in determining success in language learning. Children who are more outgoing and who are prepared to take risks tend to be better language learners. Shy, quieter and less adventurous children may be less successful [12.1:x]. Further, emotional issues may inhibit a child learning. If a child is unhappy because of experiences she/he has been through, is worried about friends and relatives left behind in another country or has not settled well into the school, inevitably this will get in the way of effective learning.

A safe and welcoming environment

It is important that all children feel safe and supported within their school. Because some EAL pupils have little English and some may be obviously different from other children in terms of skin colour, hairstyle or dress, they may be picked on, bullied or isolated from other children. You need to be aware of this and work with the school to follow the advice offered below on supporting children new to the school [12.2:ii]. Ensure you know the school procedures for dealing with bullying and racist incidents. Children who are bullied may suffer low self-esteem and their attendance at school may also suffer.

Teaching styles

Children who arrive in school from overseas may have had a very different experience of schooling. Some may have gone to schools with a similar education system to ours but others may be used to what might be termed a more 'traditional' system. There might have been a lot of learning by rote, little expectation that the pupil should contribute to lessons and very little pair or group work. Children may take a little while to adjust to a different system [12.1:vii].

Beginner EAL and bilingual children

Don't panic

You will find that in some schools panic will set in when a child arrives who speaks little or no English. How do we communicate with him/her? Will he/she understand anything? In other, usually inner-city, schools staff see this as par for the course and indeed in some nurseries the vast majority of children have little English when they arrive.

At the admission interview which should normally occur with the parent or carer, important information should be found out by the school about the child. You may have been involved in the admission procedure or, if not, you should then find out as much as you can. Hopefully an interpreter will have attended the interview to support both the parent/carer and the school (this may have been you if you are bilingual yourself). Good admissions practice will usually mean that the child will not start school immediately, so you and other members of staff can be ready for the child's arrival.

How do you prepare? If you know what language the child speaks it may be possible for you to learn a little bit of that language, such as greetings or 'What is your name?' You may assist the class or form teacher to identify a buddy or buddies to look after the pupil when he/she starts. This may include someone who speaks the child's language – this can obviously help the child settle in fairly quickly, although sometimes the buddy child may not want to do this – be sensitive to this. Often the best buddies are those who you know will be supportive and friendly. You may find out some information about the country the child has come from and, with the class teacher, conduct a short input on this with the class or form. This could include looking at how to help someone in school if they don't speak English and how it might feel to be in that position.

If you speak the child's language and are familiar with the culture, you may prepare some school and classroom signs in the child's language or even (with the class teacher's permission) teach the other children some greetings in the new language [12.1:2 & 3]. You could talk to the class teacher/s and to the class about the new child's country and culture and any key differences to do with religion or food. You could even find some posters for a display about the country the child has come from.

Having everything prepared for when the child arrives is also very important. In primary schools this will mean, for example, ensuring there is a place to sit, books ready and tray labelled. In secondary schools, it may mean having exercise and textbooks available and a school diary. Make sure you know how to pronounce the child's name correctly and you know the child's first or calling name. Children have been known to go through school being called by the wrong name or having been given an 'English' name instead. If you have been asked to support the child, it can be very useful to establish who the home contact is – and, in primary settings, to establish contact with the person who brings the child to school. As with all the strategies you use, talk to the class teacher about this [12.1:1; 12.2:2 & 3].

When the child starts school

This can be quite a daunting experience for some children. Try to imagine how it might feel. Spend a minute or two thinking about this and make some notes about what might be different and how you might feel [12.1:vii & x].

> You enter an institution in a strange country, where no one or few people may speak your language and you can't speak theirs. You have no friends, people may be a different colour to you and look different, you don't know the rules (written and unwritten) of the school and you don't know what to expect in lessons. It may

be that you didn't even want to come here – it was your parents' decision or you had to leave! You may be missing your home and your friends. Because of this, it is important that the school is as welcoming as possible. The teaching assistant should:

- Be prepared (see above)
- Show the pupil around the school – where the toilets are, dinner hall, etc.
- Introduce the child to his/her buddy and make sure the child is looked after at break and lunchtimes
- Introduce him/her to a supportive child, perhaps an older child, who also speaks his/her language
- Establish a home contact
- Smile and be friendly and relaxed! Talk to the child normally (don't be slow and halting) and use clear, simple language.

In lessons, the child may not say anything at all to start with, even if they do know some English. This is quite normal and is often known as the 'silent period' – the child will be listening and learning but not necessarily speaking [12.1:3 & iii]. This can continue for some time – perhaps for a couple of weeks or even up to six months. Monitor this but do worry too much. If a child is outgoing, they are much more likely to start talking earlier – character obviously plays a role.

You may be asked to work with a newly arrived pupil in induction sessions separate from the rest of the class for the first half term to term [12.1:1 & 4]. These may be every day for half-an-hour to an hour, although this varies considerably from school to school. Work should be set for you to do by the class teacher or EAL teacher [12.1:5 & 6; 12.2:2,3 & 4]. It is important that you liaise with these staff on an ongoing basis about the lessons and the progress pupils make. If you do speak the child's first language, this can be ideal time to talk to the child in this language about how school is going and establish rapport. This can be a great relief for some children who may be struggling to communicate and succeed in school [18.3:viii].

Supporting the child in the classroom

You will need to talk to the class teacher about the best ways you can support the EAL child in lessons; further guidance may be provided by EAL staff. There is some very helpful further reading listed at the end of this chapter. Being prepared is essential. One very important strategy is to use visual aids to explain ideas and concepts which are vital in the early stages [12.1:7]. For example, a child may know a lot about volcanoes because there are volcanoes 'back home' or because she/he has studied them in school. If the lesson has no visual aids or the introduction is just 'talked' or in plain text, the child is not likely to learn much from the lesson. It is essential for you and the class teacher to discuss what is needed before the lesson to make it accessible [12.1:1;12.2:iii].

There is a danger that in the first part or introduction to a lesson, the early stage learner of English may gain little from the teacher's explanation, unless it includes the use of relevant visual aids [12.1:8 & iv]. Whispering to the pupil to try to help in the introduction, even in the child's first language, can be very distracting for the rest of the class. If you have spoken to the class teacher beforehand, you may be able to identify some appropriate visual aids. If the lesson is the literacy hour, you could discuss with the class teacher the possibility of your using a different text at a more appropriate language level outside the classroom for the first half hour, if the school has an appropriate space – a corridor is not normally appropriate. The class teacher should plan this with you – the text needs to be age-appropriate [12.1:8; 18.1:ix; 18.2:x].

There is a wide range of activities that can be used with EAL pupils when they are following up a teacher's introduction to the lesson and these will inevitably vary according to the aims of the lesson. Some examples are matching vocabulary or sentences to pictures, matching definitions to explanations, retelling stories or doing an experiment using picture prompts, and gap-fill activities [12.1:4 & v]. Your role here would be to support pupils in understanding but, of course, not to do the activities for them! It is also important not to avoid key vocabulary items. For example, words such as 'transparent' and 'translucent' may seem difficult but are actually quite easily taught if items which have these qualities are brought into the lesson [12.1:9; 18.3:viii].

You will need to be aware that sometimes things that we assume that 'everybody knows' are not known by some EAL pupils. This is because we often make cultural assumptions about the curriculum and the prior knowledge pupils bring with them to the school [12.2:6 & vii]. A topic such as 'Going on Holiday' or 'Going to the Seaside' may be alien to some cultures, as would some fairy tales and nursery rhymes; or in higher-level texts there may be literary or historical references that the pupil does not understand. As you gain more experience, you will be able to identify these before the lesson. During the lesson it may mean that you will have to explain the topic or item, or alternatively it may be appropriate that a different task is set.

In some schools, you will be a very important language model for EAL pupils, particularly when working in small groups. This does not mean that you should speak in slow, halting language or, if the pupils don't seem to understand, speak louder. You should speak at a normal pace initially to pupils and then slow down or focus on key words as necessary [12.1:ix; 12.2:ix]. There may be specific language or vocabulary targets for the lesson which should help you focus. If you ask a child a question, allow a little more time for the pupil to respond. The child may need more time to process the question [18.3:viii].

This chapter is only a start in understanding the needs of children learning EAL. You may well want to attend further training or read more if you are going to undertake a qualification in this area or specialise in it. It can be very useful to put yourself in the child's position or reflect on your own experiences and perhaps frustrations when travelling or living abroad and what would have helped you. A useful activity you can do is to compare two EAL pupils, one who is succeeding and achieving well in school and one who is not doing so well. Find out as much as you can about these two pupils and try to work out why this is the case.

And finally, remember that EAL pupils should not be judged as having special needs just because they are learning English [20.1:vii; 20.2:vii]. The new Code of Practice on SEN makes this very clear. You should normally have high expectations of EAL pupils. If you are concerned about their learning, discuss this with the teacher or SENCO. It is usually a tremendously rewarding experience working with EAL pupils, seeing the progress they make, and it is a privilege to play a part in this.

Questions to ask yourself

- What do you know about the countries which the pupils with whom you work come from? Where can you find out more?
- Do these pupils have other educational needs as well as language problems?
- Do you know to whom on the staff and the LEA you can go to get further information about support the pupils' EAL needs?

Essential reading

Gibbons, P. (1991) *Learning to Learn in a Second Language.* Primary English Teaching Association (Australia). (Available in the UK through NALDIC, South Herts EMA Centre, Holywell School Site, Tolpits Lane, Watford WD1 8NT Tel: 01923 231855.)

Some further reading

Buxton, C. (1994) *Language Activities for Bi-lingual Learners.* London: Tower Hamlets Language Support Service: Learning Design Publications.
EMAS (2001) *Good Practice in Admission and Induction.* London: Hackney Ethnic Minority Achievement Service.
EMAS (2000) *Challenging Children.* London: Hackney Ethnic Minority Achievement Service. (Available through EMAS, The Learning Trust, Mare Street, Hackney, London E8 1GQ. Practical resource book with a secondary and KS2 focus with many practical examples of classroom materials.)
Hall, D. (2002) *Assessing the Needs of Bilingual Learners: Living in Two Languages.* London: David Fulton Publishers.

10 Working with teachers in the classroom

Roles and responsibilities

There is clear guidance in the recent proposals that, whatever happens in the classroom in terms of delegation of teaching strategies,

> qualified teachers must always **oversee** the teaching and learning process, using their training and expertise to identify learning activities and goals, and to define the pace and scope for individuals and groups [and] in doing this they may identify activities that will contribute to teaching and learning, and that in their professional judgement can be carried out entirely or partially by other suitably trained adults with an appropriate level of supervision.
>
> (DfES 2002a: 21)

TAs teach but do not take the responsibility for the direction and organisation of the learning. What this means virtually has to be re-established for each teacher and TA partnership [13.1:iii; 15.1:iii; 16.1:iii; 16.2:1]. One teacher is happy for you to change direction when working with a pupil because things are not going well, another will want you to ask him or her first. On the whole, TAs have proved a sensitive group of staff, intuitively watching each teacher and 'feeling their way' as to the limits and boundaries for each classroom. As job descriptions become more common and detailed, misunderstanding should become rarer. However, what seems to happen now is that managers negotiate a job description, but each teacher is not aware of the exact purpose of the TA in a lesson. The more you and the teacher can find time to make these implicit understandings explicit, the better you will work together [8.2:ii].

Remember, teachers have not often in the past been trained to work with additional adults in the classroom, nor have managers realised the importance of relationships and communication to the effective working of TAs. Only recently I met a newly qualified teacher in a secondary school who had three TAs turning up to some of her lessons and she did not have any idea why they had come or what they were supposed to do. She assumed they were to support three individual pupils and left it at that – what a waste of expertise and human resource! It helps if each teacher who has a TA allotted to them, as

127

in many primary classrooms now, can be involved in the drawing up the TA's job description. If this has not happened for you, ask if it could be discussed when your time for review comes. If you are going to work with a different or new teacher you must find at least a few moments to discuss the following:

- What do you particularly want me to do?
- What do I do if a pupil in your room asks to go to the toilet?
- Can I write in any pupils' books?
- What contact with parents or carers do you expect of the TA?
- Do you want me to attend consultation evenings?
- Do I take part in SEN reviews?
- Can I do anything at the request of a parent, such as change a child's reading book or search for lost equipment?
- Can I tidy the rooms? Your desks? The resources area?
- Is there anything you do not want me to do?

(Watkinson, 2002b: 63)

The classroom process: planning, preparation, performance and review

What goes on in the classroom is the centre of all the school's activities. It is here that, hopefully, pupils learn. All the other procedures are there to support that process. The teachers, the hierarchy of management, the building, books and equipment should all be directed to this purpose. You are helping this process right 'at the chalkface'. So, you see how everybody's efforts go to make up what actually happens. In any domestic or life process, the better the planning and preparation the better the event goes, and the more often the event takes place the more we learn about how to improve it – provided we review what happened. Learning in the classroom is no different. Sometimes, to a new onlooker it seems to happen effortlessly, but the more time you spend in class, the more you will realise the background procedures that have enabled the pupils to learn most effectively. Now, as an experienced TA, you will be expected not just to appreciate these but to be part of them. It is no longer possible to do your job fully by just dropping into lessons and out of them; you need liaison time with teachers, study time to understand rationales, and preparation time. You will have ideas, experience and expertise to contribute [8.1:ix]. You should be reflecting on and reviewing what you are doing constantly in your head while you do it, and you need to feed back these thoughts to someone [8.1:3]. Sometimes a newly qualified teacher, having come from college thinking they were now trained to do it all properly and then being faced with the never-ending challenge of a classroom full of pupils, will ask 'When do you get it all sorted out?' Unfortunately, or really fortunately, the answer is 'never'; the process is cyclical and changing. Even in the same room with the same teacher and class and curriculum, the changing nature of human beings means that needs change and so the classroom process will be different. A teacher or TA who is complacent and feels they have got it all 'sussed' is not going to be the best support for the pupils. Where you are still a learner, you are still thinking and form part of a learning organisation.

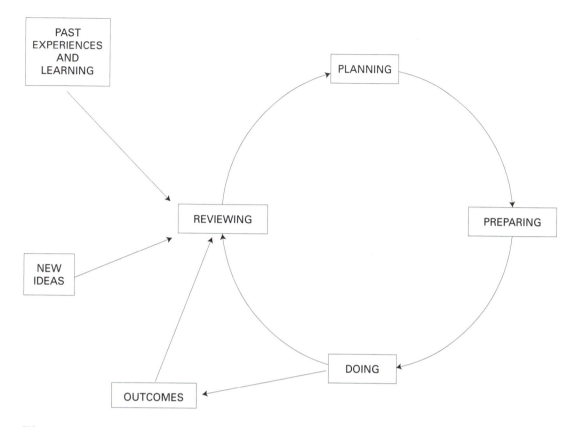

Figure 10.1   The classroom process cycle

Planning

Understanding teaching and learning policies

The school will have already decided what their approach is to teaching and learning and many schools have established policies for this area; hopefully you will have a copy [3.1:i; viii]. It will cover such things as:

- What kind of teaching methods the schools encourages
- How the school deals with children of differing ability:
  - whether pupils are to be taught in mixed-ability groups, streamed (in similar-ability classes for most of the time) or setted pupils of the same age group put together in similar-ability groups for patroller lessons)
  - how work for individual pupils is to be differentiated
  - how those with learning problems are to be supported
  - whether gifted and able pupils are to have any special treatment
- How pupils are to be involved in their own learning
- Whether particular active learning strategies or investigative/problem-solving approaches are to be used
- Whether all lessons are to be structured and planned in the same way
- How oral work is to be conducted – what expectations there are for allowing debate or discussion

- How written work is to be presented
  – who marks what and in what way
- What study skills are to be taught or encouraged
- How pupils can be rewarded for good work, and what the consequences might be for poor work, or how such pupils are to be supported
- Where staff can seek assistance, resources and ideas

As you can see from the list many of the items will affect how you work with pupils. If when you read it you do not understand the jargon – words such as pedagogy – you must ask your mentor or a class teacher to explain. 'Pedagogy' means 'any conscious activity by one person designed to enhance learning in another' (Watkins and Mortimore 1999: 3): just what your job is!

Planning and preparation

There is no substitute for good planning. This does not mean everything you are going to do has to be spelt out in a particular format on a piece of paper; it just means thinking ahead rather than thinking on your feet. Pieces of paper are needed when memory needs a jog, and when others need to know what you are going to do and it is either too complicated or too long to be able to tell them. For a TA and a teacher there may just be no opportunity for verbal communication. For too long, TAs have been paid only for pupil contact time, and teachers are busy people. Luckily for the pupils, this is changing and the need for formal and informal time with the teachers is now seen as vital to underpin good practice in the classroom [8.1:i]. It is still not the norm for you to have paid time for planning with teachers, but the benefits of such time are being recognised more, as are ways of using paper communication to compensate for the lack of human contact time [3.1:1].

It is important that teachers share their planning with you in some way, so that you know not only what you are doing but how and why [8.1:i; 8.2:i]. You may know the pupils well but you must know the teacher's intentions, their curriculum objectives for the lesson [2.1:1 & i; 13.1:2; 14.2:1 & 2]. Teachers plan for the long term so that pupils do not cover the same material year after year. Together they have developed yearly schemes of work to plan out curriculum coverage over the time the pupils are in the school. You need to have some curriculum understanding in order to fulfil the teacher's objectives, particularly if you are working in a secondary school or employed specifically to support literacy or numeracy or any other subject in the primary school. There is a brief description of the principles of supporting the curriculum below and specific chapters for literacy and numeracy, which are not only important as independent subjects but are used in virtually every other subject. You will soon recognise the differences between what goes on in each year group as you work in different classes [8.1:v].

Individual teachers, or sometimes year groups of teachers, then plan for the medium term, usually a term ahead. Medium-term plans will consider the sort of resources, events, activities and ideas which will support the curriculum objectives of the long-term plan and are practical and feasible, given the classroom circumstances [8.1.2]. These plans are usually available and you will find them helpful and interesting. Some schools are involving experienced TAs in some of the termly planning sessions for the medium-term plans. By working with them, or even just looking at them, you will know what kinds of thing will be coming up in the term and whether there are any ideas you could contribute [8.1:5 & ii].

Teachers then produce short-term plans covering the detail of each week's work, and how they are adapting the curriculum to the needs of the pupils, including those with IEPs and other individual targets, and how the pupils have been dealing with the work up to now [2.1:1 & i; 8.1:vi & vii]. These plans should incorporate your role in supporting the pupils' learning [8.1:vi]. Within these short-term plans, teachers will produce some individual lesson plans. These should contain the learning objectives and some indication of the teacher's expectations of what the outcomes will be [3.1:ii]. They may contain some indication of how you can tell whether the objective has been achieved – success criteria – but this is unusual unless the lesson includes a test [8.1:1]. This is the kind of thing you can talk about regularly with the teacher you work with or your mentor.

Examples of good practice

A TA in one school came up with the first draft of a planning/recording sheet for the pupils with whom the TAs worked. The teachers saw it as supporting them in their work, and appreciated a mechanism for the TAs to report back to them about the progress of children during a session. Another school allocated a shared planning time on a Thursday. Another recommended that TAs had a copy of the teacher's planning on a Monday morning, and were given time to work on differentiation for their pupils on a Monday afternoon. Another school made the long- and medium-term planning of all teachers available in a folder in the staffroom. In yet another school, the TAs' personal planning was done by them at home at the weekend, after the teachers had given them their plans on a Friday. In this same school the TAs were linked with specific teachers and spent time with them over the summer holidays on the long-term planning. Some schools just encouraged the teachers to leave their planning out on their desks and the TAs looked at it as they went into the room to work. The teacher admitted that if the TA was late it could throw her, but nevertheless the preparation and rapport previously established enabled the TA to pick up instantly what was wanted.

Teachers may have separate plans for the TAs, or give them copies in which the TA role is spelt out. Some teachers use an exercise book to write down tasks for the TAs, who then write their comments before leaving the book on the teacher's desk when leaving the room. There are some good examples of

Date .... Teacher .... TA ....

Lesson ....

Learning objective

Activities
Introduction

Group work

Plenary

Resources

Children					
Individual needs					
Feedback comments					

Any general comments:

Figure 10.2   A possible planning sheet for teachers and TAs to use

systems in use in Balshaw and Farrell (2002: 67–73), and one possibility is shown in Figure 10.2.

You may make your own plans – 'shopping lists' of resources or equipment you will need to find or make, books to look out for, or special clothing to take with you [8.1:6 & xi]. You will also be thinking of varying the strategies to match the requirements of the teachers and the needs of the particular pupils with whom you work. When you know things beforehand, you can think of different ways of presenting the same objectives. This is particularly important with slow learners, who need a lot of repetition to grasp concepts but need to be kept interested and motivated to learn. You will also have your own resources – pictures, books, artefacts, people you know – which can add a different and interesting slant on the teacher's ideas. Do remember: if in doubt, check with the teacher first that they agree to you using your own ideas or equipment.

Preparation

It is important that you have time, both to prepare things for the teacher and to make your own preparations. Still too often planning and preparation are done in your own time. Do try to negotiate some paid time for this. The section on working with practical subjects should also be read before undertaking any practical work to ensure you have taken all the necessary health and safety precautions.

The learning environment

Chapter 4 talked of the broad concept of a 'healthy school' being more than just a clean, hygienic and safe one but needing the good relationships of those who worked there to provide a good working climate. It also indicated that schools should be 'providing not only an environment which is safe for exploring and growing bodies but also a learning environment for enquiring minds' [5.1:1 & vii]. The surroundings in which learning takes place influence the quality of the learning. You know yourself that having things where you know you can find them – materials or tools – makes a job easier [17.1:i]. Having the right lighting, or a comfortable chair at the correct height makes a difference to how long you can persist at a task [5.3:ii; 16.1:6]. Sharp tools are usually safer than blunt ones. A jigsaw with lost pieces is useless, blunt pencils will not produce good handwriting, paper with curled edges does not encourage good presentation. A welcoming room or building encourages its use [13.1:3; 14.1:3; 16.1:3].

You are responsible for all the equipment or materials you use, and should provide a role model in your use of them. You will need to find out where items are kept that you will be using and how to use them properly [17.1:i]. This will include knowing about storage facilities, what to do if you or pupils you are with break or spill anything, and how to dispose of waste of any kind [5.2:ii; 10.1:6 & viii]. This goes for pencils, paper and scissors as well as televisions, audio or computer equipment, scientific equipment or chemicals, tools, toys and books [17.1:3 & iii]. Check *before* a lesson that you have correct and sufficient materials for a task; never leave your pupils to go to get something, particularly if they are young and away from their class base [5.2:3 & 5].

Chapter 5 touched on the use of music, the company of others or silence, and the freedom from fear or anxiety to create a learning atmosphere. The teacher will set the scene of their classroom, creating resource centres, setting out the furniture appropriately and putting up displays to create the atmosphere they feel is most conducive to the tasks to be performed there; the management will decide about the more public places and the budget to be spent on various items. You may be given a particular role in maintaining the environment, such as display or plants and animals, and there may be other people doing other things, such as art media and books, or specialist technicians for science or ICT equipment or equipment to support SEN, so you need to know how you fit into the scheme of things [5.1:ii; 13.1:3]. You also need to be able to adjust the working environment to provide appropriate lighting, heating or ventilation, if this changes while you are in that location [5.3:1]. Make sure the pupils you are with are safe and can move about adequately, if they have to, and use the space appropriately. This may mean ensuring they stay with you if you go out into the grounds or do not charge about if suddenly released into a large space, such as a hall [5.3:2]. It may be advisable to shut any windows which you have opened, after use, for security reasons; check the procedures for your school. Your example in maintaining a tidy, organised personal work area, with the proper tools decently maintained – from paper and pencils to large expensive equipment – will be a powerful role model for the pupils. If you are asked to get things ready for a lesson [17.1:1], or to spend time supporting the teacher in maintaining the classroom environment, this should be paid time, as you will have to do it when the pupils are not there. You might need to adjust your timetable to enable you to do this, but you should be able to negotiate this with the teacher or your line manager [2.1:5; 5.2:7].

Display

Whatever is displayed on school walls, and the manner in which it is displayed, gives messages to pupils and adults about what is valued. If displays become faded and tatty, the message is 'Who cares?' If it is part of your role to renew or create displays for the teacher, you can find more advice in Watkinson (2003).

Making and maintaining equipment, resources and materials

It may also be part of your role to ensure that things are ready for the pupils' use with the teacher [5.1:1; 17.1:4]. You should have paid time to do this, especially if, as the new proposals are designed for, you are to relieve the teacher of some of the tasks that teachers should not routinely be expected to do. You can make specified workcards and worksheets, given a prototype, make and mend equipment and books, or sort and organise classroom resources and equipment, according to the wishes of the teachers [5.2:3 & 5]. There may be specialised equipment used to support particular elements of the curriculum or particular SEN [17.1:2]. Do check you know how these are to be used to best effect – things such as counting apparatus, word banks and computer programmes. At NOS Level 3 you should be aware of the rationale behind the design of some of the simple apparatus, and be able to assess its quality and suitability for the task and report your ideas back to the teacher. You may become responsible for stock maintenance and reordering; do follow the school procedures and report any problems you have [5.3:5].

Check with the teacher if you have any doubts over what to use, or how much of a particular medium or material you should use – it just could be they were saving that bit of gold paper for a special decoration for a festival, or that was the paint to be used for the forthcoming examination, or someone had ordered that set of floppy disks especially! [5.2:1; 16.1:4]. Pupils of differing ages and stages of development will need different apparatus and you should be able to recognise this [14.2:4]. A useful tip, if working with pupils with learning difficulties, is to spend some time in classes of pupils at least two years younger than the ones you work with [5.1:1]. Sometimes courses ask you to do this as part of your training. So, if you are in an infant school, ask to spend time in a nursery class or school; in a junior school, go to the infant department or school; and secondary school TAs should spend some time in a primary school. This can be done by arrangement with the managers of each establishment, but do go with a particular agenda in mind; for instance, to see the mathematics apparatus. Going with a focus means you will not be immediately distracted by the wealth of other things going on in a different school, but in any case you will find you will come away with many more ideas than those you set out to get. You should be able to maintain resource banks so that the right quantity is available. This could apply to workcards or ICT accessories, depending on the responsibilities which have been delegated to you [3.1:2; 17.1:2]. You do need time to prepare special resources – find reference books of pictures, locate the games or counting blocks that are shared between classes, and check that the audio-visual equipment or new software programmes work. If you have not used equipment before, check how it works, how it is maintained and how to use it safely and effectively [5.2:i; 5.3:i].

Remember that the pupils should help with some equipment preparation and maintenance [5.1:ii]. You must encourage all pupils to use their classroom, school premises, equipment and materials carefully and safely, with the least wastage [5.1:4; 5.2:4; 5.3:v]. You must guide them in the safe use of equipment [17.1:2]. They should be able not only to get out but also to clear up equipment and resources, if they are accessible, and leave them safe and ready for others [5.3:3 & 4; 17.2:8]. Paintpot washing is the classic example. It is said, 'If TAs are helping with teaching and learning, who washes the paintpots?' – my answer is 'the pupils!'[16.1:5]. If four- and five-year-olds can do this at the end of a session, supervised by a TA, there should not be a problem for most other pupils. This is a matter of time management; you must allow sufficient time at the end of a task for the pupils to clear away books, paper and pencils properly, check the floor and return equipment to its places [15.3:4]. You are not their servant. Carry a few sharp pencils, a pencil sharpener and spare pens by all means, but make it clear it is the responsibility of every pupil to know where to find them or to carry them with them. Do tell the teacher or line manager if you have any problems with materials or equipment – its allocation, location, quality, availability – or even the space you have to work in; if you do not say, people will presume all is well [8.1:4; 17.1:6 & iv]. Also tell the teacher if pupils break anything; there may well be a policy of pupils paying for replacements if it was deliberate. Dealing with broken glass or spilt liquids needs to be done safely and you may need to summon help.

Live animals can still be kept in schools but clearly some are more suitable than others, and the proper procedures, safety codes and hygiene facilities should be in place. Micro-organisms such as fungi can be grown in schools but there are proper ways of doing it and of disposing of finished cultures. Yeast growth, yoghurt cultures and examining pond algae are likely to be the extent of work in primary schools, but safe procedures should still be followed. In secondary schools, cultures on special media such as agar will take place and you need to understand the proper ways of dealing with this equipment and its safe disposal. Plants are often grown in schools, both inside and outside. Some are hazardous in causing allergies or producing poisonous seeds or leaves. The schools will have comprehensive guidance for taking pupils out of schools on visits, whether to static displays in museums, on fieldwork or on activity trips. The guidelines must be followed implicitly.

Performance and feedback form such a large part of your role that the whole of the next chapter is devoted to them.

The curriculum

The curriculum is everything that goes on in school. There is the formal explicit part; the informal part, which covers all the bits everybody knows go on between lessons, in the corridors or the playground, assembly or clubs; and the hidden curriculum, covering the bits about relationships and climate, the way you feel when you work in or visit a place.

You need to be familiar with the NC for the subjects and ages with which you work, remembering that overall there should be breadth and balance, coherence and consistency, relevance and differentiation. These words are written into the legal descriptions of the NC. All schools will have copies of the documents and it is well worth reading the introductory pages (DfEE 1999a; DfEE 1999b: 10–13) on 'Values, aims and purposes', and the requirements made of schools and teachers, including its structure and timing. The latest revision, published to begin in September 2000, stated the aims of this NC as:

> Aim 1: The school curriculum should aim to provide opportunities for all pupils to learn and to achieve . . .

Aim 2: The school curriculum should aim to promote pupils' spiritual, moral, social and cultural development and prepare all pupils for the opportunities, responsibilities and experiences of life. . . . The four main purposes of the National Curriculum: To establish an entitlement, to establish standards, to promote continuity and coherence and to promote public understanding.

(DfEE 1999a; DfEE 1999b: 13)

The documents lay out the subjects which have to be studied in England: English, mathematics and science, which were denoted as the core, and the foundation subjects of DT, ICT, art, music, PE, history and geography, and after age 11 a modern foreign language. RE was included in a basic curriculum; Welsh is an additional subject for pupils in Wales. Spiritual, moral, social and cultural education, citizenship and environmental education are now more closely defined by the new Curriculum 2000. There is still revision as to what is compulsory after the age of 14, the end of KS 3, as the whole curriculum and examination structure post-14 is still being examined. If you are in a secondary school, ask the teacher you work with or your mentor what is being taught in your school, how and why. Refer to a copy of the NC for the age group you are working with; most TAs get themselves a personal copy for their particular phase. Look at the programme of study for the relevant key stage, and at the attainment targets at the end of the NC book (DfEE 1999a; DfEE 1999b). Level 2 will describe the achievement of an average 7-year-old, level 4 an average 11-year-old, level 5 an average 13-year-old and level 6 a GCSE equivalent. This will give you some insight into what to expect when you work with pupils. For instance, try looking at the NC for ICT [17.2:vii].

Briefly, the NC indicates that children in Year 1 and Year 2 will be exploring the use of equipment to become familiar with it. They need to become confident that they can operate machines properly and safely, and start to develop their own ideas [17.2:ix]. Key Stage 1 children can gather information about their peers and make graphs, enter and store information, plan work and give instructions to things such as turtles, and can use a variety of tools and outputs such as art programmes, simple databases with lots of pictures. They can describe what they are doing and relate it to what people do outside school in a shop or the home, share their ideas, and review and present their work in a variety of ways. You can encourage all of this activity.

By Key Stage 2, children can use a wide range of tools and sources, and begin to use research skills. They should be questioning the plausibility of the information they get, and its quality. They can consider the audience of any work they produce; say, if using a camera or recording a playlet or a song. They will be able to create databases, classify, check, interpret and think about the information they use. They can organise a variety of sources such as word processing and photographic images for simple desktop publishing, monitor different dimensions in the environment, ask 'what if?' questions of simple spreadsheets by changing values – they can get different patterns and

Table 10.1 To show the referencing of items repeated in the curriculum sections of the NOS

Aspect of subject teaching	ICT	English/literacy	Literacy across the curriculum	Mathematics/numeracy	Numeracy across the curriculum	Chapter or section in this book with a fuller description
	NOS 3–17	NOS 3–18	NOS 3–20.1	NOS 3–19	NOS 3–20.2	
Following legislation and policies	2:ii	1:i,ii; 2:i,ii 3:i,ii	1:i,iii	1:i,iii; 2:i.	2:i,iii	4
Working under the direction of a teacher	1:1	1:1,3; 2:1,3	1:2	1:1,2,4; 2:1, 2,4	2:2	10
Knowing learning objectives, plans and intended outcomes and activities			1:2, ii	1:1; 2:1	2:2,ii	10
Knowing the basic principles of learning the subject		1:iii; 2:iii				5
Knowing which pupils you are working with and how this will be organised in relation to what the teachers and other pupils will be doing		1:1, 2:1		1:2, 2:2		10
Understanding expectations for age	2:vii	1:iii		1:ii; 2:ii		5, 6, 12, 13
Having accurate and up-to-date information on pupils in subject areas			1:1, vi	1:3, iv; 2:3, iii	2:1, iv	7, 8, 10, 12, 13
Knowing pupils' learning needs or SEN		1:2; 2:2 1:iv; 2:iv: 3:viii	1:v	1:v; 2:iv	2:v	6, 7
Supporting pupils with EAL		1:x; 2:x; 3:vii	1:vii; 2:vii			
Knowing the sort of problems that might occur		1:x; 2:xi	1:x	1:x; 2:ix	2:x	5, 6, 7
Equipment and resource location and provision	1.2	1.4, vii; 2:4, viii		1.5, vii; 2:5, vi	2:viii	10

Table 10.1 Continued

Aspect of subject teaching	ICT	English/ literacy	Literacy across the curriculum	Mathematics/ numeracy	Numeracy across the curriculum	Chapter or section in this book with a fuller description
	NOS 3–17	NOS 3–18	NOS 3–20.1	NOS 3–19	NOS 3–20.2	
Knowing and agreeing support strategies for pupils	2:3, viii	1:3,v; 2:3; 3:iii	1:3, vi	1:4, iv; 2:4, v	2:3, vi	7, 8, 9
Obtaining resources needed for agreed support strategies		2:4		1:5		10
Implementing strategies correctly		1:5; 2:5	1:3	1:6; 2:6		10
Using praise, maintaining interest and feeding back		1:vii; 2:ix; 3:v	1:7, ix	1:7, 9, viii, ix; 2:7, vii, viii, ix	2:7, ix	6, 11
Supporting pupils' self-confidence and self-esteem, motivating and interesting, dealing with difficulties in this area	2:4	3:7	1:8	1:8, viii; 2:8, vii	2:8	6
Monitoring pupils and modifying activities if necessary		1:6; 2:6	1:5	1:9; 2:9	2:5	7, 11
Providing information for records and reports		1:7; 2:7		1:10; 2:10		11
Reporting problems		1:8; x8; 2:8, xi	1:6, x; 1:9	1:11, x; 2:11, xi	1:6, 9; 2:6, 9, x	8, 9, 11

relationships. They should be able to share and exchange ideas, and query different ways of doing things.

By Key Stage 3 they are independent users of much ICT equipment, and should be becoming systematic and selective in its use, able to analyse and reflect on what they are doing. They can use different media for testing or problem solving, and produce good-quality presentation fit for their purpose. They will e-mail and format websites, explore the continually evolving forms of communication and suggest improvements.

Key Stage 4 pupils should have developed a holistic approach to using all the various methods currently available, mixing and matching them, and be easily ICT literate in the world outside school.

Supporting pupils in curriculum areas

Whatever the subject, certain strands or aspects of teaching and learning reappear in the NOS for that subject, most of which have been dealt with in the chapters up to this point and will not be repeated. Table 10.1 shows the items and their NOS references.

These strands or aspects of teaching and learning apply whatever the subject but do have some subject-specific elements to them. These aspects also apply to working with practical subjects such as science and DT, as well as all the other subjects taught in school, although the standards do not make reference to these. For instance, all your work needs to be done within the confines of national legislation and the policies laid down for the school, but there will be subject-specific legislation in the NC and subject-specific policies. All that you do is under the direction of or with the permission of the teacher of the class in which you are working. You need to understand the learning objectives of the teacher and the strategies they wish you to employ in gaining those objectives. There will be differing strategies to support different subjects, and you need the appropriate resources for the subject you are teaching. You need to observe the health, safety and security precautions related to the area you are in, the subject (whether it is a practical one) and materials and equipment you are using. All the classroom procedures should take place with a view to maintaining and developing the pupils' self-confidence and self-esteem, using appropriate praise and things to interest them. If the pupil finds a particular part of a subject difficult, such as spelling or the concept of capacity or working in three dimensions, it is particularly important to deal with such problems in a way to maintain interest and self-esteem [19.1:8]. You need to access records and contribute to their maintenance with all the provisos of confidentiality and accuracy mentioned in the previous chapter. You particularly need to know and understand what special needs the pupils with whom you are working have and how they will best be supported in the subject you are involved with.

The subject-specific detail also comes into understanding the subject for yourself, using the correct vocabulary and procedures for that subject; for instance, how to use special apparatus properly or how to subtract by the currently approved methods [18.3:5]. If you had difficulty with a subject at school, this does not mean you will have difficulty helping pupils and supporting teachers in that subject; in fact, it may be the opposite – you may well understand the problem the pupil is having better than someone who is an expert in that subject.

Another aspect of curriculum development, which makes life complicated, is that subject divisions are not as clearcut as the NC sometimes makes them look. Life actually does not work in neat bundles, though it does help to organise thinking in that way and all the things that go with this, such as books, resources, curricula, departments, faculties, personnel; even schools and universities specialise. English and mathematics, particularly, go across the curriculum. Science can easily be seen not to exist without language and number, art needs the scientific information from the study of materials, and so on [20.1:vi]. Knowledge is holistic. In primary schools, for some years, teachers were encouraged to plan without specific reference to subjects, and used what became known as the 'topic' approach. Most schools retained the subject records and resources but for some children this vagueness meant they did not learn anything properly, hence the legal definition of the curriculum subject matter in the NC. But computation methods learnt without context, the rote learning of things such as tables without any relevance to everyday life is pointless and actually is more difficult. How many of you have helped your pupils or your own children learn their spellings only to find the same words mis-spelt in a letter or an essay? [20.1:4]. This recognition of the need to apply learning across the curriculum, particularly English and mathematics, is the reason for a whole NOS [20] being dedicated to it. Pupils who cannot communicate their understanding or understand what is being taught clearly have a great disadvantage. This may be due to having English as an additional language or to learning problems [20.1:vii & 2:vii]. If this is so, you will need to refer to the EAL and SEN chapters and units as well as the class teachers and SENCO.

Supporting practical subjects

The general principles of supporting any curriculum subject apply to practical work, but with the added component of making sure you are aware of the safety measures you and the pupils need to take [10.1; 17.1:3]. Usually pupils enjoy any kind of practical work, whether it means using tools or media or working with their own bodies as in PE or drama. However, some pupils, particularly as they get older, become very self-conscious about expressing themselves, or being slower or less competent than others, things such as dexterity or clumsiness being more obvious in these subjects. It is important, therefore, to maintain the fun element of such activities and to be alert to the possibilities of low self-confidence or poor self-esteem.

You need to know the learning objectives of the activity you are supporting in the same way as for any lesson. The activity should have a shape – introduction, the activity itself and review. You will need to plan and prepare, participate, and ensure completion and clearing up by the pupils in your group. Practical subjects will have elements of skill, knowledge and understanding, just as the more formal activities do. If you are unsure of any of these, do ask. You should be trained by the teacher in any skills with which you are unfamiliar, and if you are supporting pupils at a higher level, say for external examinations, you may well feel more secure if you undertake the qualification yourself. Have a look at the relevant parts of the NC and any textbooks used by the teacher, seeing how diagrams are reproduced for recording or certain procedures are carried out. You need to know the degree of accuracy required for measuring purposes, whether preparing materials, measuring with the pupils or recording. You must familiarise yourself with any tools or apparatus to be used *before* you work with the pupils.

Electrical safety and security

You will certainly be using electrical equipment at some time in your school work and it is especially important that you follow the safety precautions and instructions for such equipment. There are a very useful couple of pages in *Be Safe* (ASE 2001: 22–3) and a full account of dealing with electrical matters safely in *Safeguards in the School Laboratory* (ASE 1996: 57–64), which should be found in every school.

Mains electricity must always be treated with care and you should be constantly alert and regularly check for faulty switches, broken sockets or plugs, frayed flexes and any defects in apparatus which could lead to problems [17.2:6]. They should never be used. You should label them as dangerous, take them out of use and report them immediately [17.1:6,7 & iv; 2:xi]. Pupils should be trained from the outset how to use apparatus properly and how to deal with sockets, switches and connections according to the policy of the school. Pupils should be taught from an early age that water and electricity are dangerous together, so wet hands or floors are to be avoided when dealing with any of this equipment. Make sure you know where the nearest fire extinguisher for use with electrical equipment is, and where master switches are in cases of accidents. **Always switch off the power**, if necessary at the mains or the meter, before dealing with any incident or breakdown. If there is an electrical incident, send for help. If you have to act without turning off the power, insulate yourself by standing on a pile of dry paper and use a wooden pole or chair to get the victim away from the source of power.

Batteries need replacing or recharging and may contain toxic materials. Recharging should be done with care, and dud batteries disposed of where indicated by any school procedures. Bulbs are made of fragile glass, a possible hazard in itself. Appropriate storage is important both for the equipment and for things such as batteries, film, tape and bulbs [17.2:9, xii & xiii]. It needs to be safe *and* secure, as most electrical items are expensive and sought after.

All these items will have come into school with a handbook for their safe and proper use [17.1:3; 5.2:2]. Much of the equipment you may already have at home and be familiar with, except perhaps for the overhead projector (OHP).

It is still worth checking that the school equipment is similar. Switches may be in different places or the sequence of operations different. Always use the appropriate consumables [17.2:7]. Cheap tape or paper can be damaging for some machines. Follow the setting up and operating instructions indicated for the machine you are using; again some actions can damage equipment. For instance, OHPs should not be moved until the bulb cools down, as doing so will certainly shorten the life of the bulb and can even cause it to explode. This is particularly true of PowerPoint projectors, where a certain routine for switching off is essential to prevent damage.

In order to minimise risks, also be alert for things such as the use of correct furniture [17.1:4]. Using low chairs for computers can cause eye or back strain; trailing flexes through furniture can be hazards. The flexes of OHPs are often encased in rubber treads where they go across the floor, to prevent people tripping; computers, screen and printers should be near the power source. You may need to talk politely to the teacher in charge of the ICT lesson or the ICT coordinator if you have a concern [17.2:x].

Preparing yourself

Before you work with pupils using any equipment there are several things to do, but particularly when dealing with ICT equipment you should check your job description to see what is expected of you and make sure you have any copies of policies or procedures [17.2:i]. Somewhere there will be instructions as to storage and maintenance, the use of various sorts of equipment by pupils (or not), who has access and when, how equipment or consumables are allocated and what requirements the school has of anybody using the equipment [17.1:i,ii & iii; 2:xii & xiii]. There may be signing out procedures for tape recorders, for instance, or a booking procedure for the video camera. The policy should also have references to the legislation of which users should be aware, and how the school deals with such matters [17.1:ii]. For instance, software CDs are often used under licence; you should never use your own disks from home, unless they are approved by the school. The same copyright procedures used for photocopying may be indicated for scanning and printing materials using a computer. The Data Protection Act covers any use of data for compiling databases, say in a class survey. While most schools will operate a firewall preventing inappropriate incoming data getting to the pupils from the Internet, there may be child protection issues when pupils start communicating with each other or with other schools. Ensure you understand the school policies and procedures for dealing with virus control and any kind of Internet or e-mail access, use of passwords and other possible sources of problems [17.2:ii & iii].

You will need to spend a little time in self-tuition in the use of any equipment with which you are not familiar, and if you are supporting ICT in the secondary school you may need to undertake further study at a local college. While pupils with developmental problems in secondary schools may be operating at levels more usually found in primary schools, one of the requirements of the secondary curriculum is increasing independence and some of the sophisticated uses of data logging, spreadsheets, e-mail, creating websites, video-conferencing, even film-making may require you to understand such techniques.

You may need to familiarise yourself with programmes used by the school. If you do not have a computer at home, ask if you can borrow one for a limited time or use the school machines for practice. Remember there may be a problem with insurance, as such equipment is valuable and portable; do check. If you are not familiar with fax machines, using the Internet or sending e-mails, see if there are ways of practising. Try out equipment such as tape or video recorders before you use them; nothing is more embarrassing than being given a task which the pupils will be really keen to do and then finding something does not work, or a battery is flat, or you have run out of film [17.2:v].

Questions to ask yourself

- What did you enjoy most about your lessons when you were at school?
- Which classrooms were most welcoming? Why?
- Which areas of your current school workplace seem inviting? Why?
- Do you leave yourself enough time to think about what you are going to do before you do it? At home? At school?
- Do you present a good role model in the way you organise yourself and the resources you are going to use with the pupils?
- Are you sure of the learning objectives of all the lessons in which you are involved?
- Have you got your own copy of the NC? Have you seen the long-term plans for the curriculum in the subjects with which you are most closely involved? Have you seen the teacher's medium-term planning? Are you part of the short-term planning?
- Do you need to do any further study in any curriculum area in order to support the pupils properly in those lessons? How are you going to do this? Who can help you?

Essential reading

ASE (1996) *Safeguards in the School Laboratory*, 10th edn. Hatfield: Association for Science Education.

ASE (2001) *Be Safe: Health and Safety in Primary School Science and Technology*, 3rd edn. Hatfield: Association for Science Education.

DfEE (1999a) *The National Curriculum: Handbook for Primary Teachers in England; Key Stages 1 and 2*. London: DfEE and QCA.

DfEE (1999b) *The National Curriculum: Handbook for Secondary Teachers in England; Key Stages 3 and 4*. London: DfEE and QCA.

DfES (2002a) *Developing the Role of School Support Staff* (Consultation DfES/0751/2002). London: Department for Education and Skills.

Some further reading

Babbage, R., Byers, R. and Redding, H. (1999) *Approaches to Teaching and Learning*. London: David Fulton Publishers. (Especially Chapters 2 and 3.)

Balshaw, M. and Farrell, P. (2002) *Teaching Assistants: Practical Strategies for Effective Classroom Support*. London: David Fulton Publishers.

Lee, V. (1990) *Children's Learning in School*. London: Hodder and Stoughton for the Open University. (Especially Parts 2 and 3.)

Any subject curriculum handbook for teachers which accompanies any published scheme being used in the school by your class or teachers you work with.

Belair publications on display or creating learning environments for various subjects (Belair Publications Ltd, PO Box 12, Twickenham, TW1 2QL, England).

11 Performance and feedback

Performance

The three-part lesson

Most lessons are in three parts – an introduction, beginning or exposition; a middle, often practical or small group session; and a concluding, summarising or plenary part. This was set out in some detail in the literacy and numeracy strategies and its formality seems to have ended any attempts at lengthy periods of work such as could be seen in infant schools in the 1970s. Your role in each of the three parts of the lesson needs to be clarified with both your line manager and the teacher, and possibly the SENCO [13.1:4]. Different schools have differing philosophies or needs for your presence. While it may be valuable for you to sit, apparently doing nothing during the teacher's introduction or exposition, too often it appears that you need that time to understand the purpose of the lesson because of lack of planning and preparation time allocated to you; it may be a more valuable use of your time to be allocated to a specific task elsewhere. You may be needed in that introductory time to keep some pupils in the room, or prevent their attention from wandering or encourage them to respond to questioning. You may need to interpret the teacher's words in sign language or in simpler words, or use the time collecting information for the teacher on particular pupils' responses. Whatever it is, it should not just be an ignored time. You are too valuable.

Your role is usually more obvious during the middle, more active part of the lesson, which is more frequently planned for by the teacher and is often considered the 'meat' of the lesson, when the main learning is done. The end part of the lesson, the recap or plenary, reviewing what has been learnt, sometimes get shortened but is really valuable in reinforcing with pupils what they were in the lesson for. You might be able to use that time for completing any records or writing a few comments for the teacher, or you may be given other tasks to do, such as photocopying or even marking books.

Photograph 3   Helping the teacher at the introductory part of the lesson

Teaching

TAs definitely teach, but this statement has caused some of the problems with the teaching unions about their status.

> Although no one should pretend that teaching assistants are teachers, when they are most successful they show many of the skills characteristic of good teachers: an understanding of children and their needs and behaviour; an ability to interact effectively with them to promote learning; and the ability to assess where pupils are in their learning and what they need to do to make further progress. Making the most of such abilities should certainly not threaten the professionalism of teachers; rather it should be encouraged and developed to the full.
>
> (Ofsted 2002: 18) [8.1:ii]

The problem seems to be the meaning of words: teach, teaching and teacher. Parents teach their children, brothers and sisters teach each other and our friends teach us. By 'teachers' most people seem to mean adults with Qualified Teacher Status (QTS). The new proposals attempt to be more specific, but admit

> In practice, the difference between the contribution of a qualified teacher and a higher level teaching assistant, or a cover supervisor, will not be defined in terms of simple words but by the quality of what each member of staff can reasonably be expected to demonstrate. It is not reasonable to look to a teaching assistant to demonstrate the full subject expertise and professional judgement of the qualified teacher.
>
> (DfES 2002a: 19–20)

You must act under the direction of qualified teachers at all times, and they take responsibility for the teaching and learning of the pupils in their class.

Effective performance

I am sure you have watched teachers with whom you work to see how they approach their teaching. Teaching is a performance, an act. Some teachers still do not like another adult in the room, because they feel they are being watched by a possibly critical audience. Acting needs courage, forethought and practice; so does teaching. You need confidence to show sufficient authority to perform effectively. You must speak clearly, grammatically correctly if possible, and with a confident, but not loud, tone of voice. You will notice that quieter teachers tend to have quieter classes. Watch yourself in a mirror and, if possible, allow yourself to be videoed. Your gestures – non-verbal communication – are very significant [2.1:4; 2.2:1]. Much behaviour management can be achieved without a word, such as by raising an eyebrow, signalling 'turn it down' and, above all, maintaining eye contact. If you sit looking bored this will signal to pupils that the lesson is boring – it may be, but you must act not bored.

Strategies

There are many strategies that you can use to support learning, and through experience you will realise which ones work best for which circumstances and which pupils [3.1:vi]. You can enable the pupils to read instructions, explain, instruct or listen; ensure they take turns or share; and ensure the quietest gets a time to speak and the extrovert gives way to the others at times [14.1:5]. You can explain a task to enable the pupils to do it more successfully themselves [3.1:4; 12.2:5]. You can keep them on task without being aggressive, praise their progress, comment on success, and assist only where necessary – show by example rather than doing it for them [2.1:v; 3.2:5; 14.1:6]. You can make things interesting and relevant to their world [3.2:3]. You can use words they will understand, and remind them of what the teacher has said [2.1:viii]. Your use of language and vocabulary will be a role model for the pupils. If you adapt or modify any of the teacher's instructions because the pupils need something different in order to achieve the teacher's objectives, don't forget to tell the teacher what you have done and why [3.1:ix]. You might need to go through a piece of work more than once to make sure the pupils have learnt what was expected and, instead of doing the same thing twice, you change the order of the words or the colour of the paper or play a game instead of making lists – your ideas are usually only too welcome [16.2:ix]. At the end of a session, try to leave time to go through with the group of pupils you have been with what they think they have learnt or achieved. If things went wrong, or they did not finish, make sure they have worked out why it went wrong and what they can do better next time.

Questioning and challenging
This is a very important way to help children learn, achieve, think and question for themselves [3.2:iii; 3.2:5; 14.2:8; 18.3:iii]. Education is partly about imparting knowledge, and without it there is no context for understanding, but the process by which we acquire and digest that knowledge is as important. Without questioning either by you or, hopefully, by the pupils, we cannot be sure they understand or make any progress [18.3:1]. Asking questions purely to check knowledge and understanding is a common teaching strategy. It relieves the monotony of the one voice and enables the pupils to feel part of the lesson. The teacher will ask questions of various levels of difficulty (differentiated) to encourage all the children to feel able to answer and be part of the class. Questions can be closed, needing only 'yes' or 'no' answers, or open, sometimes called 'higher order' questions, where the answers can be varied. Open questions are not so often used in a large class situation because there is not enough time for them, but you could use them with a small group. The actual asking of the questions needs the same kind of clarity, eye contact, and

structure as an exposition, and practice [18.3:2]. One of the things you can do to prepare for a lesson is to make a list of possible open and closed questions.

> With the agreement of the teacher, note the teacher's questions.
>
> * Can you categorise them into open and closed?
> * Who answers which ones?
> * Do the same pupils always answer?
>
> Talk this over with the teacher after the lesson.

Intervention and non-intervention
You may be doing this instinctively; it is about enabling the pupils to do as much as possible for themselves. You may need to interpret, scribe, repeat instructions, give an example, or show a skill on a separate piece of material or apparatus. It is no good handing in a piece of work that you have dictated to the pupil; this gives the teacher a false impression of the pupils' capabilities and the pupil has merely learnt how to manipulate you. You need to be mobile, so that you do not just sit alongside a particular pupil waiting to wait on them. Praise them, encourage them, comment on their work and assist them, but try to do it at appropriate moments [3.1:6; 16.1:5].

A busy teacher may find it easier to give answers to some pupils' questions or do things for them. A TA has that much more flexibility so they can answer questions such as 'How do you spell elephant?' or 'Where can I find something about deserts?' or 'Can you cut this out for me, please?' with 'Have a try – sound it out', 'Where did we look for information yesterday?' and 'Have a go on a spare bit of material; look, I'll show you on this scrap piece first, then you try' [16.1:5; 16.2:xiii].

Active listening
Listening to pupils is a very valuable way to spend time. It is not just a matter of hearing what they say but responding, internally taking note of things of importance to their well-being or learning, encouraging them to communicate their needs and ideas and above all encouraging their thinking [2.1:iv & 3; 2.2:ii; 3.2:4 & 6; 9.2:i; 15.3:i]. Eighty per cent of the time in school the teacher or you can be giving out and only twenty per cent of the time the pupils actively participating. Pupils have to engage with their learning; it is not a passive exercise.

> In the morning, read a short article in the newspaper which contains some statistical information. After a week, try to remember as much detail as you can of what you read. Then repeat the process with a different subject; this time, within an hour of reading the article, tell someone the contents. Then see how much of the second article you remember the next week. Usually the very act of trying to tell someone about a subject fixes it better in the memory.

Try explaining a complex idea you have had to a friend. It could be a way of redesigning your garden or sorting out a domestic problem or an educational project you are involved in. Ask them to comment and then argue or discuss the idea. You may not change you mind or ideas, but you will feel more confident that you understand what you are about to do or how you feel about it.

Sensitivity and response

All the time you are working with pupils you need to keep aware of how they are tackling the task set. While in class your concentration must not slip, so that you know when to intervene or modify what is happening. Sometimes something unusual or unplanned happens [3.1:9]. It could be a fire practice, when you have to respond as you have been trained, making sure the pupils you are with understand what to do. It could be a rainbow from a rain shower or even from a sudden shaft of light unexpectedly hitting bevelled glass. This will distract the pupils, and you can decide whether to use the moment to admire the colours and talk about cause and effect, or try to get the pupils to ignore it. It will all depend on the pupils you are with and the importance of the task they are supposed to be doing. These special moments are unplanned but can be used to appreciate natural phenomena and stimulate interest and curiosity.

An example of good practice

Sheila, a TA, works with Barbara, a Year 1 child who has Down's Syndrome. During a literacy hour, Sheila is sensitive to the needs of Barbara, able to give mild reproach, to comfort or to sit back as appropriate, and so enables Barbara to complete a simple task. Sheila is firm, the boundaries of the situation are clear for both, she repeats phrases such as 'birthday – b'. She challenges, using words such as 'quickly', 'no', 'you do know', 'come on – don't show off' along with 'I'm pleased', 'well done'. She bends to Barbara's level, she concentrates all the time, she is physically close, and her hand and eye movements are particularly significant. She is not static, seated alongside Barbara the whole time, but frequently gets up to help other children when she can, and so lets Barbara have space and time to complete what the teacher has set her. Sheila is sensitive to Barbara when she fidgets, even offering to change chairs with her. She is very persistent and will not let Barbara leave a task of which she feels Barbara is capable. Barbara knows that she has to try on her own. While Sheila works with other children, her body language clearly says 'I am not with you at the moment', although she watches her out of the corner of her eye. She uses a lot of 'what for?' and 'why?' questions with the other children, also Year 1.

Skills teaching

Wherever possible, *do not do* the activity for the pupil. Do a separate one and show the pupil how you did it. This goes for everything, from cutting out for the youngest pupils to sophisticated science experiments [10.1:4]. Practical skills can only develop by the pupil doing it for themselves.

All the suggestions made for group working – getting pupils organising, planning, talking, questioning, thinking, reviewing and evaluating – hold for practical activities. The booklet *Primary Design and Technology* (DATA 1996) has some useful tips for showing children how to do something, talking to children while they are working, supporting practical work, supervising a group (including clearing away), organising and maintaining resources and creating a display. The following are some of their tips for helping children in practical work (p. 19):

- Don't do things for them that they can do for themselves, *e.g. fetch materials, clear away, use tools*
- Encourage them to think about what they are doing and to work carefully
- Remind the children about safe working
- Follow the same rules as the children when using tools or they will soon copy bad habits
- Encourage them to keep their work area tidy, *e.g. return tools and equipment which are no longer needed, put unusable scraps in the bin, rearrange equipment and materials on the table so that it is easier to work*
- Encourage them to be as accurate as possible, *e.g. cutting carefully, measuring food ingredients, marking the position before punching a hole or sticking something down*
- Watch how the children are holding tools and how they have positioned themselves and suggest changes if necessary, *e.g. 'you might find it easier to stand up to do that', 'try holding it like this', 'use this finger to guide it/keep it still'*
- Make sure that girls and boys have equal access to tools and equipment – sometimes that is true in theory but not in practice!
- If you need to show a child how to do something, use a spare piece of material rather than their work
- Use the correct names for tools, equipment and materials and help the children to remember them.

Working with individual pupils, groups or the whole class

Some of your work will necessarily be at an individual level, particularly where the pupils have physical needs, in order that they can take part in class activities [3.1:4]. Hopefully these needs will be spelt out in statements or IEPs. This whole area of dealing with the individual needs of those with SEN is dealt with in Chapter 8, and there are many books and sources of information. The SENCO in the school will help you best in this area, as they will also know what particular support you can get locally, such as computer aids or lifting gear. All pupils benefit at some time from having individual attention, but a teacher with a whole class to teach and monitor can rarely spare time for this. You should have time to explore ideas and listen to individual stories, to develop appropriate individual strategies for learning, and to catch the learning moments and boost self-esteem, provided it does not create a dependency culture [3.1:3]. Some schools make sure that different TAs are allocated to a pupil at different times of the week. This means, if you are ill or if there is a personality clash, the pupils still receive help.

An example of good practice

Angela had a genetic wasting muscular condition which meant she was a wheelchair user from the age of six. She had a TA, Jean, who was with her all day but worked all over the classroom under the guidance of the class teacher, unless Angela required help getting equipment or going to the loo. She had a different TA at lunchtime, but she became very fond of Jean. The two met after school sometimes, and Jean became friendly with Angela's mother. Angela's parents bought her an electric wheelchair, enabling her to get around the building or playground on her own. During her primary years, Angela was introduced to computers, then to a laptop and so was able to complete her school work independently. By the time Angela was ten, she was rather heavy to lift, and secondary school was looming, so another TA, Beryl, was appointed to share Angela's needs, and both Jean and Beryl did other TA tasks in the school. When Angela went on to secondary school, Jean and Beryl went with her on the visits but decided not to transfer with her. The transition went well, and Jean still remained a family friend. Angela later went to university away from home, with a full-time carer for her physical needs, able to study and have fun just like any other student. In the holidays, she and Jean still met up for tea and to share news.

Sometimes, under the teacher's instruction, you may be asked to monitor the work of the class, while the teacher works with an individual. Do make sure you feel capable of doing what the teacher asks, and that he or she is within call, if not eye contact, if you do this. A common practice is for a TA to take a story-time with younger pupils while the teacher goes over something with one or two other pupils. Another is where all the pupils are set a task which they should be able to get on with, while the teacher works with one pupil or a group. It just needs someone to walk round the class and check that everyone is occupied on the task set. Unfortunately, the introduction of TAs to many schools was done as a result of earmarked funding for individual pupils, and the funding came in multiples of pupil contact hours associated with particular pupils. Still some parents and pupils think that they have to have so many hours' one-to-one support each week. The Code of Practice clearly states 'that this may not be the most appropriate way of helping the child' (DfES 2001b:

53). It should not be the case that the least qualified and trained member of staff always works with the pupils with the most complex needs.

Do talk with the class teacher about the particular needs of individual pupils. You will also be able to fill in some of the detail for the class teacher. This element of exchanging information is essential for you to be able to do the best for individual pupils. Klaus Weddell, who was not only a retired teacher but also a retired educational psychologist, trained in diagnosing and helping pupils with SEN, became an LSA in his retirement. He wrote an account of his experiences in O'Brien and Garner's (2001) book *Untold Stories:*

> it can be quite difficult to get specific information about what the teacher finds a child can and cannot do – and under what conditions. It is usually more difficult to obtain information about what a child can do than about where the child is failing. There is a similar problem about discovering the particular situations in which a child performs better than in others, so as to get an idea about teaching approaches.
>
> (Weddell 2001: 92)

Sometimes teachers have a concern about the confidentiality of such information, or it may be that when a pupil does well it is easier to miss it than when they do something wrong.

One of the points of discussion that occurs frequently is whether pupils should be withdrawn from class for special help. Various research projects have investigated this, and much of the emphasis of the move towards inclusion has been in the direction of increasing group work over individual help, and including pupils in the whole class rather than withdrawing them. Clearly, some support, such as special exercises for a particular condition, may have to take place in special rooms or with particular apparatus, and the same argument could hold for special learning exercises. However, the social context of learning is also important. Learners need language and social interaction to aid them; you can facilitate this, but keep the talk on the subject. Sometimes the argument for withdrawal is not equipment but a quiet place to enable an easily distracted pupil to have a time away from their peers, and even sometimes to allow the rest of the class or the teacher to have a bit of respite from the interruptions of those who find the subject matter beyond them. It is a matter of balance, and the final decision must be with the class teacher, who themselves will be working within the policies of the school. If you have a problem with the decision, discuss it carefully with the teacher or SENCO.

Make sure, when working with a group, that you are clear as to whether the group is to work together, or whether they are just doing individual work and sitting together [16.2:ii]. It is tempting, particularly in a primary classroom, to think that because children are sitting in groups they are working in groups. This is not always so. If the pupils are completing individual tasks, social contact needs to be minimal – only asking for help or clarity. The low level of chat which frequently surrounds group work can often be conversation about trivia – football, television programmes, other people. This is the type of gossip found on an assembly line in a factory where routine and boring tasks are being completed. School work should not be like that. Most individual tasks do benefit from group discussion beforehand and after completion and at appropriate times in-between – sharing ideas, helping pupils who are 'stuck', giving encouragement, and so on. You should exercise judgement over the helpfulness of communication when pupils are sitting close together, engaged in apparently independent tasks.

Alternatively the task may be a collaborative one, or include a combination of collaboration and individual work [2.2:iii; 15.2:2]. The brainstorming sessions at the beginning of a writing task need cooperation; the individual writing task, concentration and preferably silence. Games, sharing equipment in a science experiment, debates all need the skills of group work, and your job is to act like a facilitator in a conference group or a good chairperson. Set the scene; put in suggestions at appropriate times; try not to influence the thoughts but enable them to be expressed; keep the group focused on the task; ensure that all contribute and that no one person dominates; ensure that thoughts are gathered together, possibly ordered in some way; keep an eye on the time [2.2:5; 9.1:1]. Dip into Dunne and Bennett's (1994) book if it is on your staffroom shelves; it has many ideas for looking at the way in which pupils work and learn in groups [18.3:6].

You may have to develop group rules, such as when playing a game or even to get pupils to talk in turns [2.2:2]. Learning to work cooperatively in a group is part of growing up, and the more you can get the group not only to act responsibly while working together but also to take responsibility for the group, the more you will help the pupils [2.2:6]. If you are working with a group or individual in a teacher's class, you should take care over voice levels of your pupil or group: stop talking and stop them talking when the teacher asks for silence or makes any whole-class announcement. It can be very distracting for the teacher who wants to say something to the class, even though it is not meant for your group, if someone is still 'chuntering on' in the background.

Occasionally, TAs have been asked to take a whole class instead of the teacher, as a supply teacher, say. You may know the way the class works, the characteristics of the pupils in it and what is planned for the day by the teacher, and be an experienced TA and quite capable of doing the job better than a stranger. It is the biggest area of dispute in the work of TAs in schools. The new proposals indicate that TAs, with the new suggestion of a higher-level teaching assistant (HLTA) qualification, will be able to take a class without a teacher present. These HLTAs could cover classes in the case of short-term absence of the teacher

> for example when teachers are ill or undertaking professional development or planning, preparation and assessment (PPA) activities. A member of support staff with appropriate training and skills, who knows the pupils' needs and school procedures, may be a more appropriate choice to undertake cover than another qualified teacher or a supply teacher.
>
> (DfES 2002a: 21)

the previous chapter should always be observed. You may be using chemicals that could be dangerous if eaten, or handling soil or pond water. Precautions for doing these activities should be observed, such as covering open cuts with lightweight gloves and ensuring proper hand washing after use. A list of suitable chemicals for primary schools, as well as those that are dangerous, is included in *Be Safe* (ASE 2001: 19), although it is not comprehensive. The international hazard warning symbols (ASE 2001: 21) could be displayed and taught to children. It is the duty of all staff to point out to a more senior member of staff any hazards noticed in equipment or procedures [17.2:5].

Good pupil behaviour is essential when doing practical activities; you need to monitor this, intervene and, if necessary, tell the teacher in charge if you have any concerns about any of the pupils you are working with. Usually, pupils are more interested in 'doing' than in listening, reading or writing and so often behave better in such lessons, but they can get excited when new activities are introduced. Be clear in your intructions to the pupils [17.2:iv]. There are many false rumours about what is safe practice – or not. The important thing is that parents should be aware of the nature of activities that will be carried out, the safety precautions that will be taken and the risk assessments that will be carried out, particularly in secondary activities. These will all be spelt out in prospectuses and policies to ensure the school staff are both protected and able to provide an appropriate breadth of experience for pupils.

For instance, it is perfectly possible to heat things in primary science lessons, but some sources of heat are not recommended, such as spirit lamps and picnic stoves. Nightlights, hot water, electric rings, microwave ovens, hair dryers and kilns are all suitable for use in primary schools, but must be used with proper procedures and adult supervision, or only by an adult, e.g. the kiln.

Use of glass should be avoided in primary schools, but even here accidents can happen and children need to be taught the hazards of glass and what to do if they find something broken. You should know how and where to dispose of broken glass and, where glass is more widely used, as in secondary science lessons, the first aid procedures for dealing with cuts. Knowing the first aid procedures for dealing with foreign objects or chemicals in the eye when in a laboratory or workshop would also be good practice.

Some lessons include using ourselves or animal parts, such as bits of skeletons. Here you must be aware of sensitivities about differences between pupils, e.g. shape, colour or size. Tasting and feeling and smelling things should be done hygienically. Examining soft body parts, such as offal, is both permissible and safe provided they are fresh and fit for human consumption; eyes of pigs can be used, but not those of sheep, cows or goats. You may find some pupils dislike this kind of handling, or have cultural or ethical reasons for not taking part. They should never be put under pressure to take part, and the teacher should be told of any problems.

Difficulties

In class you are likely to get into difficulties for several reasons [3.1:x]. It may be your fault – you may have forgotten a particular resource, not understood the teacher yourself, arrived late for the lesson or actually not understood the content of the lesson. Do not try to cover up either with the teacher or with the pupils. If you have forgotten something, you can either get it if it is in the room, or improvise or change direction. You cannot leave your group if you are working with them outside the classroom. If you have a good relationship with the teacher and the occurrence is unusual, a quick word with the teacher will probably allow you to solve the problem and go and fetch the missing item. If there is something you do not know or understand then say so, as you should not pass on incorrect information to the pupils. You can either find out together with them by consulting a textbook or just ask the teacher what to do.

Problems with the pupils are less worrying personally, but still need attention. If it is a matter of their lack of understanding, feed back to the teacher at the end of the session in one of the ways described below. If it is a safety matter, report the incident to the teacher immediately. The most likely problem is that the pupil or the group gets out of hand because they are seeking trouble or they are bored. Do read the sections on behaviour management in Chapters 3 and 6 [3.1:11].

Monitoring, assessment and feedback

Observation strategies

If you are undertaking a course it is very likely that you will be expected to make some structured observations of pupils learning, or a teacher may ask you to watch a pupil for a particular purpose. You need to understand the purpose of the observation – just interest, or concern over progress, or concern over social interactions within a group [7.1:ii]. Even if you are not asked to observe, it is always worth spending a little time watching pupils. In this way you will begin to broaden your concept of the normal range of responses and behaviours briefly described in Chapter 5 [7.1:i; 7.2:i]. You should ask the class teacher of the pupils you want to watch first, and find time to discuss the issues and protocols of observation before you start anything formal, as well as spending time with them afterwards discussing your observations [7.1:2].

As with looking at the use of apparatus, you can notice all sorts of things at random, just by being in a class with small children or young people, but it will sharpen your perceptions if you do this with some organisation. You should write down some things in as structured a way as possible, and this means you would be making records on someone else's child, for whom a class teacher is responsible [13.1:9]. It means taking time either out of your paid time or doing it voluntarily. It is important that your observing does not become intrusive for the pupil or disrupt any other class activity [2.1:vi; 7.1:4,5 & iii]. You need some agreed ground rules [7.1:1].

Possible protocols to consider for classroom observation [7.1:viii]

The following need to be discussed between the TA and the class teacher where any observation is to take place:

- The purpose of the exercise is to . . . e.g. understand more about . . .
- The adults involved will be . . .
- The pupils involved will be . . .

The head teacher/department head/line manager has been told what is happening, and has agreed. It needs to be checked that:

- anything written is to be shared first with each other, so that comments can be made and points of accuracy checked
- any comments to be seen by others will be anonymised, or amalgamated with others to preserve confidentiality
- the main audience of any summary written material will be . . . e.g. the other members of a course, or an outside reader
- the people observed or interviewed can have a copy of the notes made if they so wish
- you know what will happen to any written records
- the intended outcome of the activity is . . .
- you know what you will do if the observation shows up anything within the classroom or school that someone wishes to address or celebrate
- if others get involved, they will be covered by the same sort of protocols
- someone seeks permission of the parents of the children closely involved.

Either side should be able to make comments at any time in the process if there is any discomfort or suggestion about what is taking place or being said.

(Watkinson 2002: 39)

There is much more detail about observing in Wragg (1994), although this was written for teachers. Harding and Meldon-Smith (1996) was written for NVQ students in Child Care and Education and so is a more helpful book for TAs. While it was intended for those working with young children, its principles hold good throughout school phases, and the suggested forms are very useful. These books cover why, what, where and how to observe. They also look at things that can be measured about learning and things that cannot but are equally important.

Observing

You can use a sheet of A4 paper on a clipboard, a spiral-bound memo pad or an exercise book. Focus on one area of interest, one pupil, and observe at regular times, e.g. every 30 seconds or every minute. Decide on a part of their body which is of interest, such as their hands. What they are saying?

Do this for five minutes.

- Did they keep still? Did they touch any resources? Did they touch another pupil? Whom did they speak to? Was it about their work?
- Did this tell you anything more about the pupil, the table or desk they are working on, or the children they are with? Repeat the exercise with a different pupil at the same desk/table, or the same pupil in a different context or classroom.
- Did the same thing happen? How was it different?

OR

Note every five minutes what they are doing, and, if they are talking and you can hear what they say, put that down.

- What have you found out about this pupil?

THEN

- What did the pupil do during that period?
- Was it anything to do with what the teacher intended or not?
- Did the pupil learn anything new during the time you were watching?
- Did they understand anything better?
- Did they practise anything that they had done before?
- Did anyone talk to them or help them? Were they the pupils sitting near them or adults?
- Could you have made things easier for them if you had been sitting there, or if they had been in a different place, or had different resources? In what ways?

Find an opportunity to talk through what you saw with the teacher.

You can develop grids with names and headings of what you are particularly looking for, such as asking or answering questions, or with time markers. If you are going to question the pupils, you can prepare some questions beforehand.

Feedback to pupils and teachers

You need to monitor, even informally, how the pupils are progressing and what achievement they make in a lesson, often to make adjustments to what you are doing as you go along, but also then to feed back to the teacher [3.1:8; 13.2:8; 14.1:7; 16.2:x]. Assessment information is best when gathered against the objective for the session, so it is doubly important that you know what this is [3.1:12]. It would also be useful for the teacher to know how well pupils are progressing towards their targets, particularly in literacy or in an IEP, as these are likely to be specific and short-term; what their behaviour is like, especially if a behaviour programme is in place; and what unexpected things you noticed [2.1:6]. Feedback can be much more informal than the planning process;

sometimes just a verbal comment, at the end of a lesson before the TA and teacher separate, in the corridor on the way to the staffroom, or even in the car park on the way home, can help the teacher plan the next step for the pupils with whom the TA has been working. You may have already alerted the teacher if you have had problems during the lesson, but it is better, if you can, not to interrupt him or her and just leave your comments to the end [14.1:8]. In one school, the TAs themselves devised a separate written feedback system that would have some consistency for the teachers. Another school had a diary system for noting improvement and problems. TAs also use teachers' assessment forms, after training and guidance, which can be ticked when things are achieved. You could stick a polite Post-it note on the teacher's desk when you leave the room, or in the pupil's workbook if the teacher is going to see it – not if it is going home. Make time voluntarily to chat, and gradually your contribution will be recognised, meetings will be convened and paid planning time will be instituted. Feedback can usually be done on the move. This has happened in many schools already [14.1:9; 16.1:9].

Feed back informally to pupils, saying 'Well done, you finished today', or 'It looks better than yesterday' or 'You remembered to spell . . . correctly' [16.2:ix]. Give the pupil something to aim for next time, such as 'Let's see if you can do that without my help tomorrow'. You should have established whether you are to write directly in pupils' books and the approved method of doing this: red or black pen, comments or ticks, correction procedures, etc. You can say 'You tried hard', or 'That is well done for you', particularly if it fulfilled the teacher's targets for those pupils for that lesson. Saying things are marvellous, when clearly they are not, is not helpful [12.1:viii; 12.2:viii & 9]. If the work is careless, particularly if you know the pupils well and they can do better, get them to do it again, or if there is not time, at least to recognise that they can do better [3.2:v & vi]. Maybe they are having an 'off' day. Try to ensure they finish the task set, giving them a warning as time gets short. If they finish early, they should have some kind of follow-up task to do [3.1:10]. You may need to help them complete a homework diary.

Formative and summative assessment – evaluation

All the time teachers work with pupils they inwardly make small judgements. Those with QTS recognise this as informal **formative** assessment. TAs will also judge, but without training they may not recognise what they are seeing. As you increase in understanding of how learning takes place, and of the needs of pupils and the content of the curriculum, you will be increasingly useful in helping teachers in making more formal formative assessments [8.2:i]. You will recognise what is realistic to expect of certain pupils, and what is a fair judgement [8.2:1]. You should spend time with the teacher making sure you agree about what you are looking for, and what lesson or part of the lesson would be best to watch for what the teacher is hoping to see [8.2:1 & 2]. The feedback from TAs can be as important as the in-class support they are providing to the pupils, and teachers need to make arrangements to obtain

Photograph 4   Carrying out an assessment activity for the teacher

this. You can also see there is the potential for disagreement with the teacher as you get more experienced. You may be convinced a pupil has real difficulties where the teacher could have assumed they were just being lazy, or you might consider a pupil was pretending to be slow in order to get your extra help. You must deal with this professionally, be certain you can justify what you are saying and have evidence to support you; and where relationships between you and the teacher are good, and you have pre-agreed the method and criteria to be used, there should not be a problem [7.2:3; 8.2:5].

You may be asked to complete more formal assessment sheets as part of your job. If so, do ensure you have complete instructions as to what you are to observe and what to write [7.1:3]. This may become evidence in a reporting process. Sometimes TAs who have worked closely with pupils with special needs are asked to write their own report of what they are doing, and how their charges have progressed (or not) [8.2:v]. Again, get full instructions about what is required, ensure you look for strengths as well as weaknesses, and be brief, concise and accurate [7.1:8; 7.2:2 & iii; 8.2:3]. If possible, get the document typed, but only by a member of the school staff. Always date any such record and sign it.

It might seem easier to observe and measure what is learnt over a period of time than to try to watch it actually happening; but beware, it has its pitfalls.

This is called **summative** assessment. Test results depend very much on how questions are asked, particularly where understanding is needed as well as memory, such as in science. Pictures, or seeing and handling the actual materials about which questions are asked, and being able to enquire about the meaning of the questions, all influence how correct the answers will be. Many of us can remember taking tests or examinations when we did not feel very well or the weather was exceptionally hot. These things can all affect our recall and performance, and thus our test results [7.1:iii].

The things that teachers want to assess are the knowledge gained, the understanding that has developed, the skills learnt, and the attitudes to learning that are influencing the pupil. Some of these factors are easier to see or measure than others. Tests and examinations tend to test knowledge and understanding; practical skills have to be observed in action as well as by examination of an end product, and are more usually seen as part of a vocational competence assessment [8.2:iii]. Attitudes are really only seen in the way pupils cope with learning as it happens. In all of these assessments some kind of standard has to be established and then monitored in order that results from one teacher or class or school are comparable with those from other places. Individual observers will differ – their observations will be subjective. Tests with limited aims can be repeated by different people with similar results; the more people who use them and check them, the more reliable the results. However, there is always the question of whether a particular test is the valid one to assess a particular area of learning – just as the old IQ tests are now considered invalid because the concept of intelligence has changed [7.1:v; 7.2:ii]. Methods used will also vary with the age of the pupil. Clearly pre-school children will not undergo written examinations, and there is still some concern about the formal testing procedures inflicted upon seven-year-olds with the Standard Assessment Tests or Tasks (SATs). Science is not tested externally until Year 6, and even here there is much debate about how investigative, experimental and explorative work can be tested by written tests. Practical work is not tested until secondary school, and there is still much contention about the use or misuse of project work. Many teachers brought up by a formal academic examination-based route still have problems with the competence observation and portfolio approach of NVQs [7.1:iv; 7.2:1].

Any kind of assessment procedure needs careful handling by those conducting it, whether it is an informal observation for interest or a formal external examination. If you think back to your own experiences, you may remember a lot of 'hype' among your peers, stern faces from your teachers, the classroom furniture all rearranged so that you would not cheat. The fuss did not make you feel confident and give of your best. You need to minimise the disruption to normal school life, yet ensure quietness and freedom from interruptions [7.1: 4 & 5]. Even simple assessments, such as hearing pupils read in the infant class, can achieve better results in a calm, friendly atmosphere. Most teachers will welcome questions and suggestions you have about procedures to get the best from pupils, provided you offer them in the usual spirit of constructive support [7.2:4; 8.2:4]. Some families and cultures are particularly keen on examinations and will create tension in the home, and many schools now practise for external tests, sometimes to the detriment of covering the curriculum in other areas. The tension can be counterproductive. Some pupils (and adults) are very sensitive about being observed, hence the need for protocols and care about your presence in the room doing something unusual [7.1:vii]. In some cases you will be given the examination guides to follow, giving a certain procedure. It is important for validity that you follow these instructions, but you can do this without being officious [7.1:7; 7.2:1]. Particularly if you are supporting a pupil with SEN, you may be asked to read a test paper to a pupil, or encourage a small child to respond to particular questions. Again, the calm, friendly approach will enable the pupils to give of their best [7.1:6].

As well as ensuring the pupils do their best in any kind of assessment or test, you must always remember that you have to operate within the framework of the school policies and under the guidance of the teachers. Confidentiality about the process and the results is really important [7.2:5 & iv].

Recording and reporting

Formats and confidentiality

It is particularly important, if you write anything, that it should be accurate, concise, legible and dated and be kept in an appropriately confidential and secure place [6.1:6]. Photocopiers can be a particular snare – important documents easily get left under the cover. Be careful about taking anything home [6.1:7]. Most of the points mentioned in the section above about assessment procedures will apply to the keeping of records, as the written outcomes of assessments form the bulk of records kept. Records should be reliable, valid, sufficient and informative [6.1:ii & v]. They will vary in nature according to the purpose for which they are kept. Some records will be kept just by the teacher – daily reading records, weekly spelling tests, progress in understanding of certain concepts or comments about attitudes, problems. Most teachers, especially in secondary schools, have mark books which look like registers, with the names of pupils down the margin and a different page for each kind of assessment or test they are conducting. Marks for assignments or completion of tasks, money for trips, and absences can all be entered on this kind of grid [6.1:i]. Some teachers will just hand you their mark book and explain how they want it completed; others will want you to keep separate records and enter what they want in their mark books.

More formal, end-of-term or end-of-year records will often be kept in a central, secure place and the contents of the files determined by the policies of the school [6.1:vii; 6.2:i & iii]. Parents are able to request to see the file of their own child or children, giving notice; they cannot see other pupils' records and they do not need to see the day-to-day mark book type of record [6.2:iv]. Sometimes these teacher records are idiosyncratic to the teacher, and sometimes school procedures are in place. The type of record keeping expected, the purpose, organisation, storage and security will all be determined in school policies and there will be specific ones for both assessment procedures and record keeping [6.1:2,5 & iv]. All records pertaining to pupils with SEN will be kept or maintained by the SENCO, especially any documentation about School Action, School Action Plus and statements, and all the IEPs and review documentation that go with such action [6.1:viii]. Other records will be collated by heads of departments or year group leaders to ascertain whether a group of students as a whole are progressing, either in a subject or over a period of time. This monitoring is essential for standards to be kept up. You do not have any right of access to records, except of course your own, unless this is specified as part of your role – you could be responsible for typing data from tests or examinations into a computer, for instance. However, it is often useful for you to see some records, such as the background of a pupil with whom you work who has a difficult or different home background. You must be very careful when handling school records of any kind: confirm your role and responsibility, ask permission if at all in doubt and always return records promptly as agreed [6.1.1:3 & ii; 6.2:ii].

Increasingly computers are used to store records, both numerical and word data. The school must conform to the Data Protection Act and so computer records are as accessible to parents as paper records; that is, they would not be able to see the collection of numerical data, but would be able to have a copy of anything written about their children [6.2:4]. Schools do pass on some aspects of the collated numerical data, such as the percentages of pupils reaching certain levels in SATs or GCSE examinations. Sometimes the sheer volume of data which can be collected seems overwhelming in this age of computers. It has become tempting to collect and manipulate as much as possible, as if the problem is solved once it is recorded. While you must comply with what is asked of you, you can still make suggestions for improvement; you should not just be doing things blindly, without questioning [6.2:2,3,6 & v]. Report any difficulties and clarify any concerns you have with the teacher with whom you are working [6.1:4 & 8]. This will include concerns you have about the location of records as well as the actual record keeping process, particularly if you feel records are being misused [6.1:vi; 6.2:3].

Increasingly, parents and pupils themselves are being asked to contribute to records as well as see them. Their views on the pupil's progress, attainment, attitudes to learning or interests can be most helpful, in addition to the standard sort of data kept in school records, such as birth date, serious illnesses and schools attended.

Moving forward

Things do not always go smoothly in class or in the school. Sometimes the resources are not sufficient, the procedures seem cumbersome, time runs out, or somebody's patience is not what it should be. Do not worry about this. Just remember what would have made it go better; talk to someone about it, your TA colleagues or the class teacher; and maybe change what you do the next time. Make suggestions for improvements, enter into any consultation process. We learn more from mistakes than from doing things correctly.

Questions to ask yourself

- Which teachers did you relate to well in your own school? Why?
- Are you sure of what you are supposed to be doing for all parts of the lessons in which you are involved?
- Are there any skills which you should practise?
- Have you got all the relevant policies?
- Are you sure about your ability to communicate what you know about other people's children?

Essential reading

ASE (1996) *Safeguards in the School Laboratory*, 10th edn. Hatfield: Association for Science Education.

ASE (2001) *Be Safe: Health and Safety in Primary School Science and Technology*, 3rd edn. Hatfield: Association for Science Education.

DATA (1996) *Primary Design and Technology: A Guide for Teacher Assistants*. Wellesbourne: The Design and Technology Association.

DfES (2001b) *Special Educational Needs Code of Practice*. London: Department for Education and Skills.

Some further reading

Alexander, R. (1994) 'Teaching strategies', in A. Pollard and J. Bourne (eds) *Teaching and Learning in the Primary School*, pp. 142–56. London and New York: Routledge.

Brown, G. and Wragg, E. C. (1993) *Questioning*. London and New York: Routledge.

DfES (2002a) *Developing the Role of School Support Staff* (Consultation DfES/0751/2002). London: Department for Education and Skills.

Dunne, E. and Bennett, N. (1994) *Talking and Learning in Groups*. London and New York: Routledge.

Dunne, R. and Wragg, T. (1994) *Effective Teaching*. London and New York: Routledge.

Fisher, R. (1995) *Teaching Children to Learn*. Cheltenham: Stanley Thornes.

Fullan, M. and Hargreaves, D. (1994) 'The teacher as a person', in A. Pollard and J. Bourne (eds) *Teaching and Learning in the Primary School*, pp. 67–72. London and New York: Routledge and the Open University.

Harding, J. and Meldon-Smith, L. (1996) *How to Make Observations and Assessments*. London: Hodder and Stoughton.

Kyriacou, C. (1991) *Essential Teaching Skills*. Cheltenham: Stanley Thornes.

O'Brien, T. and Garner, P. (eds) (2001) *Untold Stories – Learning Support Assistants and their Work.* Stoke on Trent and Sterling, USA: Trentham Books.

Ofsted (2002) *Teaching Assistants in Primary Schools: An Evaluation of the Quality and Impact of their Work* (HMI 434). London: Ofsted.

Watkinson, A. (2002) *Assisting Learning and Supporting Teaching.* London: David Fulton Publishers.

Wragg, E. C. (1994) *An Introduction to Classroom Observation.* London and New York: Routledge.

Wragg, E. C. and Brown, G. (1993) *Explaining.* London and New York: Routledge.

12 Supporting literacy

Developing literacy skills

Speaking and listening, reading and writing are the most important skills that children will develop in school. They use these skills to communicate their needs, to find out information, to express a range of emotions, to help them structure and form their ideas. They need and use these skills all day long for every part of the curriculum. In school our role is about helping children to develop these skills and to use them to the best effect in school and in their lives. Children's literacy development is dependent on all these skills. They are not separate strands of development but weave together, and children's development in one area contributes to their development in another. Children need to talk to express an idea before they attempt to write it down. Reading text helps them to understand the conventions of writing and aids their own experiments in writing text. Your role in school is to be aware of opportunities throughout the day when you can support children in extending their skills.

Speaking and listening

Speaking and listening are skills that children depend on in every aspect of their lives. Chapter 5 refers to linguistic intelligence, the importance of communication as a dimension of brain activity, but more particularly to the importance of language development as a special vehicle for thought. On arrival at school children have normally already learnt an enormous amount about language, more than they will in the rest of their lives. They have mastered a wide vocabulary and the structures of our language and are able to express quite complex ideas. Some are ready to talk and contribute their ideas and opinions very readily. Their enthusiasm is obvious and they benefit from the teacher's attention and response. Others are much more reticent and reluctant to speak in front of the class for a variety of reasons. Any delay in development of speaking and listening through deafness or other physical or emotional reasons is likely to create delays in starting reading and writing [18.3:4]. The TA is well placed to notice these children, to come alongside them and help them to gain the confidence to attempt to answer the teacher's questions or contribute to discussion. A TA's role can be just the link needed to promote understanding for a pupil who has a limited vocabulary, or a teacher who has limited time to explain [20.1:viii]. Sometimes shyness or just plain quietness is all that is preventing development, and you can give that one-to-one attention that can overcome any problem. You may be the one who spots that there is a deeper-seated problem than is obvious in a large class situation. Repeating the question, pointing out a helpful picture, making a mistake that makes the child laugh and relax, all of these strategies can support the shy or reticent child.

You need to consider the type of question you are asking, particularly when the purpose is to encourage speaking and listening. The questioning strategies mentioned in the previous chapter are particularly important. Closed questions are those with only one answer and often that is a one-word answer: 'Where was the dog?', 'What colour was the girl's coat?' Open-ended questions are those with a variety of answers, where children are encouraged to try out an idea and give a reason for what they have said: 'How do you think Jo felt at the party?', 'Why do you think that?' This type of question means that children are developing an idea, trying out a theory and then presenting the evidence that took their thoughts in a particular direction. Give them time to answer; do not jump in too soon. Children need plenty of opportunities to prepare their thoughts and speak at length to the class, so that they develop the skills of communicating effectively. The adults in the classroom should not be the only ones asking questions. Children should have the opportunity to question and contribute their ideas to discussion.

Children use adults as role models. They need to hear language structures being used before they will attempt them in their own speech. They need to hear ideas being expressed in a particular way before they will try it for themselves and eventually try it in their own writing. This modelling is an important aspect of the work in the classroom and its importance cannot be stressed enough. Modelling is also an excellent way of helping to extend children's vocabulary. Take any opportunity to use an alternative word or a precise adjective rather than 'nice'. 'What is the right time, *exactly* the right time?' 'That red flower – is it scarlet or crimson?' Here we are using any occasion to extend children's knowledge of language.

Reading development

You already know a great deal about children as readers. You will have heard very competent readers, reading with accuracy, fluency and enthusiasm to the class or in assembly. You will have sat with children who are just beginning to learn to read and are working out the text word by word. At Level 3 you need to know the basic principles of how children learn to read and develop from that early struggling stage to become fluent, enthusiastic readers. We will cover this briefly in this chapter and refer you at the end to a number of books which will provide you with more detailed information.

Reading strategies

There are four main strategies that we use as readers and these are the strategies that children use to become readers. They are illustrated in *The National Literacy Strategy Framework for Teaching* (DfEE 1998c) and are represented as a set of searchlights, each illuminating the text. The more searchlights the child is able to use, the more successful they will be and there will be no danger of being left in the dark with a text that cannot be deciphered.

The importance of all these strategies has only been realised in the last fifteen or so years. Before that, teaching reading went through a series of fashions where teaching the use of one strategy predominated. In the 1940s the teaching of phonic skills was regarded as the way to teach reading. This was followed by an approach that was built on teaching children to recognise whole words. Children were taught words such as 'aeroplane' that they learnt by shape. This was followed by an approach that encouraged children to learn to read through hearing stories and gradually learning to do what the teacher was doing. Children relied heavily on contextual strategies to become readers. The National Literacy Strategy (NLS) is built on the need for children to be able to use all these strategies to become successful readers and writers.

The four main reading strategies are:

Word recognition and graphic knowledge
It is necessary to be able to recognise words by sight, by how they are written. Many words in English that are used very frequently have irregular or difficult spellings, e.g. 'was', 'half', 'after'. Children need to recognise these words by sight, so that they are able to get pace and accuracy into their reading; this is difficult if they rely on sounding the words each time they meet them. Children use word recognition skills in very early reading books when one word on each page changes: 'I like the red car', 'I like the blue car.' They will learn words through the repetition in the book and be able to use those words in other contexts. Pictures on each page help with the new word. The NLS Framework (pp. 60–1) provides a list of the high-frequency words that children should be able to read, both in and out of context, by the end of Year 2. List 2 (pp. 62–3) details the medium-frequency words that children should recognise and be able to spell by Years 4 and 5.

Phonic (sound and spelling) knowledge
Children need to understand that words are made up of letters in different combinations that correspond to spoken sounds. They require this knowledge to be able to decode unfamiliar words or words that they have not met before.
They need to be taught to

- identify sounds in spoken words;
- recognise the common spellings for each sound (phoneme);
- blend phonemes into words for reading;
- segment words into phonemes for spelling.

They will learn the vowel and consonant phonemes and the more usual ways of writing them and the skills of segmentation and blending. Segmenting is hearing the individual phonemes within a word, e.g. 'train' – t-r-ai-n – has four phonemes. Blending means merging phonemes together to make a word. To read a word we do not know we give a phoneme to each letter or letter combination, then merge the phonemes together to make the word.

The NLS publication *Progression in Phonics* (DfEE 1999c) provides detailed information on a suggested progression for learning the phonic skills. It also includes a wide range of games to use in teaching phonic skills.

One very important principle to remember in working with young children on their phonic skills is to be sure that you sound phonemes as purely as possible. Try to sound consonants so that they do not have a vowel on the end. Do not sound out 'b-u-t' so that it sounds like 'ber-u-ter'. In phonic games and activities the focus is always on children hearing and discriminating sounds. Activities that involve colouring in objects that begin with the same letter can take quite a long time but do not enhance a child's ability to hear and discriminate different phonemes.

Knowledge of context

As adults, we use this skill all the time when we are reading; in fact we rely on it so much that it is difficult to realise that we are using it. When we pick up a cookery book we automatically know that it will contain very different information and vocabulary from a romantic novel. We expect to find words such as 'ingredients', 'measure', 'fry' and 'casserole' and are ready to follow a set of instructions. Our expectations of the text have led us in a certain direction. The same thing happens with children. This is a strategy that adults encourage them to use so that, as they open a book, they know what vocabulary and type of text to expect. A frequent question asked is 'What do you think this book will be about?' In discussing a book the young, inexperienced reader benefits from being encouraged to use words that they will meet in the text. The book with a fairy-tale castle on the front will be very different from the book that has photographs of farm animals. It is likely to start 'Once upon a time . . .' and contain words such as 'giant', 'princess' and 'witch'. Through their knowledge of books, children learn to prepare themselves for a certain type of text.

This skill is used within sentences as well. The child who reads 'I saw the boat in the harbour' when the text says 'I saw the ship in the harbour' is not demonstrating that they cannot read the word 'ship'. They are showing that they have made an intelligent guess about the sentence and, because the word they have substituted makes sense, they most probably are quite unaware that they have made a mistake.

Grammatical knowledge

Knowledge of the way language works also helps the reader to decode a text. Very young children, in learning to talk, show how much they have learnt about language structures. The child who says 'I taked the apple' is not mimicking adults. They are experimenting with the relationship they have already heard between 'talk' and 'talked', 'walk and 'walked', and applying it, this time incorrectly to 'take'. Gentle correction from sympathetic adults will soon help the child to sort out 'take' and 'took'. When reading, the child who is struggling to sound out 'swam' will know the word is not 'swim' because the text is in the past tense. Using grammatical strategies or cues is most difficult for children who are learning English as an additional language. They have to learn these grammatical structures before they can use them in decoding a text.

Good teaching equips children to use as many of these strategies as possible. If a child is heavily reliant on one strategy, he is going to be stuck if that one fails. Children at different stages use some strategies more than others [18.1:iii]. For example, children in the early stages are encouraged to read and re-read familiar and predictable texts. In doing this, they come to rely on the use of contextual and word recognition cues. This can create difficulties later on, when the child is exposed to a wider range of unfamiliar texts, often at the beginning of Key Stage 2. Now the child needs to pay attention to sounds and the spelling of words but they have not secured their use of phonic skills, because of their earlier reliance on contextual and word recognition skills.

The successful and confident reader is able to tackle texts from both ends: they read from the text down, having a good understanding of the overall structure and context of the piece, and from the words or sounds and spellings up, using these word skills as necessary. This balance is important, with every child having a range of strategies that they can call on as needed [18.1:vi].

Teaching reading

Shared reading

Shared reading is a main part of the literacy hour that focuses on developing pupils' skills as readers. The teacher uses this time to make the children familiar with books, discussing the author ('Do you remember we read a book by this author last week?'); the features of a book – spine, cover, title; and the type of book – fiction or non-fiction. The teacher with the children reads the pictures, guiding the children to search out the meaning. At this early stage it is the teacher who carries the main responsibility for reading the text. He/she is modelling what readers do and talking about what he/she is doing as a reader, so that the children can learn from observing a reader in action. The teacher reads the text for the children, dramatising the text, whispering or shrieking as the text requires. The teacher avoids word-by-word reading, helping the children to get the flow of the story. He/she may move a pointer or his/her hand under the text to demonstrate reading from left to right and sweeping back to the left at the end of the line. Through discussion and questioning the teacher helps the children to understand the story – 'What would you do?' On re-reading the text he/she will encourage children to join in parts of the text that they recognise or remember so that they begin to act as readers. Gradually, as they gain confidence and their knowledge of text grows, children will play an increasing part in the reading and will read along with the teacher.

The teacher will use this time to pick up phonic information and point out (or ask the children to point out) words that begin with a particular sound. They may also search for words that they recognise by sight. Gradually the teacher decreases his/her contribution to the reading while encouraging children to take more and more opportunities to join in. You will recognise that the teacher is encouraging the use of the strategies outlined earlier in this chapter. The children are encouraged to think about context, they use opportunities to reinforce phonic and word recognition skills and they hear grammatical structures through the reading. By watching the teacher use these strategies you will ensure that your use is correct.

Word work

Another important part of the literacy hour is the section devoted to word work. In Reception and Key Stage 1 this will focus on phonic knowledge and skills. Children will learn to discriminate a range of sounds. Then they will concentrate on hearing phonemes in the initial position – at the beginning of a word. They will move on to hearing phonemes in the final position – at the end of a word. The vowel sounds that occur in the medial position – in the middle of a word – can be more tricky, as the sounds can be quite similar. At this point children will begin to blend and segment consonant-vowel-consonant words – CVC words, such as 'cat', 'leg', 'lip', 'dog' and 'cup'. They will play a range of games to reinforce this knowledge. They will then progress to blending and segmenting, reading and spelling CCVC or CVCC words so that they learn the common consonant blends, e.g. 'flag', 'drum', 'plug', 'king', 'duck' and 'bell'. They then move on to vowel phonemes that are made with a combination of letters, e.g. 'ai' as in 'rain', 'ee' as in 'seem', 'oa' as in 'boat'. Finally, they will meet the wide range of vowel phonemes that occur in English: 'ey', 'ea', 'igh', 'air', etc. Children will secure this knowledge in Key Stage 1 and will use it increasingly in their reading as they grow in independence. *Progression in Phonics* (DfEE 1999c) covers this in detail and provides templates for the materials needed for a wide range of games and activities.

In this part of the literacy hour the focus is on reading from the words up. The teacher is providing the children with an important strategy for tackling unknown words. Teaching assistants play an important role in phonic work. They may work with a group who need reinforcement of a particular skill. In games and activities they observe with the teacher to identify children who are uncertain about particular phonemes.

Guided reading

In the third part of the literacy hour the class work in groups and a group of children will work with the teacher on guided reading. The focus here is on independent reading rather than the teacher modelling the reading process.

The teacher works with about six children of similar ability who all have a copy of the same book, a book that they are able to read with some support. Guided reading sessions follow a common pattern.

The teacher:

1. introduces the book through discussion with the pupils. Is it fiction or non-fiction? Have we read a book by this author? Have we read a book about these characters? What is the title? What do we think it will be about?;
2. draws the children's attention to any new or difficult vocabulary in the book and any more difficult ideas or concepts in it;
3. reminds the children of the strategies they will use in reading the text if they come across a word they do not know – 'sound it out, use the pictures, read the sentence again to the end and see if you can work out the word';
4. asks one or two questions that the group will discuss when they have read the story.

The children then all read their book and the teacher moves around and provides support and help as needed, often praising children for a really good effort and providing the unknown word as little as possible. The support he/she provides is helping the children to use the strategies they know to work out the word. When the group comes back together, the teacher discusses their reading and the questions that he/she has asked them to think about. In guided reading the children are reading at a level where they have considerable independence but are benefiting from a sustained period of teaching that is extending their range of skills.

Supported reading

In supported reading the teaching assistant repeats the guided reading session with the same group of pupils. The TA will be reinforcing what the children learnt in their guided session with the teacher. The TA carries out the session in the same way, focusing on particular details that the teacher mentions. Supported reading will occur most often with children who are experiencing some difficulty in reading; more able readers do not often need this reinforcement.

Independent reading

All this focus on reading is leading to a stage when the child is reading fluently, accurately and independently. The child now often reads on their own and the more they do this the more able they are to teach themselves about reading. This is identified in the NC as Level 3:

> Pupils read a range of texts fluently and accurately. They read independently, using strategies appropriately to establish meaning. In

responding to fiction and non-fiction they show understanding of the main points and express preferences. They use their knowledge of the alphabet to locate books and find information.

(DfEE 1999a: 5)

At this stage children have a good mastery of basic reading strategies and the focus of reading tends to shift to exploring the meaning and grasping main points within a text. We have from the start recognised the importance of children understanding what they are reading. Now the focus is on extending children's interaction with a variety of texts. They build on three basic components of reading:

- *reading the lines*
  This means that we work on the text at a literal level. The children talk about what happens in the story – what Goldilocks does and what the bears say when they come home. Children gain information from the text on the page and can use this in discussion;
- *reading between the lines*
  Here we are asking children to deduce things that the author does not actually say. When the text states 'He walked across the park, the street lamp lighting his way' we encourage the children to deduce that it must be night though the author has not written this. 'The boy gobbled his food' infers that he was greedy but the text again does not actually state this;
- *reading beyond the lines*
  When children are thinking about characters' motives and making judgements about the text, they are operating at this level. They realise that the brothers in the book they are reading are continually fighting because they are jealous of each other. They bring their own experience and experience from other books they have read to bear on the text.

As children move through Key Stage 2, shared and guided reading focus more and more on these levels of comprehension. Children are encouraged to present their views and support what they are saying with evidence from the text.

Take a few moments to read some of the books that the children in Year 6 are reading. It is amazing the complexity of texts that they are able to handle when we consider their halting efforts a few years ago.

Literacy support programmes

Considering what a complex process it is to become a reader, it is not surprising that some children have difficulties with reading. There will be a number of reasons why they do not make progress at the same rate as their peers and are in danger of being left behind by their classmates. The NLS has developed four support programmes for children of different ages, designed to improve their reading and writing skills and to bring these children into line with the rest of their class. TAs have a significant role to play in these programmes and specific training is provided by local authorities.

Early Literacy Support

This programme is designed for pupils in Year 1 whom the teacher assesses as not making the progress that will enable them to achieve Level 2 at the end of Key Stage 1. About six pupils are identified and given thirty minutes' additional literacy teaching each day for twelve weeks. This extra teaching is provided by a trained TA who works with a detailed plan of work and is supported by the class teacher. The activities that the pupils are involved in relate to the work of the class and the children's progress is assessed regularly through the twelve weeks. Some teachers question introducing this programme so early in Year 1 and feel pupils are being labelled at an early age. Others recognise the benefit of acting early to provide support for children so that they do not experience the longer-term effects of failure.

Additional Literacy Support

Designed for pupils in Years 3 and 4, this programme revises work on phonics and is taught by trained TAs. Supported reading and writing are a significant part of this work. Again the principle is to secure the children's skills and keep the children in touch with the work of the rest of the class.

Further Literacy Support

This is designed for pupils in Year 5 who are experiencing difficulties. The programme provides three sessions of additional teaching each week. TAs provide additional literacy teaching which focuses on specific reading and writing skills which are linked to the work of the rest of the class.

Literacy Progress Units

These units are designed for pupils in Year 7, the first year in the secondary school. Their aim is for pupils to achieve Level 4 by the end of the year. Pupils are withdrawn to work in small groups on the units of work that they need.

The resources to provide all of these programmes will be available in your school, and teaching assistants will receive training to enable them to work on these support programmes. Further training courses should be available from your local authority.

Resources for reading development

You will need to know about the resources in your school for supporting reading development. These will be arranged according to the decisions that the school has made. The language coordinator should be able to explain to you where resources are kept, how they are organised, how you will be expected to use the resources that are appropriate for the children you are working with, and how progress is tracked and recorded.

The school will have a range of books, graded in terms of difficulty, that are used as children work towards becoming confident, independent readers. These books may be predominantly one reading scheme that the school uses with the majority of the children. It may be that the school has a range of books across several schemes that it has banded or graded according to difficulty. These bands are often colour-coded. This system makes more books available to the children at each level. It also means that the children are reading a wide range of books, fiction and non-fiction, right from the beginning and not reading just about one set of characters and their adventures. You will need to know how the school system works so that, if you are responsible for working with some pupils, you know what level they are on and which band of books they are reading. You also need to know about the process of moving children from one band to another: is that your responsibility, or do you need to consult the teacher?

There is likely to be a home reading scheme, with children taking books home on a regular basis to read with parents or carers. Again you will need to know how this scheme works. Some schools keep a separate collection of books for taking home; in others, children take home their current reading book and perhaps a library book that is designed to be read with an adult. It may be your responsibility to monitor this scheme, to check on children's progress and to ensure that they are taking books home – and bringing them back.

It is likely that there is a range of resources for children who have the most difficulty in learning to read, those with special educational needs. The SENCO should be able to discuss these resources with you and explain how you will be using them to meet the particular needs of the children you are working with.

Problems in supporting reading development

You will experience a number of problems in your work but most of these can be resolved through discussion with teachers, the language coordinator, the SENCO or the headteacher. You will be concerned about children who are experiencing difficulty with the process of becoming a reader.

Think about the children you are working with for a moment. It is likely that a significant number of pupils with reading difficulties also have behaviour problems. These may be a cause or a consequence of their learning difficulty. The child who knows that they are not making the same progress as others in the class may turn to being disruptive to cover up their perception of failure and their low opinion of themselves. On the other hand, restless children who find it hard to concentrate may well find learning to read difficult because of their poor concentration. You will need to discuss these children with your colleagues and work out a programme to help the children bring their behaviour under control so that they can begin to make progress. A reward system can be a great incentive. Clear, achievable targets give the child a sense of purpose and can help them to recognise that what is being asked of them is possible. Good communication ensures the child receives praise and recognition as their literacy and social behaviour improve.

Motivation can be an important factor in a child's development as a reader. The resources in the school may be ones that are of little interest to the child. If the child has come to school with little knowledge of books, they can lack the motivation to get involved in an activity that means little to them. This is a good reason for having as wide a range of books as possible available in order to be able to capture children's interest.

Writing development

Writing is closely related to reading. The two activities reinforce each other. A great deal of what has been said about reading also applies to writing. The four main strategies that are used in reading apply to writing as well. Two of the strategies, knowledge of context and grammar, are used when the child is involved in composition – making decisions about their writing, planning its content and organisation. The other two, phonic knowledge and word recognition, are about the process of transcription, when the child is thinking about how to write their ideas down.

Knowledge of context

The child's knowledge of different texts, how they are constructed and the type of vocabulary that is used, will come into play as the child creates their piece of writing. They will know from their reading that a story starts in a different way from a piece of information writing. This knowledge of context will support the child in deciding whom their writing is for and what its purpose is. A letter to a friend about a recent holiday has a very different tone and uses different language from a formal letter to the council complaining about broken pavements. As the child's knowledge of text grows they will be able to make more and more sophisticated decisions about their writing.

Grammatical knowledge

In constructing their writing the child is reliant on what they know about how language works. Their writing will contain sentences and paragraphs that depend on their knowledge of how written text is organised. They will gain this information from their reading and opportunities to discuss its content and structure.

Phonic knowledge

The child needs this knowledge to help them to write the words that they need for their particular purpose. In learning to identify the phonemes, children also need to know how each of these phonemes is commonly spelt. They also need to be able to segment words into phonemes for spelling. If they are mastering these key skills they have moved a long way towards developing their skills as independent writers, because they have the basic rules for most regularly-spelt words.

Word recognition skills

The more mastery a child has of a range of words that they are able to write independently, the more confident they will feel. This knowledge will support the child in dealing with words that are not spelt regularly.

Teaching writing

In the past, the explicit teaching of writing has not had sufficient emphasis. Children were given many opportunities to practise writing but much less teaching on how to write. The NLS has provided good guidance for teachers on how to expressly teach the transitional and compositional skills of writing. An important book for you to read about teaching writing at Key Stage 1 is *Developing Early Writing* (DfES 2001c) which covers this topic in considerable detail, with many examples of activities to help children to develop their writing skills. This publication should be available in your school; all Reception and Key Stage 1 teachers should have a copy. This book emphasises two important things that teachers do in teaching writing. Firstly, they demonstrate for pupils what writers do as they prepare to write and what they do as they write. Secondly, they provide scaffolds for children's first attempts at writing. They do these things with children at the early stages of writing, but they also demonstrate and scaffold for older independent writers when they are learning something new.

Shared writing

The teacher makes the links between reading and writing explicit. Working from a text he/she will explain and discuss what the author has done to create the particular type of text that the class is working on. With the class he/she will make a list of the features of the text to show the choices that the children need to make to write a text of that particular type.

The teacher then models writing for the class. He/she explores and discusses the choices he/she is making as he/she prepares to write and then as he/she is writing his/her sentence or paragraph. He/she makes reference to the list and checks that he/she is including the features the class has identified. He/she demonstrates the process of composition. At a suitable point he/she will ask the children to contribute and help with his/her piece of writing. As he/she prepares the children to write, he/she will provide an opportunity for the children to rehearse what they are going to write. In pairs the children identify one or two sentences that they are going to write. The TA may work with a shy or reticent pupil or one who is experiencing difficulty to help them to compose their sentences. The teacher will provide a scaffold to support their early efforts in attempting to write independently. This may be the beginning of the sentence. It may be words or phrases that the children will use in writing their text. As he/she works, the teacher may make the occasional deliberate mistake to give the children an opportunity to demonstrate their learning and to check their understanding.

Beginning writers

With beginning writers in Reception and Year 1, there will be an emphasis on learning transcriptional skills so that the children develop accuracy and speed and skills become automatic. This does not only happen in shared writing; when working on their phonic skills children will be practising how to spell phonemes and will soon be joining these phonemes into words. Spelling and handwriting need to be taught systematically with regular opportunities for children to practise and learn the correct conventions. To quote from *Developing Early Writing* (DfES 2001c: 12), 'Transcriptional skills need to be practised and "over-learned" to a point where they become habitual – and correct! In order to secure this, teaching should be little and often – at least 15 minutes per day'.

You will need to know the style of handwriting that your school uses and become proficient in using it. You need to know how to form and join each of the letters and to be able to support children in forming good writing habits right from the start. The child who in the early stages forms their letters incorrectly will have enormous difficulties later on when children need to be able to write legibly and at speed. Correct pencil grip and letter formation need to be secured as early as possible. Think about the needs of left-handed children; talk to the SENCO about how you can help them.

At this early stage, the skills of transcription and composition should have an equal weighting. As children become more confident in the transcriptional skills, the process of composition takes the dominant role.

Writing at Key Stage 2

At Key Stage 2, the NLS publication *Grammar for Writing* provides detailed information on supporting pupils to become increasingly independent writers. Every teacher in Key Stage 2 should have a copy. As they move through the key stage, pupils become increasingly confident in their knowledge about language and are able to talk about nouns, verbs, adjectives, adverbs, active and passive verbs and complex sentences. This can be intimidating, as it is quite possible that you did not learn to talk about language in this way when you were at school. These terms are all explained in a glossary at the back of

Grammar for Writing. You should know what terminology is going to be introduced from the teachers' planning, so you should be able to do some preparation. Do ask the children to explain; it will help to see whether they understand the terminology that they are using.

In Key Stage 2, the emphasis in teaching shifts from phonics to more focused teaching of spelling strategies, conventions and rules. This work will build on the phonic knowledge that children have developed and will be hindered if this knowledge is not secure. The NLS publication *Spelling Bank* (DfEE 1999d) covers all of the spelling objectives that are set out in the Framework for each year from Year 3 to Year 6. It contains useful word lists that exemplify each rule and an explanation of the rule or convention as well. Again, each Key Stage 2 teacher should have a copy.

Questions to ask yourself

- Have you read the school policy on the teaching of English and identified the literacy or English coordinator or head of department?
- How secure are your own skills of language, reading and writing?

Essential reading

DfEE (1998c) *The National Literacy Strategy Framework for Teaching*. London: Department for Education and Employment.

DfEE (1999a) *The National Curriculum: Handbook for Primary Teachers in England; Key Stages 1 and 2*. London: Department for Education and Employment and the Qualifications and Curriculum Authority.

DfEE (1999c) *The National Literacy Strategy – Phonics: Progression in Phonics: Materials for Whole Class Teaching*. London: Department for Education and Employment; Standards and Effectiveness Unit.

DfEE (1999d) *The National Literacy Strategy: Spelling Bank*. London: Department for Education and Employment.

DfES (2001c) *The National Literacy Strategy: Developing Early Writing*. London: Department for Education and Skills.

Some further reading

Edwards, S. (1999) *Reading for All*. London: David Fulton Publishers.

Frater, G. (2000) *Securing Boys' Literacy*. London: The Basic Skills Agency.

Guppy, P. and Hughes, M. (1999) *The Development of Independent Reading*. Milton Keynes: Open University Press.

Meek, M. (1982) *Learning to Read*. London: The Bodley Head.

13 Supporting numeracy

Numeracy or mathematics

It is beyond the scope of these few pages to look at all you should know and the ways in which you should assist in mathematics, or what is more frequently referred to now in primary schools as numeracy. TAs, parents and teachers may well have not enjoyed mathematics at school and it is much more socially acceptable to say 'I never could do maths' than, for example, 'I never could read.' All appropriate methods are outlined in the National Numeracy Strategy (NNS) handbook (DfEE 1999e). Each class teacher has one, many TAs have their own and you should have ready access to a copy within the establishment. Two other books produced by the NNS are essential: *Teaching Mental Calculation Strategies* (QCA 1999a) and *Teaching Written Calculations* (QCA 1999b). You must be able to use the methods, formal or informal, currently being employed with the class. Do watch and listen to the teachers in your school and ask about anything you feel unsure of.

Vital to your success is the correct use of language and vocabulary. An excellent publication, the NNS *Mathematical Vocabulary Book* (DfEE 1999f) lists most of the vocabulary the pupils need; it is age/stage-related and new words are highlighted within the text. The *Handbook for Leading Mathematics Teachers* (DfEE 2000c) takes discussion on use of questions further, looking at prompting, probing and promoting questions. Many schools involve TAs in the delivery of catch-up programmes of the NNS such as Springboard 4 and Springboard 7 and you will have to ask where and when these are used in your school.

The mathematics/numeracy policy

All schools should have their own policies for teaching and learning of mathematics [19.1:i;19.2:i; 20.2:i]. Explicit in these policies will be how the NNS is to be used. The NNS radically changed the teaching of mathematics in many schools and it will almost certainly be very different from the way you were taught at school. In order to understand the scope of the learning objectives you need to be fully aware of the developments that have taken place within mathematics in recent years [19.1:ii; 19.2:ii].

- TAs operating in the Foundation Stage need to be fully conversant with the Foundation Stage curriculum, including Early Learning Goals, as well as having a working knowledge of the Key Stage 1 curriculum.
- TAs working in Key Stage 1 need a working knowledge of the Foundation and Key Stage 2 curriculum and to be fully conversant with the Key Stage 1 curriculum.
- TAs working in Key Stage 2 need to be fully conversant with the Key Stage 1 and 2 curriculums and have some knowledge of Key Stage 3.
- All TAs need to be able to use and understand the range of methods, both mental and written, that children are expected to use.

You need to be aware of:

- The informal methods for subtraction, the use of the empty number line for counting up which leads to counting up using a vertical method.
- The formal written method for subtraction (decomposition) and the use of the expanded form. This method might well be familiar to many people but the understanding comes in the use of the expanded form.
- The grid method of multiplication and how to move children to the standard written format.
- Chunking for division and the use of the standard written method.
- The variety of mental methods that children could use to approach a calculation.

Developing numerate pupils

There are some children who seem to have a good grasp of the mathematics involved in any given situation. This is often called having a good 'feel for number'. They seem to know automatically if they have done something wrong or which strategy is suitable for calculations. For example, in KS1 if a child who is asked what 93 – 89 is equal to realises that the numbers are very close together they will approach the calculation in a very different way from the child who just sees two numbers that bear no relationship to each other.

The aim of the NNS is for all children to have a 'feel for number' and to be numerate. To be numerate a person needs to know more than just the four rules. A key point would be being able to apply their knowledge. Being numerate includes knowing algebra, shape and space, measures and data handling. Mathematics is essentially a social, practical activity and as such should involve pupils in using practical apparatus and enjoying problem-solving activities [19.1:viii; 19.2:vii]. These types of activity can present more difficulties than the more straightforward practice of calculations.

The daily mathematics lesson

This is now firmly established within the primary phase and is becoming increasingly common within Key Stage 3.

Oral and mental starters (OMS)

Within the OMS, you should work primarily with those pupils needing greatest support. Model with these pupils the activity being run by the teacher. You should have any resources needed readily to hand, such as

- white boards and marker pens
- number cards
- hundred squares
- calculators
- counters
- number lines.

Your involvement greatly assists the teacher in maintaining pace and in providing a brisk, interactive and meaningful start to the lesson; the interaction between the teacher and TA is seamless. The TA usually sits at the back of the class with a cohort of less able pupils. Other pupils who are not always very confident tend to gravitate towards the TA, dipping in and out of the support as and when necessary. This prevents the distinctive 'labelling' of pupils. All the class see you as a resource to be used. It is important that the support is confidence-building or strategy-giving, not doing the work for the pupils by giving the answers.

The main part of the lesson

It is here that there is most variance in practice. In lessons with a substantial teaching element, that is where a new topic is being introduced, you can sit with and assist the less able group of pupils, modelling for them the teaching being delivered. Once the direct teaching part of this type of lesson is complete and the pupils are engaged upon some other activity (written or other) you will probably remain as direct support for the less able pupils. In this way there is a significant support structure in place for those very pupils who need most support when learning new concepts or skills.

If the lesson is a follow-up lesson or a consolidation lesson, with minimal input from the teacher at the start of the second phase, you should not be restricted to working with the less able pupils. There is a requirement that the class teacher works with all pupils within a class and this means that the teacher has to spend at least one of the week's mathematics lessons working more closely with the least able pupils. On such occasions you should operate with other groups, including the most able. Sometimes you could even hold a watching brief over two groups, thus providing less intensive support but monitoring and intervening as and when appropriate.

You need to pay particular attention to:

- ensuring children are using the appropriate mental strategies and formal written methods for calculation;
- ensuring that the children fully understand the mathematical reasoning. For example, when multiplying by ten many children will say 'add a nought' but this will not work with decimals;

- extending children's knowledge by effective use of open questions and allowing children to spot patterns and rules;
- ensuring that calculators are being used appropriately (schools should have a policy on the use of calculators, but it is often under-use rather than over-use that is the problem) [19.1:iii];
- enabling children to estimate the answer and use appropriate strategies for checking the results of calculations.

During each week all pupils need time to work unaided, as they need to develop as independent learners. One of the most recent changes in education policy has been the change to the national key stage tests (SATs). From 2003 more using and applying questions will be used. You need to allow children to explain their answers verbally and in writing – usually in that order. Make sure that you have seen exemplar questions from the national tests in order to familiarise yourself with the expectations.

The Plenary

One of the main purposes of the plenary is that it provides the teacher with an opportunity to assess the learning that has taken place during the lesson, and you can assist the teacher in this objective. You need to use the plenary to obtain and use information about a pupil's ability to understand and use number. You can also, by use of questions and prompts, help these children to cement the learning of the lesson, to firm up their ideas and to help cancel out any misconceptions which have arisen during the work part of the main teaching activity.

Good use of language, questions and vocabulary are clearly vital and you may need the same sort of resources as in the OMS, plus blank paper for jottings and vocabulary cards to assist the children with formulating answers using the correct words.

Assessing understanding in mathematics [19.1:iv; 19.2:iii]

One method of obtaining information about a child's ability is observing and taking notes during the oral and mental starter or the plenary. Another is to analyse children's SATs. These tests cover the range of work that children are expected to do in a year. The tests are statutory in Years 2 and 6 and optional in Years 3, 4 and 5. The drawback is that these tests only give information about what a child does or does not know. But what you really need to be aware of is why a child is getting something wrong. You should be aware of how teachers use the two days' 'assess and review' lessons at the end of each half term to carry out assessments. The NNS has produced a useful book called *Using Assess and Review Lessons* (DfEE 2000d). As the lessons are activity based rather than pencil and paper tests, they enable the teacher or assistant to ask the children questions which help gauge their understanding.

Central to all the activities is the role of discussion and the importance of children's explanations. Valuable insights are provided by children explaining how they arrived at the correct answer (or the incorrect answer). On many occasions, what seems like a completely wrong answer is hiding a misconception, which, when corrected, will enable the children to get the right answer. For example, when calculating 48×16, the child might give the answer 336. It is only by asking the child how they did it that you would ascertain that the child was multiplying 48 by 1 rather than 10 (then adding it to 48×6).

A point you need to be aware of is that children's ability in number can vary widely from their ability in shape, space and measures. It is not uncommon to find an able child who finds it difficult to look at a shape and, for example, work out whether it has a right angle, particularly if the shape is orientated differently from usual.

Mathematics resources [19.1:vii; 19.1:vi; 20.2:viii]

Most schools have a maths area where large resources are kept; for example, different types of scales, trundle wheels, metre sticks, weights and capacity jugs. Class teachers often have smaller resources either in their year group or their classroom. You should have your own box of resources, including devices to develop understanding of shape and space. Particularly useful would be geoboards or pegboards for children to make 2D shapes.

An excellent resource is the Springboard materials. These are intervention programmes that are used to support children who are falling slightly behind their peers but are not on the SEN register. These materials only support number work and complement the daily lesson. Most schools are using these intervention strategies and you will find the materials useful to look at, particularly as they include video demonstration of lessons.

Strategies for supporting mathematical development [19.1:vi;19.2:v; 20.2:vi]

Possibly the most crucial strategy is enabling children to experience practical activities [19.1:viii; 19.2:vii]. This starts off in Reception classes when using cubes for addition and subtraction. However, there can be a danger that children will rely on the physical object for too long. For example, rather than committing to memory the number bonds to ten, children often continue to use their fingers.

Practical activities are also vital when working on shape and space. Children need to have experience of making shapes on geoboards and then drawing them. You must be very clear about the properties of shapes as this is an area of common confusion. For example, a square is a special rectangle. Purchasing a mathematical dictionary would be a good investment or *Mathematics Explained For Primary Teachers* (Haylock 2001).

Do be aware of how powerful the use of the empty number line is to model and explain various mental strategies, for example when working out $93 - 19$:

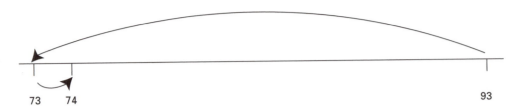

Figure 13.1 Number line showing – 20 then + 1

The number line is also used to show repeated addition and subtraction with its links to multiplication and division.

In terms of mathematical development the most important aspect of primary and early secondary teaching is children's understanding of the number system. For this, children need to be able to see, and you need to help them see, the connections between various areas of mathematics. For example, children need to see and use the relationship between ¾, 75% and 0.75.

Estimation is a key developmental point. There are problems in estimation. Children are often conditioned to get the correct answer and can see estimation as the teacher wanting them to get the answer deliberately wrong. Using measures is an excellent way to teach estimation and it is crucial that children have plenty of experience of practical measuring activities. Once estimating skills are established they can be extended to areas of number. For example, a child estimating 43 × 56 could work out that the answer would be somewhere between 2000 (40 × 50) and 3000 (50 × 60) and then hone it down to estimate that the answer would be about halfway between the two numbers.

The most difficult but potentially the most rewarding lessons for TAs are those involving the solving of problems. With the classroom teacher, think very carefully about the questions you both will ask children and the type of recording children will use to solve the problem. The intervention questions need to be carefully graded in order that the answer is not virtually given to the child. They should give the child who is stuck a clue which enables them to independently access the task. This is particularly appropriate for children with different learning needs.

Problems in mathematical development [19.1:x; 19.2:ix; 20.2:x]

Some of the difficulties that occur as children develop mathematically are ironed out as they get older but there are some key areas that hinder their progress.

The first of these is the issue of place value. Children need a thorough and regular grounding in place value work. Part of the original intention of the oral and mental starter in the NNS was to include regular counting activities. While these are still regular occurrences in classrooms, TAs need to be aware of the purpose of counting. Just as in any other part of mathematics, areas of misconception should be targeted. For example, most children by Year 2 can count in twos and tens (starting from zero) up to quite large numbers, but the area of misconception would be counting in tens, starting from a non-multiple of ten, and crossing the hundreds' boundary, e.g. 171, 181, 191, 201, 211, etc. It is often counting in tens that confuses children and you need to deliberately target this in your support.

Another area of common confusion, and possibly the most important, is how children learn mental strategies and how they move to written calculations. There is a difference between rapid recall of facts and mental strategies. Rapid recall is the calculations that children are expected to just 'know', whereas mental strategies are calculations that need to be specifically taught and applied according to the situation. For example, double 35 = 70 is a fact that should be known by Year 4 whereas knowing that a quick way to calculate 35 + 36 is to double 35 and add 1 would be a strategy that needs to be applied. The booklet *Teaching Mental Calculations Strategies* (QCA 1999a) is an excellent resource and explains all the strategies and age expectations.

Parents (and some teachers) often comment that children are expected to learn too many strategies. You should understand why there is this expectation. If one was presented with the following calculations: £8 − £ 2.99, 45 + 46, 16 × 7, 55 + 37, 135.4/10, 428 × 2, 900 − 500, 36 − 18, 78 − 32, one would reasonably expect that they could be answered mentally, but the strategies used would all be different. Children need to be taught different strategies and then, crucially, when it is appropriate to apply them. For example, if you were supporting pupils in a lesson that was concentrating on using near doubles, you would give the children practice examples that were appropriate for this strategy, e.g. 30 + 31, 24 + 25, but at some point in the lesson you could ask the child what 55 + 37 is. Using near doubles would obviously not be a good strategy to work this out. What you are doing is leading the child to look at the numbers first and see if there is any connection between them before attempting the calculation.

It is a clear intention of the NNS that by the end of Key Stage 1 children should be able to *mentally* answer any two-digit addition or subtraction question. When children move into Key Stage 2, the focus switches to *written* calculations. The intention of the NNS is that by the end of Key Stage 2 children should have a standard written method for all four rules of number. This means one standard written method for each operation.

The difficulty that children experience is how they move from mental to written calculations, particularly in Years 3 and 4. *Teaching Written Calculations* (QCA 1999b) explains this in detail. You can support this movement from mental to written by ensuring that the children think about what method they are going to use. For example, if a child was given 2001 − 1999 to calculate, it would be inappropriate and inefficient to set it out as a written calculation when the child could easily count up 2. The first question to ask when supporting a child with a calculation is 'Can you do it in your head?' If the calculation is inappropriate to work out mentally, the child should use a standard written method at Key Stages 2 and 3.

Another problem that could arise is recognising when it is appropriate to use a calculator. Guidance is given on the role of the calculator in the NNS framework (DfEE 1999e: 8).

Links between mathematics and other subjects

In the Foundation Stage it is commonplace for links to be made between mathematics and other subjects. This becomes less commonplace in Key Stage 1 and certainly by Key Stages 2 and 3. Excellent guidance is given in the introduction to the NNS framework (DfEE 1999e: 16). All secondary schools in spring 2002 were supposed to devote a day's training to numeracy across the curriculum. You may have been able to attend this; if not, do ask the head of mathematics for any useful information to help you in your work.

Questions to ask yourself

- How did you feel about learning mathematics at school?
- Are you confident in supporting pupils in mathematics? Do you need to further your own knowledge and skills outside the school scene?
- Are you able to participate in the school INSET programme for the numeracy strategy? If not, why not? If your circumstances are the problem, can you reorganise some regular events in your life in order to be able to understand the school mathematics practices better?

Essential reading

DfEE (1999e) *The National Numeracy Strategy* [Framework for teaching mathematics]. London: DfEE.

DfEE (1999f) *The National Numeracy Strategy: Mathematical Vocabulary Book*. London: Department for Education and Employment, Standards and Effectiveness Unit.

DfEE (2000c) *Handbook for Leading Mathematics Teachers*. London: Department for Education and Employment.

QCA (1999a) *The National Numeracy Strategy: Teaching Mental Calculation Strategies: Guidance for Teachers at Key Stages 1 and 2*. (QCA/99/380). London: Qualifications and Curriculum Authority.

QCA (1999b) *The National Numeracy Strategy: Teaching Written Calculations: Guidance for Teachers at Key Stages 1 and 2*. (QCA/99/486). London: Qualifications and Curriculum Authority.

Some further reading

Aplin, R. (1998) *Assisting Numeracy*. BEAM, The National Numeracy Project and the London Borough of Tower Hamlets.

Askew, M. (1998) *Teaching Primary Mathematics: A Guide for Newly Qualified and Student Teachers* (with additional contribution by M. Selinger). London: Hodder and Stoughton.

Burton, L. (1994) *Children Learning Mathematics: Patterns and Relationships*. Hemel Hempstead: Simon and Schuster Education.

DfEE (2000d) *Using Assess and Review Lessons*. London: Department for Education and Employment.

Fox, G. and Halliwell, M. (2000) *Supporting Literacy and Numeracy: A Guide for Learning Support Assistants*. London: David Fulton Publishers.

Haylock, D. (2001) *Mathematics Explained for Primary Teachers*, 2nd edn. London: Paul Chapman.

Headington, R. (1997) *Supporting Numeracy*. London: David Fulton Publishers.

Liebeck, P. (1984) *How Children Learn Mathematics: A Guide for Parents and Teachers*. London: Penguin Educational.

14 Future prospects

Developing as a professional TA

The profession of teaching assistance

Teaching is a professional activity, where teachers are considered professionals alongside lawyers and clergy. It is high time that teaching assistance was considered in the same light, a profession in the world of education, drawing a parallel with the nursing profession in the world of medicine.

Teaching assistance as teaching is a reflective activity, a feature that this book has encouraged in you from the start (Calderhead 1994). By studying at Level 3 you now also have acquired a body of specialised knowledge about pupils and their learning methods and needs, teaching methods and curriculum content which you will rely on in your everyday work. You know about learning development and what affects it. You are also 'goal orientated'; that is, you aim to fulfil the learning objectives of the teachers for the pupils with whom you work, to enhance their learning and to support the ethos and aims of your school. You are accountable to these pupils and to your colleagues for the quality of your 'performance'. Your context is, as that of teachers, often complex and you have to use your personal judgement to analyse what is going on and what to do about it, with the interests of the pupils uppermost in your mind. You also have a body of developed skills, based on your experience and learning, which you adapt to the context in which you find yourself. It is only a matter of time before this knowledge, understanding and skills base is defined as a pedagogy similar to but different from that of the teaching profession. Already we have the NOS at Levels 2 and 3 and the draft standards for HLTAs (DfES and TTA 2003).

It remains for you to have your own professional association, recognising those characteristics and supporting their development, and possibly registration as a recognised member of the profession. There may well come a time in the next few years when you will be required to be registered, as teachers and nurses are, with entry requirements or qualifications for each level. As things are, anyone can be appointed to any TA job, provided they are cleared by the police. Management and parents have no clear idea of who is suitable for what jobs. There should come proper recognition in terms of pay and conditions of service, although this might mean clearer job boundaries and fewer people doing the more specialised jobs. Already the teacher and support staff unions (apart from the National Union of Teachers) are debating some of the pay concerns with the National Joint Council for Local Government Services, following the agreement signed on 15 January 2003. The Workforce Agreement Monitoring Group is preparing to issue joint guidance notes to help schools with implementation of the proposed contractual changes for teachers. If you are interested in following these developments, use the DfES website or one of the union sites given at the end of this chapter.

Taking charge of your own development

Part of the process of professional development is about being a life-long learner. Learning is like the scientific process, the plan–does–review cycle; it never stops. Each time you do something and reflect upon it, you refine how you do that particular thing the next time. A critical, questioning approach is not about being negative. If something does not work for you or mean a lot, then find something that does. We can learn more from our mistakes than from getting things right. Be prepared to change. As you become a reflective practitioner, taking responsibility for your own development, building on the contributions of others to both the reflection and the development, you will provide better support for other learners and greater job satisfaction for yourself.

Being a professional also has an element of responsibility in it. One of the reasons people say they like being TAs is the lack of responsibility. But even if you do not have the ultimate responsibility for pupils' learning, you do have a responsibility to do your best for them, a responsibility of care, a responsibility to your colleagues and to the school. By retaining the power to be an active learner yourself, you will empathise more with those you help and work with. Plan your own pathways, set yourself realistic goals or targets with a realistic timeline, and recognise milestones of achievement as you progress [4.2:2].

Development does not all depend on available courses, nor will any course provide all the answers. A lot of your development will depend on your own initiative, making the most of any opportunities. Also, it is salutary to remember that your efforts may not 'pay off' in terms of increased pay or opportunities for advancement, but they will definitely increase your job satisfaction, your value to the school and the pupils with whom you work, and should provide you with transferable skills for other roles you may undertake in your life. Young people training to be nursery nurses, when later having their family, have found that their knowledge and understanding of child development is invaluable. Honing your team skills can spin off into a club activity. Any course of study sharpens your mind and gets the brain working.

Keeping up to date or going further up the career ladder

You do not have to decide immediately what lies in the future for you – your personal circumstances may change anyway – but do keep your learning up to date. There is no magazine or website servicing just your needs, although articles appear from time to time in the teachers' journals. The weekly newspaper for teachers, the *Times Educational Supplement*, found in many staffrooms, has a regular resources section as well as news and teachers' jobs. The monthly magazines for special education, child education (Key Stage 1) and junior education (Key Stage 2) are purchased by some schools. All the subject associations have their journals; the Association for Science Education, for instance, has several, one general, one for primary teachers and one for technicians among others, along with many of their own publications and their own website. Some LEAs send out newsletters to TAs but some authorities, with long-established delegated management strategies, do not even know how many TAs there are in their schools. Maybe, if there is ever a national TA association, they will publish their own materials to support TAs.

One way of keeping up to date is to attend local meetings of TAs; this also enables you to share practice and ideas with TAs from other schools. If you have not got a group like this, one of your development points could be to start one.

Starting a local group

Get your headteacher to agree to you meeting in your school, probably in the evening (you may have to pay a hire charge). Contact your cluster schools, or the half-dozen geographically nearest to you. Invite their TAs to come. Try to get a free speaker to come to start you off – maybe

- one of the SENCOs
- an EP
- a local tutor
- a local adviser
- a therapist.

Lay on tea and coffee and biscuits. Charge the minimum to cover your costs. Get a representative from each school to be on a steering committee. Arrange to meet in one of the other schools next term – you have a local association in formation!

From these little acorns, the national tree could grow.

You may be considering specialising but staying as an experienced TA. Look around for local courses in the area you are interested in. Look for websites belonging to associations in the area you want – an SEN area or curriculum area, say – and see what is on offer. Try to visit other schools and talk to local advisers in the area you like.

An example of specialisation

One TA decided to specialise in speech and language development. Her school had several children with poor skills in this area, so the SENCO timetabled her to support all those with this particular need. She contacted the speech therapist and found resources and associations to help. The speech therapist has since left the area and so this TA is a vital part of the school's provision. The school has purchased books for the TA to study and use, and is encouraging her to visit specialist speech and language units in the authority. The recent Ofsted report singled out this provision for special praise and commended the practice to others.

You could consider moving schools, just taking a different job which may or may not be on a different pay scale. This would broaden your experience, particularly if was a different phase of education or served a different catchment area. All schools are different, whatever the apparent background, and you could easily be helping a different age range or taking groups instead of supporting one particular pupil. Try talking about the differences with colleagues from other schools, if you have a network meeting or go on a course. The next step up the ladder is to consider a foundation degree (two-thirds of an honours degree) in teaching assistance or the HLTA training which, it is proposed, will be developed after the standards are finalised (DfES 2002a).

   You may be considering teaching, but whatever way you approach this you will still have to get a degree, and in it must be included an element of curriculum understanding and knowledge. If you are considering this route, you should look on the Teacher Training Agency (TTA) website or the DfES 'canteach' site for what is available and what the entry requirements are. Contact your local higher education provider to see what they can do (not all have Initial Teacher training departments) and your LEA – some areas have School-based Initial Teacher Training (SCITT) schemes. Talk to your headteacher as well, as your school may be willing to support you through training in order to 'grow their own' teacher.

Check out the following [4.2:i]:

What people can help you?
- In school:
    - Mentor
    - Line manager
    - The headteacher; other senior managers, especially the SENCO or subject leaders
- Outside school:
    - Networks
    - Advisers
    - College tutors or assessors

What books do you have or have access to?

- Texts like this one, published by David Fulton Publishers
- Copies of the NOS
- DfES, Ofsted, QCA and Teacher Training Agency (TTA) publications relating to TAs
- Guidance from DfES or the LEA regarding TAs
- School textbooks which accompany any schemes used in school, including the NLNS materials
- School guidance and policies – see Chapter 4

In-house training

- Training days, staff meetings, team meetings
- Informal meetings

Off-site training

- Provided by the LEA
- At a local college or university
- Distance learning – Open College or Open University opportunities

Computer resources – websites

- DfES, Ofsted, QCA and TTA
- LGNTO and the Employers' Organisation (EO)
- Awarding bodies
- Unions – Unison and GMB

Opportunities for informal and formal observation of good practice in others [4.2:ii]

Opportunities to participate in any school based research initiative.

Your values

Whatever way forward you decide to go, you must be sure why you want to continue working in schools. While you must consider whether you just wish to consolidate your learning and improve your performance at Level 3, or whether to continue in your studies to become an HLTA or even a teacher, it will be worth your while to spend a little time considering what your basic values are. Level 3 is about no longer being just adequate but contributing, being consistent, having effective communication and working relationships with your colleagues; being part of the team building, the ethos and climate development; and showing initiative and undertaking responsibility, while recognising the constraints of being a TA and the responsibilities of the teacher.

> Take a look at the Values and Principles which underpin the NOS (in the Appendix).
> Read them through carefully.
> Can you agree with these?
> If you were asked to 'sign up' to them could you?

The NOS Values and Principles are similar to some others and, instead of just reading the Appendix and thinking they are fine, try the following examples as well. While TAs do not yet have a professional association or a code of ethics, some of those already published do come near to one. Barber (1996: 237) talks of a code of ethics for teachers:

Commitment to the development of children and young people who become increasingly independent;

a commitment to foster learning and understanding of learning among parents and other adults;

a commitment to refine and develop professional skills as an individual and to assist that process among other members of the profession;

a commitment to the promotion of learning and education in the development of healthy communities and democratic society;

and finally, a commitment to the notion that learning has a part to play in the growth of global understanding and the sustenance of the planet.

Consider how far you can uphold the professional values and practice required of qualified teachers. The standards of those awarded QTS include the professional code of the General Teaching Council for England. Teachers should demonstrate that:

1.1 They have high expectations of all pupils; respect their social, cultural, linguistic, religious and ethnic backgrounds; and are committed to raising their educational achievement.

1.2 They treat pupils consistently, with respect and consideration, and are concerned for their development as learners.

1.3 They demonstrate and promote the positive values, attitudes and behaviour that they expect from their pupils.

1.4 They communicate sensitively and effectively with parents and carers, recognising their role is in pupils' learning and their rights, responsibilities and interests in this.

1.5 They contribute to and share responsibly in the corporate life of schools.

1.6 They understand the contribution that support staff make and other professionals to teaching and learning.

1.7 They are able to improve their own teaching by evaluating it, learning from the effective practice of others and from evidence. They are motivated and able to take increasing responsibility for their own professional development.

1.8 They are aware of and work within the statutory frameworks relating to teachers' responsibilities.

(DfES and TTA 2003: 6)

Obviously, some of the phrases in the above statements refer only to those with QTS. The HLTA consultation standards are clearly based on the QTS standards:

Those meeting the Higher Level Teaching Assistant Standards must demonstrate all of the following:

1.1 They have high expectations of all pupils; respect their social, cultural, linguistic, religious and ethnic backgrounds; and are committed to raising their educational achievement.

1.2 They treat pupils consistently, with respect and consideration, and are concerned for their development as learners.

1.3 They demonstrate and promote the positive values, attitudes and behaviour they expect from the pupils with whom they work.

1.4 They work collaboratively with colleagues as part of a professional team, and carry out their roles effectively knowing when to seek help and advice from colleagues.

1.5 They reflect upon and seek to improve their own practice.

1.6 They work within school policies and procedures, and are aware of legislation relevant to their role and responsibilities in the school.

1.7 They recognise equal opportunities issues as they arise in the school, and they respond effectively, following school policies and procedures.

(DfES and TTA 2003: 5)

Take the sets of values set out above and see where they overlap.

Identify where you can see they relate to your job and yourself.

Draw up a set of TA values for yourself.

Suggest your colleagues try the same.

Discuss your set with those of your colleagues.

Can you agree a code of practice for TAs, remembering that teachers take the final responsibility for teaching and learning of pupils and TAs are always working under their direction and supervision?

Does it vary depending on the level of competence?

And now finally . . .

Questions to ask yourself as you think ahead

How did you feel when you first picked up this book or went to your first course session?

Have things changed at home or in your school since then?

How do you feel now?

What was the most interesting? What was the most challenging?

What changes have you made to your practice?

What else do you want to

- learn more about
- think about
- tell somebody
- read
- explore further?

Why?

Do you need anyone or anything else to do these things?

When can you do them?

Start planning now! Enjoy!

Essential reading

The Appendix

Some further reading

Barber, M. (1996) *The Learning Game: Arguments for an Education Revolution.* London: Victor Gollancz.

Calderhead, J. (1994) 'Teaching as a professional activity', in A. Pollard and J. Bourne (eds) *Teaching and Learning in the Primary School.* London and New York: Routledge with the Open University.

DfES (2002a) *Developing the Role of School Support Staff* (Consultation DfES/0751/2002). London: Department for Education and Skills.

DfES and TTA (2003) *Standards for Higher Level Teaching Assistants: Consultation Document April 2003* (Consultation). London: Department for Education and Skills and Teacher Training Agency.

Useful websites

www.canteach.gov.uk
www. teachernet.gov.uk

The unions mainly used by TAs

GMB: www.gmb.org.uk
Professionals Allied to Teaching (PAtT): accessible via www.pat.org.uk
Unison: www.unison.org.uk

The main awarding bodies

CACHE: www.cache.org.uk
City and Guilds: www.city-and-guilds.co.uk
Edexcel: www.edexcel.org.uk
Oxford and Cambridge and RSA examinations (OCR): www.ocr.org.uk
The Open University: www.open.ac.uk

15 Appendix: Values and principles underpinning the National Occupational Standards for Teaching/Classroom Assistants

The National Occupational Standards for teaching/classroom assistants are built upon the following set of agreed values and principles of good practice.

Working in partnership with the teacher

It is the teacher whose curriculum and lesson planning and day-to-day direction set the framework within which teaching/classroom assistants work. The teaching/classroom assistant works under the direction of the teacher, whether in the whole class or on their own with an individual or a small group of pupils. Teaching/classroom assistants, therefore, need to be fully briefed about the teacher's plans and intentions for teaching and learning and her/his contribution to these. Ideally, teaching/classroom assistants will be involved by teachers in their planning and preparation of the work.

Working within statutory and organisational frameworks

Teaching/classroom assistants are an integral part of the school staff team and as such have a responsibility for working to agreed school policies and procedures. In turn, the day-to-day work of the school takes place within a wider legislative framework affecting the content and delivery of the curriculum, health and safety, child protection and other aspects of school life. Teaching/classroom assistants need to be aware of these school and statutory frameworks, particularly those that directly impact on their own work with pupils.

Supporting inclusion

The principles underpinning inclusive education are those of setting suitable learning challenges, responding to pupils' diverse learning needs, and overcoming potential barriers to learning. Many teaching/classroom assistants are employed with specific responsibilities to work with individual pupils, others are given more general classroom responsibilities. Both roles are key to supporting inclusion by facilitating participation and learning, helping to build confidence, self-esteem and independence so that all pupils are enabled to reach their full potential alongside their peers.

Equality of opportunity

Teaching/classroom assistants have an important role in ensuring pupils' equal access to opportunities to learn and develop. Some pupils need additional or different support in order to have equality of opportunity and teaching/classroom assistants are often employed to provide this for individuals or small groups of pupils. Sometimes, working under the direction of the teacher, teaching/classroom assistants will work with the whole class in order to free up the teacher to work with individual pupils who need special attention.

Anti-discrimination

Teaching/classroom assistants must not discriminate against any individual or group on the grounds of gender, racial origins, religion, cultural or social background, disability or sexual orientation. They must comply with legislation and school policies relating to discrimination and should practise and promote anti-discriminatory practices in all interactions with pupils and colleagues.

Celebrating diversity

Teaching/classroom assistants should demonstrate their valuing of pupils' racial and other personal characteristics in order to help them develop self-esteem and a sense of identity, as well as promoting an understanding and appreciation of different belief systems and cultures in all pupils.

Promoting independence

In providing support for individual or groups of pupils, teaching/classroom assistants will encourage independence by helping them to develop self-esteem, self-reliance and learning skills as well as increase their subject-related knowledge, understanding and skills. Pupils should be given opportunities to make their own decisions and take responsibility for their own actions.

Confidentiality

Teaching/classroom assistants must adhere to the school policy for the confidentiality of information at all times. This requirement covers information about pupils and colleagues and extends to communications with others in social as well as work-related situations.

Continuing Professional Development

Teaching/classroom assistants will take advantage of planned and incidental self-development opportunities in order to maintain and improve the contribution that they can make to raising pupil achievement. Asking for advice and support to help resolve problems should be seen as a form of strength and professionalism.

References

Abbott, J. (1996) 'The critical relationship: education reform and learning'. *Education 2000 News*, March, 1–3.

Abbott, J. (1997) 'To be intelligent'. *Education 2000 News*.

Alexander, R. (1994) 'Teaching strategies', in A. Pollard and J. Bourne (eds), *Teaching and Learning in the Primary School*. London and New York: Routledge, pp. 142–56.

Aplin, R. (1998) *Assisting Numeracy*. BEAM: The National Numeracy Project and the London Borough of Tower Hamlets.

ASE (1996) *Safeguards in the School Laboratory*, 10th edn. Hatfield: Association for Science Education.

ASE (2001) *Be Safe: Health and Safety in Primary School Science and Technology*, 3rd edn. Hatfield: Association for Science Education.

Askew, M. (1998) *Teaching Primary Mathematics: A Guide for Newly Qualified and Student Teachers* (with additional contribution by M. Selinger). London: Hodder and Stoughton.

Babbage, R., Byers, R. and Redding, H. (1999) *Approaches to Teaching and Learning*. London: David Fulton Publishers.

Baginsky, M. (2000) *Child Protection and Education*. London: NSPCC.

Balshaw, M. (1999) *Help in the Classroom*, 2nd edn. London: David Fulton Publishers.

Balshaw, M. and Farrell, P. (2002) *Teaching Assistants: Practical Strategies for Effective Classroom Support*. London: David Fulton Publishers.

Barber, M. (1996) *The Learning Game: Arguments for an Education Revolution*. London: Victor Gollancz.

Bastiani, J. (1989) *Working with Parents: A Whole-school Approach*. London: Routledge and NFER-Nelson.

Blamires, M., Robertson, C. and Blamires, J. (1997) *Parent–Teacher Partnership*. London: David Fulton Publishers.

Blatchford, P. and Sharp, S. (1994) *Breaktime and the School: Understanding and Changing Playground Behaviour*. London and New York: Routledge.

Brown, G. and Wragg, E. C. (1993) *Questioning*. London and New York: Routledge.

Bruce, T. and Meggitt, C. (1996) *Child Care and Education*. London: Hodder and Stoughton.

Bruner, J. S. (1966) *Towards a Theory of Instruction*. Cambridge, Mass. and London: The Belknap Press of Harvard University Press.

Burton, L. (1994) *Children Learning Mathematics: Patterns and Relationships*. Hemel Hempstead: Simon and Schuster Education.

Buxton, C. (1994) *Language Activities for Bi-lingual Learners*. London: Tower Hamlets Language Support Service.

Calderhead, J. (1994) 'Teaching as a professional activity', in A. Pollard and J. Bourne (eds*) Teaching and Learning in the Primary School*. London and New York: Routledge with the Open University.

Cottam, P. and Sutton, A. (1985) *Conductive Education: A System for Overcoming Motor Disorders*. London: Croom Helm.

DATA (1996) *Primary Design and Technology: A Guide for Teacher Assistants*. Wellesbourne: The Design and Technology Association.

Dessent, T. (1987) *Making the Ordinary School Special*. London: The Falmer Press.

DfEE (1996) 'Supporting pupils with medical needs in schools' (Circular 14/96). London: Department for Education and Employment.

DfEE (1998a) *Teachers Meeting the Challenge of Change* (Green paper). London: Department for Education and Employment.

DfEE (1998b) *Excellence for All Children: Meeting Special Educational Needs* (Green paper). London: Department for Education and Employment.

DfEE (1998c) *The National Literacy Strategy Framework for Teaching*. London: Department for Education and Employment.

DfEE (1998d) *Meeting Special Educational Needs: A Programme for Action* (MSENPAS). London: Department for Education and Employment.

DfEE (1999a) *The National Curriculum: Handbook for Primary Teachers in England*: Key stages 1 and 2. London: Department for Education and Employment and the Qualifications and Curriculum Authority.

DfEE (1999b) *The National Curriculum: Handbook for Primary Teachers in England*: Key stages 3 and 4. London: Department for Education and Employment and the Qualifications and Curriculum Authority.

DfEE (1999c) *The National Literacy Strategy: Phonics: Progression in Phonics: Materials for Whole Class Teaching*. London: Department for Education and Employment, Standards and Effectiveness Unit.

DfEE (1999d) *The National Literacy Strategy: Spelling Bank*. London: Department for Education and Employment.

DfEE (1999e) *The National Numeracy Strategy* [Framework for teaching mathematics]. London: Department for Education and Employment.

DfEE (1999f) *The National Numeracy Strategy: Mathematical Vocabulary Book*. London: Department for Education and Employment: Standards and Effectiveness Unit.

DfEE (2000a) *Working with Teaching Assistants: A Good Practice Guide*. London: Department for Education and Employment.

DfEE (2000b) *Teaching Assistant File: Induction Training for Teaching Assistants*. London: Department for Education and Employment.

DfEE (2000c) *Behaviour Management Module: Induction Training for Teaching Assistants*. London: Department for Education and Employment.

DfEE (2000d) *Using Assess and Review Lessons.* London: Department for Education and Employment.

DfES (2001a) *Teaching Assistant File: Induction Training for Teaching Assistants in Secondary Schools.* London: Department for Education and Skills.

DfES (2001b) *Special Educational Needs Code of Practice.* London: Department for Education and Skills.

DfES (2001c) *The National Literacy Strategy: Developing Early Writing.* London: Department for Education and Skills.

DfES (2002a) *Developing the Role of School Support Staff* (Consultation DfES/0751/2002). London: Department for Education and Skills.

DfES (2002b) *Time for Standards: Reforming the School Workforce* (Proposals DfES/0751/2002). London: Department for Education and Skills.

DfES (2002c) *The Education (Teaching Work and Registration) (England) Regulations 2002* (Draft Circular and guidance). London: Department for Education and Skills.

DfES and TTA (2003) *Standards for Higher Level Teaching Assistants: Consultation Document April 2003* (Consultation). London: Department for Education and Skills and Teacher Training Agency.

Donaldson, M. (1984) *Children's Minds.* London: Fontana Paperbacks.

Dryden, G. and Vos, J. (1994) *The Learning Revolution.* Aylesbury: Accelerated Learning Systems.

Dunne, E. and Bennett, N. (1994) *Talking and Learning in Groups.* London and New York: Routledge.

Dunne, R. and Wragg, T. (1994) *Effective Teaching.* London and New York: Routledge.

East, V. and Evans, L. (2001) *At a Glance: A Quick Guide to Children's Special Needs.* Birmingham: The Questions Publishing Company.

Edwards, S. (1999) *Reading for All.* London: David Fulton Publishers.

EMAS (2001) *Challenging Children.* London: Hackney Ethnic Minority Achievement Service.

EMAS (2001) *Good Practice in Admission and Induction.* London: Hackney Ethnic Minority Achievement Service.

Fisher, R. (1995) *Teaching Children to Learn.* Cheltenham: Stanley Thornes (Publishers) Ltd.

Fox, G. (1998) *A Handbook for Learning Support Assistants.* London: David Fulton Publishers.

Fox, G. (2001) *Supporting Children with Behaviour Difficulties.* London: David Fulton Publishers.

Fox, G. and Halliwell, M. (2000) *Supporting Literacy and Numeracy: A Guide for Learning Support Assistants.* London: David Fulton Publishers.

Frater, G. (2000) *Securing Boys' Literacy.* London: The Basic Skills Agency.

Freeman, R. and Meed, J. (1993) *How to Study Effectively.* London: National Extension College and Collins Educational Ltd.

Fullan, M. and Hargreaves, D. (1994) 'The teacher as a person', in A. Pollard and J. Bourne (eds) *Teaching and Learning in the Primary School*, pp. 67–72. London and New York: Routledge and the Open University.

Gardner, H., Kornhaber, M. L. and Wake, W. K. (1996) *Intelligence: Multiple Perspectives*. Florida: Holt, Rinehart and Wilson, Inc.

Gibbons, P. (1991) *Learning to Learn in a Second Language*. Australia: Primary English Teaching Association.

Guppy, P. and Hughes, M. (1999) *The Development of Independent Reading*. Milton Keynes: Open University Press.

Hall, D. (2002) *Assessing the Needs of Bilingual Learners: Living in Two Languages*. London: David Fulton Publishers.

Harding, J. and Meldon-Smith, L. (1996) *How to Make Observations and Assessments*. London: Hodder and Stoughton.

Hargreaves, D. H. and Hopkins, D. (1991) *The Empowered School*. London: Cassell Education Limited.

Haylock, D. (2001) *Mathematics Explained for Primary Teachers*, 2nd edn. London: Paul Chapman.

Headington, R. (1997) *Supporting Numeracy*. London: David Fulton Publishers.

Holt, J. (1964) *How Children Fail*. London: Penguin Books.

Holt, J. (1967) *How Children Learn*. London: Penguin Books.

Hook, P. and Vass, A. (2000a) *Confident Classroom Leadership*. London: David Fulton Publishers.

Hook, P. and Vass, A. (2000b) *Creating Winning Classrooms*. London: David Fulton Publishers.

Jarvis, P., Holford, J. and Griffin, C. (1998) *The Theory and Practice of Learning*. London: Kogan Page.

Kerry, T. (2001) *Working with Support Staff: Their Roles and Effective Management in Schools*. Harlow: Pearson Education.

Kyriacou, C. (1991) *Essential Teaching Skills*. Cheltenham: Stanley Thornes.

Lacey, P. (1999) *On a Wing and a Prayer*. MENCAP.

Lacey, P. (2001) *Support Partnerships*. London: David Fulton Publishers.

Lazear, D. (1994) *Seven Pathways of Learning: Teaching Students and Parents about Multiple Intelligences*. Arizona: Zephyr Press.

Lee, V. (1990) *Children's Learning in School*. London: Hodder and Stoughton for the Open University.

Leung, C. and Cable, C. (1997) *English as an Additional Language: Changing Perspectives*. Watford: NALDIC.

LGNTO (2001) *Teaching/Classroom Assistants National Occupational Standards*. London: Local Government National Training Organisation.

Liebeck, P. (1984) *How Children Learn Mathematics: A Guide for Parents and Teachers*. London: Penguin Educational.

Lorenz, S. (1998) *Effective In-class Support*. London: David Fulton Publishers.

Lovey, J. (2002) *Supporting Special Educational Needs in Secondary School Classrooms*, 2nd edn. London: David Fulton Publishers.

MacBeath, J., Boyd, B. J. R., Rand, J. and Bell, S. (1996) *Schools Speak for Themselves*. London: National Union of Teachers for the University of Strathclyde.

Maynard, T. and Furlong, J. (1995) 'Learning to teach and models of mentoring', in Kerry, T. and Mayes, A. S. (eds) *Issues in Mentoring*. London and New York: Routledge with the Open University, Milton Keynes.

Meek, M. (1982) *Learning to Read*. London: The Bodley Head.

Northledge, A. (1990) *The Good Study Guide*. Milton Keynes: The Open University.

O'Brien, T. and Garner, P. (eds) (2001) *Untold Stories: Learning Support Assistants and their Work*. Stoke-on-Trent: Trentham Books.

Ofsted (1993) *Handbook for the Inspection of Schools*. London: Her Majesty's Stationery Office.

Ofsted (1999) *Handbook for Inspecting Primary and Nursery Schools*. London: Ofsted.

Ofsted (2002) *Teaching Assistants in Primary Schools: An Evaluation of the Quality and Impact of their Work* (HMI 434). London: Ofsted.

O'Hagan, M. and Smith, M. (1993) *Special Issues in Child Care*. London: Baillière Tindall.

Pollard, A. (2002) *Reflective Teaching: Effective and Evidence-informed Professional Practice*. London and New York: Continuum.

Pollard, A. and Tann, S. (1993) *Reflective Teaching in the Primary School*, 2nd edn. London and New York: Cassell Educational, National Primary Centre and The Open University.

QCA (1999a) *The National Numeracy Strategy: Teaching Mental Calculation Strategies: Guidance for Teachers at Key Stages 1 and 2.* (QCA/99/380). London: Qualifications and Curriculum Authority.

QCA (1999b) *The National Numeracy Strategy: Teaching Written Calculations: Guidance for Teachers at Key Stages 1 and 2.* (QCA/99/486). London: Qualifications and Curriculum Authority.

Rogers, B. (1991) *'You Know the Fair Rule'*. Harlow: Longman.

Rogers, B. (1994) *Behaviour Recovery*. Harlow: Longman.

Rogers, B. (2000) *Classroom Behaviour*. London: Paul Chapman Publishing (Sage).

SCAA (1996) *Education for Adult Life: The Spiritual and Moral Development of Young People* (Discussion papers: No 6). London: School Curriculum and Assessment Authority.

Schonveld, A. (1995) *Schools and Child Protection*. Coventry: Community Education Development Centre.

Schonveld, A. (1998) *Child Protection and School Support Staff*. Coventry: Community Education Development Centre.

Smith, A. (1996) *Accelerated Learning in the Classroom*. Stafford: Network Educational Press.

Thomas, G., Walker, D. and Webb, J. (1998) *The Making of the Inclusive School*. London and New York: Routledge.

Watkins, C. and Mortimore, P. (1999) 'Pedagogy: what do we know?', in Mortimore, P. (ed.) *Understanding Pedagogy and its Impact on Learning*. London: Paul Chapman Publishing.

Watkinson, A. (2002) *Assisting Learning and Supporting Teaching*. London: David Fulton Publishers.

Watkinson, A. (2003) *The Essential Guide for Competent Teaching Assistants:*

Meeting the National Occupational Standards at Level 2. London: David Fulton Publishers.

Weddell, K. (1983) 'Some developments in the concepts and practice of special needs education', *New Horizons Journal of Education*, **24**, 99–108.

Weddell, K. (2001) 'Klaus' story: the experience of a retired professor of special needs education', in O' Brien, T. and Garner, P. (eds) *Untold Stories: Learning Support Assistants and their Work*, pp. 89–96. Stoke-on-Trent: Trentham Books.

Whetton, N. and Cansell, P. (1993) *Feeling Good: Raising Self-esteem in the Primary School Classroom.* London: Forbes Publications.

Williams, T., Wetton, N. and Moon, A. (1989) *Health for Life: Health Education in the Primary School; The Health Education Authority's Primary School Project.* Walton on Thames: Nelson.

Wood, D. (1988) *How Children Think and Learn.* Oxford: Blackwell.

Wragg, E. C. (1994) *An Introduction to Classroom Observation.* London and New York: Routledge.

Wragg, E. C. and Brown, G. (1993) *Explaining.* London and New York: Routledge.

Index